BY NASSIM NICHOLAS TALEB

INCERTO, an investigation of opacity, luck, uncertainty, probability, human error, risk, and decision making when we don't understand the world, expressed in the form of a personal essay with autobiographical sections, stories, parables, and philosophical, historical, and scientific discussions in nonoverlapping volumes that can be accessed in any order.

FOOLED BY RANDOMNESS (2001, 2004), on how we tend to mistake luck for skills, how randomness does not look random, why there is no point talking about performance when it is easier to buy and sell than fry an egg, and the profound difference between dentists and speculators.

THE BLACK SWAN (2007, 2010), on how high-impact but rare events dominate history, how we retrospectively give ourselves the illusion of understanding them thanks to narratives, how they are impossible to estimate scientifically, how this makes some areas—but not others—totally unpredictable and unforecastable, how confirmatory methods of knowledge don't work, and how thanks to Black Swan–blind "faux experts" we are prone to building systems increasingly fragile to extreme events.

THE BED OF PROCRUSTES (Philosophical Aphorisms) (2010, 2016)

ANTIFRAGILE (2012), on how some things like disorder (hence volatility, time, chaos, variability, and stressors) while others don't, how we can classify things along the lines fragile-robust-antifragile, how we can identify (anti)fragility based on nonlinear response without having to know much about the history of the process (which solves most of the Black Swan problem), and why you are alive if and only if you love (some) volatility.

SKIN IN THE GAME (2018), this volume.

INCERTO'S TECHNICAL COMPANION, consisting of academic-style papers, miscellaneous notes, and (very) technical remarks and developments.

SKIN IN THE GAME

SKIN IN THE GAME

———

HIDDEN ASYMMETRIES
IN DAILY LIFE

———

NASSIM NICHOLAS TALEB

RANDOM HOUSE | NEW YORK

Published in the United States by Random House,
an imprint and division of
Penguin Random House LLC, New York.

RANDOM HOUSE and the HOUSE colophon are registered
trademarks of Penguin Random House LLC.

Originally published in hardcover in the
United States by Random House, an imprint and division of
Penguin Random House LLC, in 2018.

Portions of this work were originally published in
different form on *Medium*.

LIBRARY OF CONGRESS CATALOGING-IN-PUBLICATION DATA
NAMES: Taleb, Nassim Nicholas.
TITLE: Skin in the game : hidden asymmetries in daily life /
Nassim Nicholas Taleb.
DESCRIPTION: First edition. | New York : Random House, [2018] |
Includes bibliographical references and index
IDENTIFIERS: LCCN 2017047111 | ISBN 9780425284643 |
ISBN 9780425284636 (ebook)
SUBJECTS: LCSH: Risk—Sociological aspects. | Risk-taking (Psychology)—
Social aspects. | Information asymmetry—Social aspects. | Uncertainty
(Information theory)—Social aspects. | Complexity (Philosophy)
CLASSIFICATION: LCC HM1101 .T35 2018 | DDC 302/.12—dc23
LC record available at lccn.loc.gov/2017047111
International edition ISBN 978-0-525-51107-6

Printed in the United States of America on acid-free paper

randomhousebooks.com

246897531

Two men of courage:

Ron Paul,
a Roman among Greeks;

Ralph Nader,
Greco-Phoenician saint

CONTENTS

———

BOOK 1

INTRODUCTION

This book, while standalone, is a continuation of the *Incerto* collection, which is a combination of a) practical discussions, b) philosophical tales, and c) scientific and analytical commentary on the problems of randomness, and how to live, eat, sleep, argue, fight, befriend, work, have fun, and make decisions under uncertainty. While accessible to a broad group of readers, don't be fooled: the *Incerto* is an essay, not a popularization of works done elsewhere in boring form (leaving aside the *Incerto*'s technical companion).

Skin in the Game is about four topics in one: a) uncertainty and the reliability of knowledge (both practical and scientific, assuming there is a difference), or in less polite words bull***t detection, b) symmetry in human affairs, that is, fairness, justice, responsibility, and reciprocity, c) information sharing in transactions, and d) rationality in complex systems and in the real world. That these four cannot be disentangled is something that is obvious when one has . . . skin in the game.*

It is not just that skin in the game is necessary for fairness, commercial efficiency, and risk management: skin in the game is necessary to understand the world.

First, it is bull***t identification and filtering, that is, the difference between theory and practice, cosmetic and true expertise, and academia (in the bad sense of the word) and the real world. To emit a Yogiberrism, *in academia there is no difference between academia and the real world; in the real world, there is.*

---

* To figure out why ethics, moral obligations, and skills cannot be easily separable in real life, consider the following. When you tell someone in a position of responsibility, say your bookkeeper, "I trust you," do you mean that 1) you trust his ethics (he will not divert money to Panama), 2) you trust his accounting precision, or 3) both? The entire point of the book is that in the real world it is hard to disentangle ethics on one hand from knowledge and competence on the other.

Second, it is about the distortions of symmetry and reciprocity in life: If you have the rewards, you must also get some of the risks, not let others pay the price of your mistakes. If you inflict risk on others, and they are harmed, you need to pay some price for it. Just as you should treat others in the way you'd like to be treated, you would like to share the responsibility for events without unfairness and inequity.

If you give an opinion, and someone follows it, you are morally obligated to be, yourself, exposed to its consequences. In case you are giving economic views:

Don't tell me what you "think," just tell me what's in your portfolio.

Third, the book is about how much information one should practically share with others, what a used car salesman should—or shouldn't—tell you about the vehicle on which you are about to spend a large segment of your savings.

Fourth, it is about rationality and the test of time. Rationality in the real world isn't about what makes sense to your *New Yorker* journalist or some psychologist using naive first-order models, but something vastly deeper and statistical, linked to your own survival.

Do not mistake skin in the game as defined here and used in this book for just an incentive problem, just having a share of the benefits (as it is commonly understood in finance). No. It is about symmetry, more like having a share of the harm, paying a penalty if something goes wrong. The very same idea ties together notions of incentives, used car buying, ethics, contract theory, learning (real life vs. academia), Kantian imperative, municipal power, risk science, contact between intellectuals and reality, the accountability of bureaucrats, probabilistic social justice, option theory, upright behavior, bull***t vendors, theology . . . I stop for now.

THE LESS OBVIOUS ASPECTS OF SKIN IN THE GAME

A more correct (though more awkward) title of the book would have been: *The Less Obvious Aspects of Skin in the Game: Those Hidden Asymmetries and Their Consequences.* For I just don't like reading books that inform me of the obvious. I like to be surprised. So as a skin-in-the-game-style reciprocity, I will not not drive the reader into a dull college-lecture-type predictable journey, but rather into the type of adventure I'd like to have.

Accordingly, the book is organized in the following manner. It doesn't take more than about sixty pages for the reader to get the importance, prevalence, and ubiquity of skin in the game (that is, symmetry) in most of its aspects. But never engage in detailed overexplanations of *why* something important is important: one debases a principle by endlessly justifying it.

The nondull route entails focusing on the second step: the surprising implications—those hidden asymmetries that do not immediately come to mind—as well as the less obvious consequences, some of which are quite uncomfortable, and many unexpectedly helpful. Understanding the workings of skin in the game allows us to understand serious puzzles underlying the fine-grained matrix of reality.

For instance:

How is it that maximally intolerant minorities run the world and impose their taste on us? How does universalism destroy the very people it means to help? How is it that we have more slaves today than we did during Roman times? Why shouldn't surgeons look like surgeons? Why did Christian theology keep insisting on a human side for Jesus Christ that is necessarily distinct from the divine? How do historians confuse us by reporting on war, not peace? How is it that cheap signaling (without anything to risk) fails equally in economic and religious environments? How do candidates for political office with obvious character flaws seem more real than bureaucrats with impeccable credentials? Why do we worship Hannibal? How do companies go bust the minute they have professional managers interested in doing good? How is paganism more symmetrical across populations? How should foreign affairs be conducted? Why should you never give money to organized charities unless they operate in a highly distributive manner (what is called Uberized in modern lingo)? Why do genes and languages spread differently? Why does the scale of communities matter (a community of fishermen turns from collaborative to adversarial once one moves the scale, that is the number of people involved, a notch)? Why does behavioral economics have nothing to do with the study of the behavior of individuals—and markets have little to do with the biases of participants? How is rationality survival and survival only? What is the foundational logic of risk bearing?

But, to this author, skin in the game is mostly about justice, honor, and sacrifice, things that are existential for humans.

Skin in the game, applied as a rule, reduces the effects of the following divergences that grew with civilization: those between action and cheap talk (*tawk*), consequence and intention, practice and theory, honor and reputation, expertise and charlatanism, concrete and abstract, ethical and legal, genuine and cosmetic, merchant and bureaucrat, entrepreneur and chief executive, strength and display, love and gold-digging, Coventry and Brussels, Omaha and Washington, D.C., human beings and economists, authors and editors, scholarship and academia, democracy and governance, science and scientism, politics and politicians, love and money, the spirit and the letter, Cato the Elder and Barack Obama, quality and advertising, commitment and signaling, and, centrally, collective and individual.

Let us first connect a few dots of the items in the list above with two vignettes, just to give the flavor of how the idea transcends categories.

Antaeus Whacked

*Never, run away from Mamma—I keep finding warlords—Bob Rubin
and his trade—Systems like car accidents*

———

Antaeus was a giant, or rather a semi-giant of sorts, the literal son of Mother Earth, Gaea, and Poseidon, the god of the sea. He had a strange occupation, which consisted of forcing passersby in his country, (Greek) Libya, to wrestle; his thing was to pin his victims to the ground and crush them. This macabre hobby was apparently the expression of filial devotion; Antaeus aimed at building a temple to his father, Poseidon, using for raw material the skulls of his victims.

Antaeus was deemed to be invincible, but there was a trick. He derived his strength from contact with his mother, Earth. Physically separated from contact with Earth, he lost all his powers. Hercules, as part of his twelve labors (in one variation of the tale), had for homework to whack Antaeus. He managed to lift him off the ground and terminated him by crushing him as his feet remained out of contact with his mamma.

We retain from this first vignette that, just like Antaeus, you cannot separate knowledge from contact with the ground. Actually, you cannot separate *anything* from contact with the ground. And the contact with the real world is done via skin in the game—having an exposure to the real world, and paying a price for its consequences, good or bad. The abrasions of your skin guide your learning and discovery, a mechanism of organic signaling, what the Greeks called *pathemata mathemata* ("guide your learning through pain," something mothers of young children know rather well). I have shown in *Antifragile* that most things that we believe were "invented" by universities were actually discovered by tinkering and later legitimized by some type of formalization. The knowledge we get by tinkering, via trial and error, experience, and the workings of time, in other words, *contact with the earth*, is vastly superior to that obtained through reasoning, something self-serving institutions have been very busy hiding from us.

Next, we will apply this to what is miscalled "policy making."

LIBYA AFTER ANTAEUS

Second vignette. As I am writing these lines, a few thousand years later, Libya, the putative land of Antaeus, now has slave markets, as a result of a failed attempt at what is called "regime change" in order to "remove a dictator." Yes, in 2017, improvised slave markets in parking lots, where captured sub-Saharan Africans are sold to the highest bidders.

A collection of people classified as interventionistas (to name names of people operating at the time of writing: Bill Kristol, Thomas Friedman, and others*) who promoted the Iraq invasion of 2003, as well as the removal of the Libyan leader in 2011, are advocating the imposition of additional such regime change on another batch of countries, which includes Syria, because it has a "dictator."

These interventionistas and their friends in the U.S. State Department helped create, train, and support Islamist rebels, then "moderates," but who eventually evolved to become part of al-Qaeda, the same, very same al-Qaeda that blew up the New York City towers during the events of September 11, 2001. They mysteriously failed to remember that al-Qaeda itself was composed of "moderate rebels" created (or reared) by the U.S. to help fight Soviet Russia because, as we will see, these educated people's reasoning doesn't entail such recursions.

So we tried *that thing* called regime change in Iraq, and failed miserably. We tried *that thing* again in Libya, and there are now active slave markets in the place. But we satisfied the objective of "removing a dicta-

---

* Interventionistas have in common one main attribute: they are usually not weight lifters.

tor." By the exact same reasoning, a doctor would inject a patient with "moderate" cancer cells to improve his cholesterol numbers, and proudly claim victory after the patient is dead, particularly if the postmortem shows remarkable cholesterol readings. But we know that doctors don't inflict fatal "cures" upon patients, or don't do it in such a crude way, and there is a clear reason for that. Doctors usually have some modicum of skin in the game, a vague understanding of complex systems, and more than a couple of millennia of incremental ethics determining their conduct.

And don't give up on logic, intellect, and education, because tight but higher order logical reasoning would show that, unless one finds some way to reject all empirical evidence, advocating regime changes implies *also* advocating slavery or some similar degradation of the country (since these have been typical outcomes). So these interventionistas not only lack practical sense, and never learn from history, but they even fail at pure reasoning, which they drown in elaborate semiabstract buzzword-laden discourse.

Their three flaws: 1) they think in statics not dynamics, 2) they think in low, not high, dimensions, 3) they think in terms of actions, never interactions. We will see in more depth throughout the book this defect of mental reasoning by educated (or, rather, semi-educated) fools. I can flesh out the three defects for now.

The first flaw is that they are incapable of thinking in second steps and unaware of the need for them—and about every peasant in Mongolia, every waiter in Madrid, and every car-service operator in San Francisco knows that real life happens to have second, third, fourth, nth steps. The second flaw is that they are also incapable of distinguishing between multidimensional problems and their single-dimensional representations—like multidimensional health and its stripped, cholesterol-reading reduction. They can't get the idea that, empirically, complex systems do not have obvious one-dimensional cause-and-effect mechanisms, and that under opacity, you do not mess with such a system. An extension of this defect: they compare the actions of the "dictator" to those of the prime minister of Norway or Sweden, not to those of the local alternative. The third flaw is that they can't forecast the evolution of those one helps by attacking, or the magnification one gets from feedback.

*LUDIS DE ALIENO CORIO**

And when a blowup happens, they invoke uncertainty, something called a Black Swan (a high-impact unexpected event), after a book by a (very) stubborn fellow, not realizing that one should not mess with a system if the results are fraught with uncertainty, or, more generally, should avoid engaging in an action with a big downside if one has no idea of the outcomes. What is crucial here is that the downside doesn't affect the interventionist. He continues his practice from the comfort of his thermally regulated suburban house with a two-car garage, a dog, and a small play area with pesticide-free grass for his overprotected 2.2 children.

Imagine people with similar mental handicaps, people who don't understand asymmetry, piloting planes. Incompetent pilots, those who cannot learn from experience, or don't mind taking risks they don't understand, may kill many. But they will themselves end up at the bottom of, say, the Bermuda Triangle, and cease to represent a threat to others and mankind. Not here.

So we end up populating what we call the intelligentsia with people who are delusional, literally mentally deranged, simply because they never have to pay for the consequences of their actions, repeating modernist slogans stripped of all depth (for instance, they keep using the term "democracy" while encouraging headcutters; democracy is something they read about in graduate studies). In general, when you hear someone invoking abstract modernistic notions, you can assume that they got some education (but not enough, or in the wrong discipline) and have too little accountability.

Now some innocent people—Ezidis, Christian minorities in the Near (and Middle) East, Mandeans, Syrians, Iraqis, and Libyans—had to pay a price for the mistakes of these interventionistas currently sitting in comfortable air-conditioned offices. This, we will see, violates the very notion of justice from its prebiblical, Babylonian inception—as well as the ethical structure, that underlying matrix thanks to which humanity has survived.

The principle of intervention, like that of healers, is *first do no harm (primum non nocere)*; even more, we will argue, those who don't take risks should never be involved in making decisions.

---

* Playing with others' lives.

Further,

We have always been crazy but weren't skilled enough to destroy the world. Now we can.

We will return to the "peacemaking" interventionistas, and examine how their peace processes create deadlocks, as with the Israeli-Palestinian problem.

WARLORDS ARE STILL AROUND

This idea of skin in the game is woven into history: historically, all warlords and warmongers were warriors themselves, and, with a few curious exceptions, societies were run by risk takers, not risk transferors.

Prominent people took risks—considerably more risks than ordinary citizens. The Roman emperor Julian the Apostate, about whom much later, died on the battlefield fighting in the never-ending war on the Persian frontier—*while emperor*. One may only speculate about Julius Caesar, Alexander, and Napoleon, owing to the usual legend-building by historians, but here the proof is stark. There is no better historical evidence of an emperor taking a frontline position in battle than a Persian spear lodged in his chest (Julian omitted to wear protective armor). One of his predecessors, Valerian, was captured on the same frontier, and was said to have been used as a human footstool by the Persian Shapur when mounting his horse. And the last Byzantine emperor, Constantine XI Palaeologus, was last seen when he removed his purple toga, then joined Ioannis Dalmatus and his cousin Theophilus Palaeologus to charge Turkish troops with their swords above their heads, proudly facing certain death. Yet legend has it that Constantine had been offered a deal in the event of a surrender. Such deals are not for self-respecting kings.

These are not isolated anecdotes. The statistical reasoner in this author is quite convinced: less than a third of Roman emperors died in their beds—and one can argue that given that only few of these died of really old age, had they lived longer, they would have fallen either to a coup or in battle.

Even today, monarchs derive their legitimacy from a social contract that requires physical risk-taking. The British Royal family made sure that one of its scions, Prince Andrew, took more risks than "commoners" during the Falkland war of 1982, his helicopter being in the front line. Why? Because noblesse oblige; the very status of a lord has been traditionally derived from protecting others, trading personal risk for prominence—and they happened to still remember that contract. You can't be a lord if you aren't a lord.

THE BOB RUBIN TRADE

Some think that freeing ourselves from having warriors at the top means civilization and progress. It does not. Meanwhile,

> *Bureaucracy is a construction by which a person is conveniently separated from the consequences of his or her actions.*

And, one may ask, what can we do since a centralized system will necessarily need people who are not directly exposed to the cost of errors?

Well, we have no choice but to decentralize or, more politely, to localize; to have fewer of these immune decision makers.

> *Decentralization is based on the simple notion that it is easier to macrobull***t than microbull***t.*

> *Decentralization reduces large structural asymmetries.*

But not to worry, if we do not decentralize and distribute responsibility, it will happen by itself, the hard way: a system that doesn't have a mechanism of skin in the game, with a buildup of imbalances, will eventually blow up and self-repair that way. If it survives.

For instance, bank blowups came in 2008 because of the accumulation of hidden and asymmetric risks in the system: bankers, master risk transferors, could make steady money from a certain class of concealed explosive risks, use academic risk models that don't work except on paper (because academics know practically nothing about risk), then invoke uncertainty after a blowup (that same unseen and unforecastable Black Swan and that same very, very stubborn author), and keep past income—what I have called the Bob Rubin trade.

The Bob Rubin trade? Robert Rubin, a former Secretary of the United States Treasury, one of those who sign their names on the banknote you just used to pay for coffee, collected more than $120 million in compensation from Citibank in the decade preceding the banking crash of 2008. When the bank, literally insolvent, was rescued by the taxpayer, he didn't write any check—he invoked uncertainty as an excuse. Heads he wins, tails he shouts "Black Swan." Nor did Rubin acknowledge that he transferred risk to taxpayers: Spanish grammar specialists, assistant schoolteachers, supervisors in tin can factories, vegetarian nutrition advisors, and clerks for assistant district attorneys were "stopping him out," that is, taking his risks and paying for his losses. But the worst casualty has been free markets, as the public, already prone to hating financiers, started conflating free markets and higher order forms of corruption and cronyism, when in fact it is the exact opposite: it is government, not markets, that makes these things possible by the mechanisms of bailouts. It is not just bailouts: government interference in general tends to remove skin in the game.

The good news is that in spite of the efforts of a complicit Obama administration that wanted to protect the game and the rent-seeking bankers,* the risk-taking business started moving toward small independent structures known as hedge funds. The move took place mostly because of the overbureaucratization of the system as paper shufflers (who think work is mostly about paper shuffling) overburdened the banks with rules—but somehow, in the thousands of pages of additional regulations, *they avoided considering skin in the game*. In the decentralized hedge fund space, on the other hand, owner-operators have at least half of their net worth in the funds, making them relatively more exposed than any of their customers, and they personally go down with the ship.

SYSTEMS LEARN BY REMOVING

Now, if you are going to highlight only one single section from this book, here is the one. The interventionista case is central to our story

---

* *Rent-seeking* is trying to use protective regulations or "rights" to derive income without adding anything to economic activity, not increasing the wealth of others. As Fat Tony (who will be introduced a few pages down) would define it, it is like being forced to pay protection money to the Mafia without getting the economic benefits of protection.

because it shows how absence of skin in the game has both ethical and epistemological effects (i.e., related to knowledge). We saw that interventionistas don't learn *because they are not the victims of their mistakes,* and, as we hinted at with *pathemata mathemata:*

> *The same mechanism of transferring risk also impedes learning.*

More practically,

> *You will never fully convince someone that he is wrong;*
> *only reality can.*

Actually, to be precise, reality doesn't care about winning arguments: survival is what matters.
For

> *The curse of modernity is that we are increasingly populated by a class of people who are better at explaining than understanding,*

or better at explaining than doing.

So *learning* isn't quite what we teach inmates inside the high-security prisons called schools. In biology, learning is something that, through the filter of intergenerational selection, gets imprinted at the cellular level—skin in the game, I insist, is more filter than deterrence. Evolution can only happen if risk of extinction is present. Further,

> *There is no evolution without skin in the game.*

This last point is quite obvious, but I keep seeing academics with no skin in the game defend evolution while at the same time rejecting skin in the game and risk sharing. They refuse the notion of *design* by a creator who knows everything, while, at the same time, want to impose human *design* as if they knew all the consequences. In general, the more people worship the sacrosanct state (or, equivalently, large corporations), the more they hate skin in the game. The more they believe in their ability to forecast, the more they hate skin in the game. The more they wear suits and ties, the more they hate skin in the game.

Returning to our interventionistas, we saw that people don't learn so much from their—and other people's—mistakes; rather it is the system that learns by selecting those less prone to *a certain class* of mistakes and eliminating others.

Systems learn by removing parts, via negativa.*

Many bad pilots, as we mentioned, are currently in the bottom of the Atlantic, many dangerous bad drivers are in the local quiet cemetery with nice walkways bordered by trees. Transportation didn't get safer just because people *learn* from errors, but because the system does. The experience of the system is different from that of individuals; it is grounded in filtering.

To summarize so far,

Skin in the game keeps human hubris in check.

Let us now go deeper with the second part of the prologue, and consider the notion of symmetry.

---

* *Via negativa:* the principle that we know what is wrong with more clarity than what is right, and that knowledge grows by subtraction. Also, it is easier to know that something is wrong than to find the fix. Actions that remove are more robust than those that add because addition may have unseen, complicated feedback loops. This is discussed in some depth in *Antifragile*.

A Brief Tour of Symmetry

Meta-experts judged by meta-meta-experts—Prostitutes, nonprosti-
tutes, and amateurs—The French have this thing with Hammurabi—
Dumas is always an exception

I. FROM HAMMURABI TO KANT

S kin-in-the-game-style symmetry, until the recent intellectualiza-
tion of life, had been implicitly considered the principal rule for
organized society, even for any form of collective life in which one en-
counters or deals with others more than once. The rule had to even
precede human settlement since it prevails in a sophisticated, very sophisticated, form in the animal kingdom. Or, to rephrase, it *had to* prevail there or life would have been extinct—risk transfer blows up
systems. And the very idea of law, divine or otherwise, resides in fixing
imbalances and remedying such asymmetries.

Let us briefly travel the road from Hammurabi to Kant, where the
rule gets refined along with civilized life.

Hammurabi in Paris

Hammurabi's law was posted on a basalt stele around 3,800 years ago in
a central public place in Babylon, so every literate person could read it,
or, rather, read it to others who couldn't read. It contains 282 laws and
is deemed to be the first codification of our rule extant. The code has

one central theme: it establishes symmetries between people in a transaction, so nobody can transfer hidden *tail* risk, or Bob Rubin–style risks. Yes, the Bob Rubin trade is 3,800 years old, as old as civilization, and so are the rules to counter it.

What is a tail? Take for now that it is an extreme event of low frequency. It is called a "tail" because, in drawings of bell-curve style frequencies, it is located to the extreme left or right (being of low frequency), and for some reason beyond my immediate understanding, people started calling that a "tail" and the term stuck.

Hammurabi's best known injunction is as follows: "If a builder builds a house and the house collapses and causes the death of the owner of the house—the builder shall be put to death."

For, as with financial traders, the best place to hide risks is "in the corners," in burying vulnerabilities to rare events that only the architect (or the trader) can detect—the idea being to be far away in time and place when blowups happen. As one old alcoholic ruddy-faced English banker told me when I graduated from school, volunteering career advice: "I give *long*-term loans only. When they mature I want to be *long* gone. And only reachable *long* distance." He worked for international banks and survived playing his trick by changing country every five years, and, from what I recall, he also changed wives every ten years and banks every twelve. But he didn't have to go hide very far or very deeply underground: nobody until very recently clawed back (that is, reclaimed) the past bonuses of bankers when something subsequently went wrong. And, not unexpectedly, it was the Swiss who started clawing back, in 2008.

The well-known *lex talionis,* "an eye for one eye," comes from Hammurabi's rule. It is metaphorical, not literal: you don't have to actually remove an eye—hence the rule is much more flexible than it appears at first glance. For, in a famous Talmudic discussion (in *Bava Kamma*), a rabbi argues that if one followed the letter, the one-eyed would only pay half the punishment if he blinds a two-eyed person, and the blind would go scot-free. Or what if a small person kills a hero? Likewise, you do not need to amputate the leg of the reckless doctor who cut the wrong leg: the tort system, through courts, not regulation, thanks to the efforts of Ralph Nader, will impose *some* penalty, enough to protect consumers and citizens from powerful institutions. Clearly the legal system might produce some irritants (particularly with torts) and has its class of rent-seekers, but we are vastly better off complaining about lawyers than complaining about not having them.

More practically, some economists have been trying to blame me for wanting to reverse the bankruptcy protection offered in modern times; some even accused me of wanting to bring back the guillotine for bankers. I am not *that* literal: it is just the matter of inflicting *some* penalty, just enough to make the Bob Rubin trade less attractive, and protect the public.

Now, for some reason that escapes me, one of those strange things one finds only in France, Hammurabi's code, a stele in gray-black basalt, resides in the Louvre Museum in Paris. And the French, who normally know about a lot of things we don't know much about, don't seem to know about it; only Korean visitors with selfie sticks appear to have heard of the place.

On my penultimate pilgrimage to the site, I happened to lecture French financiers in a conference room in the museum building about the ideas of this book, and the notion of skin in the game. I was speaking right after the man who, in spite of looks (and personality) quite similar to those found in Mesopotamian statues, epitomizes absence of skin in the game: former Federal Reserve governor Ben Bernanke. To my sorrow, when I publicly questioned the audience, using the irony of the situation, namely that almost four millennia ago we were sort of more sophisticated with these things, and that the monument was 300 feet from where I was lecturing, nobody in the room, in spite of the high culture of French financiers, figured out what I was talking about. Nobody was aware of Hammurabi beyond some player in Mesopotamian geopolitics, or suspected his connection to skin in the game and the accountability of bankers.

Table 1 shows the progression of the rules of symmetry from Hammurabi onward, so let us climb the ladder.

TABLE 1 · EVOLUTION OF MORAL SYMMETRY

FROM TALEB AND SANDIS, 2016

HAMMURABI/ LEX TALIONIS	15TH LAW OF HOLI-NESS AND JUSTICE	SILVER RULE	GOLDEN RULE	FORMULA OF THE UNIVERSAL LAW
"An eye for an eye, a tooth for a tooth" (Hammurabi, Exodus 21.24)	"Love your neighbor as yourself" (Leviticus 19.18)		"Do unto others as you would have them do unto you" (Matthew 7:12)	"Act only in accordance with that maxim through which you can at the same time will that it will become a universal law." (Kant 1785: 4:421)

Silver Beats Gold

We rapidly go through the rules to the right of Hammurabi. Leviticus is a sweetening of Hammurabi's rule. The Golden Rule wants you to *Treat others the way you would like them to treat you.* The more robust Silver Rule says *Do not treat others the way you would not like them to treat you.* More robust? How? Why is the Silver Rule more robust?

First, it tells you to mind your own business and not decide what is "good" for others. We know with much more clarity what is bad than what is good. The Silver Rule can be seen as the Negative Golden Rule, and as I am shown by my Calabrese (and Calabrese-speaking) barber every three weeks, *via negativa* (acting by removing) is more powerful and less error-prone than *via positiva* (acting by addition*).

Now a word about the "others" in *treat others.* "You" can be singular or plural, hence it can designate an individual, a basketball team, or the Northeast Association of Calabrese-Speaking Barbers. Same with the "others." The idea is fractal, in the sense that it works at all scales: humans, tribes, societies, groups of societies, countries, etc., assuming each one is a separate standalone unit and can deal with other counter-

---

*   "Do not do unto others what you would not have them do unto you" (Isocrates, Hillel the Elder, *Mahabharata*). "What is hateful to you, do not do to your fellow: this is the whole Torah; the rest is the explanation; go and learn." Rabbi Hillel the Elder drawing on Leviticus 19:18. "Do nothing to others which if done to you would cause you pain. This is the essence of morality."

parts as such. Just as individuals should treat others the way they would like to be treated (or avoid being mistreated), families as units should treat other families in the same way. And, something that makes the interventionistas of Prologue 1 even more distasteful, so should countries. For Isocrates, the wise Athenian orator, warned us as early as the fifth century B.C. that nations should treat other nations according to the Silver Rule. He wrote:

"Deal with weaker states as you think it appropriate for stronger states to deal with you."

Nobody embodies the notion of symmetry better than Isocrates, who lived more than a century and made significant contributions when he was in his nineties. He even managed a rare dynamic version of the Golden Rule: "Conduct yourself toward your parents as you would have your children conduct themselves toward you." We had to wait for the great baseball coach Yogi Berra to get another such dynamic rule for symmetric relations: "I go to other people's funerals so they come to mine."

More effective, of course, is the reverse direction, to treat one's children the way one wished to be treated by one's parents.*

The very idea behind the First Amendment of the Constitution of the United States is to establish a silver rule–style symmetry: you can practice your freedom of religion so long as you allow me to practice mine; you have the right to contradict me so long as I have the right to contradict you. Effectively, there is no democracy without such an unconditional symmetry in the rights to express yourself, and the gravest threat is the slippery slope in the attempts to limit speech on grounds that some of it may hurt some people's feelings. Such restrictions do not necessarily come from the state itself, rather from the forceful establishment of an intellectual monoculture by an overactive *thought police* in the media and cultural life.

Fuhgetaboud Universalism

By applying symmetry to relations between individual and collective, we get virtue, classical virtue, what is now called "virtue ethics." But

---

* A stance against violation of symmetry appears in the Parable of Unforgiving Servant in the New Testament (Matthew 12:21–31). A servant who has his huge debt waived by a compassionate lender subsequently punishes another servant who owed him a much smaller amount. Most commentators seem to miss that the true message is (dynamic) symmetry, not forgiveness.

there is a next step: all the way to the right of Table 1 is Immanuel Kant's categorical imperative, which I summarize as: *Behave as if your action can be generalized to the behavior of everyone in all places, under all conditions.* The actual text is more challenging: "Act only in accordance with that maxim through which you can at the same time will that it will become a universal law," Kant wrote in what is known as the first formulation. And "act in such a way that you treat humanity, whether in your own person or in the person of any other, never merely as a means to an end, but always at the same time as an end," in what is known as the second formulation.

Formulation shmormulation, fughedaboud Kant as it gets too complicated and things that get complicated have a problem. So we will skip Kant's drastic approach for one main reason:

Universal behavior is great on paper, disastrous in practice.

Why? As we will belabor ad nauseam in this book, we are local and practical animals, sensitive to scale. The small is not the large; the tangible is not the abstract; the emotional is not the logical. Just as we argued that micro works better than macro, it is best to avoid going to the very general when saying hello to your garage attendant. We should focus on our immediate environment; we need simple practical rules. Even worse: the general and the abstract tend to attract self-righteous psychopaths similar to the interventionistas of Part 1 of the Prologue.

In other words, Kant did not get the notion of scaling—yet many of us are victims of Kant's universalism. (As we saw, modernity likes the abstract over the particular; social justice warriors have been accused of "treating people as categories, not individuals.") Few, outside of religion, really got the notion of scaling before the great political thinker Elinor Ostrom, about whom a bit in Chapter 1.

In fact, the deep message of this book is the danger of universalism taken two or three steps too far—conflating the micro and the macro. Likewise the crux of the idea of *The Black Swan* was *Platonification,* missing central but hidden elements of a thing in the process of transforming it into an abstract construct, then causing a blowup.

II. FROM KANT TO FAT TONY

Let us move to the present, to the transactional, highly transactional present. In New Jersey, symmetry can simply mean, in Fat Tony's terms: *don't give crap, don't take crap*. His more practical approach is

> *Start by being nice to every person you meet. But if someone tries to exercise power over you, exercise power over him.*

Who is Fat Tony? He is a character in the *Incerto* who, in demeanor, behavior, choices under uncertainty, conversation, lifestyle, waist size, and food habits would be the exact opposite of your State Department analyst or economics lecturer. He is also calm and unfazed unless one really gets him angry. He became wealthy by helping people he generically calls "the suckers" separate from their funds (or, as is often the case, those of their clients, as these people often gamble with other people's money).

This symmetry thing happens to link directly to my own profession: option trader. In an option, one person (the buyer of the option), contractually has the upside (future gains), the other (the seller) has a liability for the downside (future losses), for a pre-agreed price. Just as in an insurance contract, where risk is transferred for a fee. Any meaningful disruption of such symmetry—with transfer of liabilities—invariably leads to an explosive situation, as we saw with the economic crisis of 2008.

This symmetry thing also concerns the alignment of interests in a transaction. Let us refresh earlier arguments: if bankers' profits accrue to them, while their losses are somewhat quietly transferred to society (the Spanish grammar specialists, assistant schoolteachers . . .), there is a fundamental problem by which hidden risks will continuously increase, until the final blowup. Regulations, while appearing to be a remedy on paper, if anything, exacerbate the problem as they facilitate risk-hiding.

Which brings us to what is known as the agency problem.

Crook, Fool, or Both

One practical extension of the Silver Rule (as a reminder, it is the one that says *Do not do to others what you don't want them to do to you*):

Avoid taking advice from someone who gives advice for a living,
unless there is a penalty for their advice.

Recall the earlier comment on how "I trust you" straddles both ethics and knowledge. There is always an element of fools of randomness
and crooks of randomness in matters of uncertainty; one has a lack of
understanding, the second has warped incentives. One, the fool, takes
risks he doesn't understand, mistaking his own past luck for skills, the
other, the crook, transfers risks to others. Economists, when they talk
about skin in the game, are only concerned with the second.

Let us flush out the idea of agency, well-known and studied by insurance companies. Simply, you know a lot more about your health than
any insurer would. So you have an incentive to get an insurance policy
when you detect an illness before someone else knows about it. By getting insured when it fits you, not when you are healthy, you end up cost-
ing the system more than you put into it, hence causing a raise in premia
paid by all sorts of innocent people (including, again, the Spanish grammar specialists). Insurance companies have filters such as high deduct-
ibles and other methods to eliminate such imbalances.

The agency problem (or principal-agent problem) also manifests itself in the misalignment of interests in transactions: a vendor in a one-
shot transaction does not have his interests aligned to yours—and so
can hide stuff from you.

But disincentive is not enough: the fool is a real thing. Some people
do not know their own interest—just consider addicts, workaholics,
people trapped in a bad relationship, people who support large government, the press, book reviewers, or respectable bureaucrats, all of whom
for some mysterious reason act against their own interest. So there is
this other instance where filtering plays a role: *fools* of randomness are
purged by reality so they stop harming others. Recall that it is at the
foundation of evolution that systems get smart by elimination.

There is another point: we may not know beforehand if an action is
foolish—but reality knows.

Causal Opacity and Preferences Revealed*

Let us now take the epistemological dimension of skin in the game to an even higher level. Skin in the game is about the real world, not appearances. As per Fat Tony's motto:

You do not want to win an argument. You want to win.

Indeed you need to win whatever you are after: money, territory, the heart of a grammar specialist, or a (pink) convertible car. For focusing just on words puts one on a very dangerous slope, since

We are much better at doing than understanding.

There is a difference between a charlatan and a genuinely skilled member of society, say that between a macrobull***ter political "scientist" and a plumber, or between a journalist and a mafia made man. The doer wins by doing, not convincing. Entire fields (say economics and other social sciences) become themselves charlatanic because of the absence of skin in the game connecting them back to earth (while the participants argue about "science"). Chapter 9 shows how they will develop elaborate rituals, titles, protocols, and formalities to hide this deficit.

You may not know in your mind where you are going, but you know it by doing.

Even economics is based on the notion of "revealed preferences." What people "think" is not relevant—you want to avoid entering the mushy-soft and self-looping discipline of psychology. People's "explanations" for what they do are just words, stories they tell themselves, not the business of proper science. What they do, on the other hand, is tangible and measurable and that's what we should focus on. This axiom, perhaps even principle, is very powerful but is not followed too much by researchers. Revelation of preferences is best understood by the betrothed: a diamond, particularly when it is onerous to the buyer, is

---

* This section is technical and can be skipped at first reading.

vastly more convincing a commitment (and much less reversible) than a verbal promise.

As to forecasting, fuhgetaboud it:

Forecasting (in words) bears no relation to speculation (in deeds).

I personally know rich horrible forecasters and poor "good" forecasters. Because what matters in life isn't how frequently one is "right" about outcomes, but how much one makes when one is right. Being wrong, when it is not costly, doesn't count—in a way that's similar to trial-and-error mechanisms of research.

Exposures in real life, outside of games, are always too complicated to reduce to a well-defined "event" easy to describe in words. Outcomes in real life are not as in a baseball game, reduced to a binary win-or-lose outcome. Many exposures are highly nonlinear: you may be beneficially exposed to rain, but not to floods. The exact argument is flushed out in this author's technical works. Take for now that forecasting, especially when done with "science," is often the last refuge of the charlatan, and has been so since the beginning of times.

Further, there is something called the *inverse problem* in mathematics, which is solved by—and only by—skin in the game. I will simplify for now as follows: it is harder for us to reverse-engineer than engineer; we see the result of evolutionary forces but cannot replicate them owing to their causal opacity. We can only run such processes forward. The very operation of Time (which we capitalize) and its irreversibility requires the filtering from skin in the game.

Skin in the game helps to solve the Black Swan problem and other matters of uncertainty at the level of both the individual and the collective: what has survived has revealed its robustness to Black Swan events and removing skin in the game disrupts such selection mechanisms. Without skin in the game, we fail to get the *Intelligence of Time* (a manifestation of the *Lindy effect,* which will get an entire chapter, and by which 1) time removes the fragile and keeps the robust, and 2) the life expectancy of the nonfragile lengthens with time). Ideas have, indirectly, skin in the game, and populations that harbor them do as well.

In that light—that of (causal) opacity and revelation of preferences—

the *Intelligence of Time* under skin in the game even helps define rationality—the only definition of rationality I found that doesn't fall apart under logical scrutiny. A practice may appear to be irrational to an overeducated and naive (but punctual) observer who works in the French Ministry of Planning, because we humans are not intelligent enough to understand it—but it has worked for a long time. Is it rational? We have no grounds to reject it. But we know what is patently irrational: what threatens the survival of the collective first, the individual second. And, from a statistical standpoint, going against nature (and its statistical significance) is irrational. In spite of the noise funded by pesticide and other technological companies, there is no known rigorous definition of rationality that makes rejection of the "natural" rational; to the contrary. By definition, what works cannot be irrational; about every single person I know who has chronically failed in business shares that mental block, the failure to realize that if something *stupid* works (and makes money), it cannot be *stupid*.

A system with skin-in-the-game requirements holds together through the notion of a sacrifice in order to protect the collective or entities higher in the hierarchy that are required to survive. "Survival talks and BS walks." Or as Fat Tony would put it: "Survival tawks and BS wawks." In other words:

> *What is rational is what allows the collective—entities meant to live for a long time—to survive.*

Not what is called "rational" in some unrigorous psychology or social science book.* In that sense, contrary to what psychologists and psycholophasters will tell you, some "overestimation" of tail risk is not irrational by any metric, as it is more than required overall for survival. There are some risks we just cannot afford to take. And there are other risks (of the type academics shun) that we cannot afford to *not* take. This dimension, which bears the name "ergodic," is belabored in Chapter 19.

---

* In fact, those who formalized the theory of rationality, such as the mathematician and game theorist Ken Binmore, more on whom later, insist that there has never been any rigorous and self-consistent theory of "rationality" that puts people in a straitjacket. You will not even find such claims in orthodox neoclassical economics. Most of what we read about the "rational" in the verbalistic literature doesn't seem to partake of any rigor.

Skin in the Game, but Not All the Time

Skin in the game is an overall necessity, but let us not get carried away in applying it to everything in sight in its every detail, particularly when consequences are contained. There is a difference between the interventionista of Prologue, Part 1 making pronouncements that cause thousands to be killed overseas, and a harmless opinion voiced by a person in a conversation, or a pronouncement by a fortune teller used for therapy rather than decision making. Our message is to focus on those who are *professionally* slanted, causing harm without being accountable for it, by the very structure of their own occupation.

For the professionally asymmetric person is rare and has been so in history, and even in the present. He causes a lot of problems, but he is rare. For most people you run into in real life—bakers, cobblers, plumbers, taxi drivers, accountants, tax advisors, garbage collectors, dental cleaning assistants, carwash operators (not counting Spanish grammar specialists)—pay a price for their mistakes.

III. MODERNISM

While conforming to ancestral, ancient, and classical notions of justice, this book, relying on the same arguments of asymmetry, goes against a century and a half of modernistic thinking—something we will call here *intellectualism*. Intellectualism is the belief that one can separate an action from the results of such action, that one can separate theory from practice, and that one can always fix a complex system by hierarchical approaches, that is, in a (ceremonial) top-down manner.

Intellectualism has a sibling: *scientism*, a naive interpretation of science as complication rather than science as a process and a skeptical enterprise. Using mathematics when it's not needed is not science but *scientism*. Replacing your well-functioning hand with something more technological, say, an artificial one, is *not* more scientific. Replacing the "natural," that is age-old, processes that have survived trillions of high-dimensional stressors with something in a "peer-reviewed" journal that may not survive replication or statistical scrutiny is neither science nor good practice. At the time of writing, science has been taken over by vendors using it to sell products (like margarine or genetically modified solutions) and, ironically, the skeptical enterprise is being used to silence skeptics.

Disrespect for the vapidly complicated, verbalistically derived truths has always been present in intellectual history, but you are not likely to see it in your local scientific reporter or college teacher: higher-order questioning requires more intellectual confidence, deeper understanding of statistical significance, and a higher level of rigor and intellectual capacity—or, even better, experience selling rugs or specialized spices in a souk. So this book continues a long tradition of skeptical-inquiry-cum-practical-solutions—the readers of the *Incerto* might be familiar with the schools of skeptics (covered in *The Black Swan*), in particular the twenty-two-century-old diatribe by Sextus Empiricus *Against the Professors*.

The rule is:

Those who talk should do and only those who do should talk

with some dispensation for self-standing activities such as mathematics, rigorous philosophy, poetry, and art, ones that do not make explicit claims of fitting reality. As the great game theorist Ariel Rubinstein holds: do your theories or mathematical representations, don't tell people in the real world *how* to apply them. Let those with skin in the game select what they need.

Let us get more practical about the side effect of modernism: as things get more technological, there is a growing separation between the maker and the user.

How to Beam Light on a Speaker

Those who give lectures to large audiences notice that they—and other speakers—are uncomfortable on the stage. The reason, it took me a decade to figure out, is that the stage light beaming into our eyes hinders our concentration. (This is how police interrogations of suspects used to be run: beam a light on the suspect, and wait for him to start "singing.") But in the thick of the lecture, speakers can't identify what is wrong, so they attribute the loss of concentration to, simply, being on the stage. So the practice continues. Why? Because those who lecture to large audiences don't work on lighting and light engineers don't lecture to large audiences.

Another small example of top-down progress: Metro North, the railroad between New York City and its northern suburbs, renovated its trains, in a total overhaul. Trains look more modern, neater, have brighter colors, and even have such amenities as power plugs for your computer (that nobody uses). But on the edge, by the wall, there used to be a flat ledge where one can put the morning cup of coffee: it is hard to read a book while holding a coffee cup. The designer (who either doesn't ride trains or rides trains but doesn't drink coffee while reading), thinking it is an aesthetic improvement, made the ledge slightly tilted, so it is impossible to put the cup on it.

This explains the more severe problems of landscaping and architecture: architects today build to impress other architects, and we end up with strange—irreversible—structures that do not satisfy the well-being of their residents; it takes time and a lot of progressive tinkering for that. Or some specialist sitting in the ministry of urban planning who doesn't live in the community will produce the equivalent of the tilted ledge—as an improvement, except at a much larger scale.

Specialization, as I will keep insisting, comes with side effects, one of which is separating labor from the fruits of labor.

Simplicity

Now skin in the game brings simplicity—the disarming simplicity of things properly done. People who see complicated solutions do not have an incentive to implement simplified ones. As we saw, a bureaucratized system will increase in complication from the interventionism of people who sell complicated solutions because that's what their position and training invite them to do.

> *Things designed by people without skin in the game tend to grow in complication (before their final collapse).*

There is absolutely no benefit for someone in such a position to propose something simple: when you are rewarded for perception, not results, you need to show sophistication. Anyone who has submitted a "scholarly" paper to a journal knows that you usually raise the odds of acceptance by making it more complicated than necessary. Further, there are side effects for problems that grow nonlinearly with such branching-out complications. Worse:

Non-skin-in-the-game people don't get simplicity.

I Am Dumb Without Skin in the Game

Let us return to *pathemata mathemata* (learning through pain) and consider its reverse: learning through thrills and pleasure. People have two brains, one when there is skin in the game, one when there is none. Skin in the game can make boring things less boring. When you have skin in the game, dull things like checking the safety of the aircraft because you may be forced to be a passenger in it cease to be boring. If you are an investor in a company, doing ultra-boring things like reading the footnotes of a financial statement (where the real information is to be found) becomes, well, almost not boring.

But there is an even more vital dimension. Many addicts who normally have a dull intellect and the mental nimbleness of a cauliflower—or a foreign policy expert—are capable of the most ingenious tricks to procure their drugs. When they undergo rehab, they are often told that should they spend half the mental energy trying to make money as they did procuring drugs, they are guaranteed to become millionaires. But, to no avail. Without the addiction, their miraculous powers go away. It was like a magical potion that gave remarkable powers to those seeking it, but not those drinking it.

A confession. When I don't have skin in the game, I am usually dumb. My knowledge of technical matters, such as risk and probability, did not initially come from books. It did not come from lofty philosophizing and scientific hunger. It did not even come from curiosity. It came from the thrills and hormonal flush one gets while taking risks in the markets. I never thought mathematics was something interesting to me until, when I was at Wharton, a friend told me about the financial options I described earlier (and their generalization, complex derivatives). I immediately decided to make a career in them. It was a combination of financial trading and complicated probability. The field was new and uncharted. I knew in my guts there were mistakes in the theories that used the conventional bell curve and ignored the impact of the tails (extreme events). I knew in my guts that academics had not the slightest clue about the risks. So, to find errors in the estimation of these probabilistic securities, I had to study probability, which mysteriously and instantly became fun, even gripping.

When there was risk on the line, suddenly a second brain in me manifested itself, and the probabilities of intricate sequences became suddenly effortless to analyze and map. When there is fire, you will run faster than in any competition. When you ski downhill some movements become effortless. Then I became dumb again when there was no real action. Furthermore, as traders the mathematics we used fit our problem like a glove, unlike academics with a theory looking for some application—in some cases we had to invent models out of thin air and could not afford the wrong equations. Applying math to practical problems was another business altogether; it meant a deep understanding of the problem before writing the equations.

But if you muster the strength to weight-lift a car to save a child, above your current abilities, the strength gained will stay after things calm down. So, unlike the drug addict who loses his resourcefulness, what you learn from the intensity and the focus you had when under the influence of risk stays with you. You may lose the sharpness, but nobody can take away what you've learned. This is the principal reason I am now fighting the conventional educational system, made by dweebs for dweebs. Many kids would learn to love mathematics if they had some investment in it, and, more crucially, they would build an instinct to spot its misapplications.

Regulations vs. Legal Systems

There are two ways to make citizens safe from large predators, say, big powerful corporations. The first one is to enact regulations—but these, aside from restricting individual freedoms, lead to another predation, this time by the state, its agents, and their cronies. More critically, people with good lawyers can game regulations (or, as we will see, make it known that they hire former regulators, and overpay for them, which signals a prospective bribe to those currently in office). And of course regulations, once in, stay in, and even when they are proven absurd, politicians are afraid of repealing them, under pressure from those benefiting from them. Given that regulations are additive, we soon end up tangled in complicated rules that choke enterprise. They also choke life.

For there are always parasites benefiting from regulation, situations where the businessperson uses government to derive profits, often through protective regulations and franchises. The mechanism is called regulatory recapture, as it cancels the effect of what a regulation was meant to do.

The other solution is to put skin in the game in transactions, in the form of legal liability, and the possibility of an efficient lawsuit. The Anglo-Saxon world has traditionally had a predilection for the legal approach instead of the regulatory one: *if you harm me, I can sue you.* This has led to the very sophisticated, adaptive, and balanced common law, built bottom-up, via trial and error. When people transact, they almost always prefer to agree (as part of the contract) on a Commonwealth (or formerly British-ruled) venue as a forum in the event of a dispute: Hong Kong and Singapore are the favorites in Asia, London and New York in the West. Common law is about the spirit while regulation, owing to its rigidity, is all about the letter.

If a big corporation pollutes your neighborhood, you can get together with your neighbors and sue the hell out of it. Some greedy lawyer will have the paperwork ready. The enemies of the corporation will be glad to help. And the potential costs of the settlement would be enough of a deterrent for the corporation to behave.

This doesn't mean one should never regulate at all. Some systemic effects may require regulation (say hidden tail risks of environmental ruins that show up too late). If you can't effectively sue, regulate.*

Now, even if regulations had a small net payoff for society, I would still prefer to be as free as possible, but assume my civil responsibility, face my fate, and pay the penalty if I harm others. This attitude is called deontic libertarianism (deontic comes from "duties"): by regulating you are robbing people of freedom. Some of us believe that freedom is one's first most essential good. This includes the freedom to make mistakes (those that harm only you); it is sacred to the point that it must never be traded against economic or other benefits.

---

* The Ralph Nader to whom I dedicate this book is the Ralph Nader who helped establish the legal mechanism to protect consumers and citizens from predators; less so the Ralph Nader who occasionally makes some calls to regulate.

IV. SOUL IN THE GAME

Finally and centrally, skin in the game is about honor as an existential commitment, and risk taking (a certain class of risks) as a separation between man and machine and (some may hate it) a ranking of humans.

If you do not take risks for your opinion, you are nothing.

And I will keep mentioning that I have no other definition of success than leading an honorable life. We intimated that it is dishonorable to let others die in your stead.

Honor implies that there are some actions you would categorically *never* do, regardless of the material rewards. She accepts no Faustian bargain, would not sell her body for $500; it also means she wouldn't do it for a million, nor a billion, nor a trillion. And it is not just a *via negativa* stance, honor means that there are things you would *do* unconditionally, regardless of the consequences. Consider duels, which have robbed us of the great Russian poet Pushkin, the French mathematician Galois, and, of course, many more, at a young age (and, in the case of Galois, a very young age): people incurred a significant probability of death just to save face. Living as a coward was simply no option, and death was vastly preferable, even if, as in the case of Galois, one invented a new and momentous branch of mathematics while still a teenager.* As a Spartan mother tells her departing son: "With it or on it," meaning either return with your shield or don't come back alive (the custom was to carry the dead body flat on it); only cowards throw away their shields to run faster.

If you want to consider how modernity has destroyed some of the foundations of human values, contrast the above unconditionals with modernistic accommodations: people who, say, work for disgusting lobbies (representing the interests of, say, Saudi Arabia in Washington) or knowingly play the usual unethical academic game, come to grips with their condition by producing arguments such as "I have children to put through college." People who are not morally independent tend to fit

---

* There is actually an argument in favor of duels: they prevent conflicts from engaging broader sets of people, that is, wars, by confining the problem to those with direct skin in the game.

ethics to their profession (with a minimum of spinning), rather than find a profession that fits their ethics.

Now there is another dimension of honor: engaging in actions going *beyond* mere skin in the game to put oneself at risk for others, have your skin in other people's game; sacrifice something significant for the sake of the collective.

However, there are activities in which one is imbued with a sense of pride and honor without grand-scale sacrifice: artisanal ones.

Artisans

Anything you do to optimize your work, cut some corners, or squeeze more "efficiency" out of it (and out of your life) will eventually make you dislike it.

Artisans have their soul in the game.

Primo, artisans do things for existential reasons first, financial and commercial ones later. Their decision making is never fully financial, but it remains financial. *Secundo,* they have some type of "art" in their profession; they stay away from most aspects of industrialization; they combine art and business. *Tertio,* they put some soul in their work: they would not sell something defective or even of compromised quality because it hurts their pride. Finally, they have sacred taboos, things they would not do even if it markedly increased profitability.

Compendiaria res improbitas, virtusque tarda—the villainous takes the short road, virtue the longer one. In other words, cutting corners is dishonest.

Let me illustrate with my own profession. It is easy to see that a writer is effectively an artisan: book sales are not the end motive, only a secondary target (even then). You preserve some sanctity of the product with strong prohibitions. For instance, in the early 2000s, the writer Fay Weldon was paid by the jewelry chain Bulgari to advertise their brand by weaving recommendations for their great products into the plot of her novel. A nightmare ensued; there was a generalized feeling of disgust on the part of the literary community.

I also recall in the 1980s some people trying to give away books for free, but with advertisements in the midst of the text, as with magazines. The project failed.

Nor do we industrialize writing. You would be disappointed if I hired a group of writers to "help" as it would be more efficient. Some authors, such as Jerzy Kosinski, have tried to write books by subcontracting sections, leading to a complete ostracism after the discovery. Few of those writers-cum-contractors have seen their work survive. But there are exceptions, such as Alexandre Dumas *père* who was said to run a workshop of ghostwriters (forty-five), which allowed him to scale his production up to one hundred and fifty novels, with the joke that he read *some* of his own books. But in general, output is not scalable (even if the sales of a book are). Dumas may be the exception that confirms the rule.

Now, something very practical. One of the best pieces of advice I have ever received was the recommendation by a very successful (and happy) older entrepreneur, Yossi Vardi, to have no assistant. The mere presence of an assistant suspends your natural filtering—and its absence forces you to do only things you enjoy, and progressively steer your life that way. (By assistant here I exclude someone hired for a specific task, such as grading papers, helping with accounting, or watering plants; just some guardian angel overseeing all your activities). This is a *via negativa* approach: you want maximal free time, not maximal activity, and you can assess your own "success" according to such metric. Otherwise, you end up assisting your assistants, or being forced to "explain" how to do things, which requires more mental effort than doing the thing itself. In fact, beyond my writing and research life, this has proved to be great financial advice as I am freer, more nimble, and have a very high benchmark for doing something, while my peers have their days filled with unnecessary "meetings" and unnecessary correspondence.

> *Having an assistant (except for the strictly necessary) removes your soul from the game.*

Think of the effect of using a handheld translator on your next trip to Mexico in place of acquiring a robust vocabulary in Spanish by contact with locals. Assistance moves you one step away from authenticity.

Academics can be artisans. Even those economists who, misunderstanding Adam Smith, claim that humans are here to "seek maximization" of their income, express these ideas for free, and boast to not be into lowly commercial profit seeking, not seeing the contradiction.*

A Caveat with Entrepreneurs

Entrepreneurs are heroes in our society. They fail for the rest of us. But owing to funding and current venture capital mechanisms, many people mistaken for entrepreneurs fail to have true skin in the game in the sense that their aim is to either cash out by selling the company they helped create to someone else, or "go public" by issuing shares in the stock market. The true value of the company, what it makes, and its long-term survival are of small relevance to them. This is a pure financing scheme and we will exclude this class of people from our "entrepreneur" risk-taker class (this form of entrepreneurship is the equivalent of bringing great-looking and marketable children into the world with the sole aim of selling them at age four). We can easily identify them by their ability to write a convincing business plan.

Companies beyond the entrepreneur stage start to rot. One of the reasons corporations have the mortality of cancer patients is the assignment of time-defined duties. Once you change assignment—or, better, company—you can now say about the deep Bob Rubin–style risks that emerge: "It's not my problem anymore." The same happens when you sell out, so remember that:

The skills at making things diverge from those at selling things.

Arrogant Will Do

Products or companies that bear the owner's name convey very valuable messages. They are shouting that they have something to lose. Eponymy indicates both a commitment to the company and a confidence in the product. A friend of mine, Paul Wilmott, is often called an egomaniac for

---

* The most skilled traders are often wealthy, but not the wealthiest; many traders trade out of passion and aren't interested in running a business. To become a billionaire, one needs an appetite for meetings, discussions with lawyers and regulators, that type of thing.

having his name on a mathematical finance technical journal (*Wilmott*), which at the time of writing is undoubtedly the best. "Egomaniac" is good for the product. But if you can't get "egomaniac," "arrogant" will do.

Citizenship de Plaisance

Many well-to-do people who come to live in the United States avoid becoming citizens while living here indefinitely. They have a permanent residence permit as a free option, as it is a right, but not an obligation, for they can return it with a simple procedure. You ask them why they don't take the oath in front of a judge, then throw a cocktail party at a waterfront country club. The typical answer is: *taxes*. Once you become a U.S. citizen, you will have to pay taxes on your worldwide income, even if you live overseas. And it is not easily reversible, so you lose the optionality. But other Western countries, such as France and the United Kingdom, allow their citizens considerable exemptions if they reside in some tax haven. This invites a collection of people to "buy" a citizenship via investments and minimum residence, get the passport, then go live somewhere tax-free.

A country should not tolerate fair-weather friends. There is something offensive in having a nationality without skin in the game, just to travel and pass borders, without the downside that comes with the passport.

My parents are French citizens, which would have made it easy for me to get naturalized a few decades ago. But it did not feel right; it even felt downright offensive. And unless I developed an emotional attachment to France via skin in the game, I couldn't. It would have felt fake to see my bearded face on a French passport. The only passport I would have considered is the Greek (or Cypriot) one, as I feel some deep ancestral and socio-cultural bond to the Hellenistic world.

But I came to the U.S., embraced the place, and took the passport as commitment: it became my identity, good or bad, tax or no tax. Many people made fun of my decision, as most of my income comes from overseas and, if I took official residence in, say, Cyprus or Malta, I would be making many more dollars. If I wanted to lower taxes for myself, and I do, I am obligated to fight for it, for both myself and the collective, other taxpayers, and to not run away.

Skin in the game.

Heroes Were Not Library Rats

If you want to study classical values such as courage or learn about stoicism, don't necessarily look for classicists. One is never a career academic without a reason. Read the texts themselves: Seneca, Caesar, or Marcus Aurelius, when possible. Or read commentators on the classics who were doers themselves, such as Montaigne—people who at some point had some skin in the game, then retired to write books. Avoid the intermediary, when possible. Or fuhgetaboud the texts, just engage in acts of courage.

For studying courage in textbooks doesn't make you any more courageous than eating cow meat makes you bovine.

By some mysterious mental mechanism, people fail to realize that the principal thing you can learn from a professor is how to be a professor—and the chief thing you can learn from, say, a life coach or inspirational speaker is how to become a life coach or inspirational speaker. So remember that the heroes of history were not classicists and library rats, those people who live vicariously in their texts. They were people of deeds and had to be endowed with the spirit of risk taking. To get into their psyches, you will need someone other than a career professor teaching stoicism.* They almost always don't get it (actually, they never get it). In my experience, from a series of personal fights, many of these "classicists," who know in intimate detail what people of courage such as Alexander, Cleopatra, Caesar, Hannibal, Julian, Leonidas, Zenobia ate for breakfast, can't produce a shade of intellectual valor. Is it that academia (and journalism) is fundamentally the refuge of the stochastophobe *tawker*? That is, the voyeur who wants to watch but not take risks? It appears so. The most important chapter of the book, and conveniently the last one, "The Logic of Risk Taking," shows how some central elements of risks, while obvious to practitioners, can be missed by theoreticians for more than two centuries!

---

* My understanding of Seneca, as expressed in *Antifragile,* is all about asymmetry (and optionality), both financial and emotional. As a risk taker, I get something impossible to convey to classicists, which makes it frustrating to see accounts of him that miss the essential.

Soul in the Game and Some (Not Too Much) Protectionism

Let us now apply these ideas to modern times. Recall the story of the architects separated from the real users. This extends to more general systemic effects, such as protectionism and globalism. Seen that way, the rise of *some* protectionism may have a strong rationale—and an economic one.

I leave aside the argument that globalization leads to a Tower-of-Babel style cacophony, owing to the imbalance in the noise-signal ratio. The point here is that workers, people who do things, have each an artisan in them. For, contrary to what lobbyists paid by international large corporations are trying to make us believe, such protectionism does not even conflict with *economic* thinking, what is called neoclassical economics. It is not inconsistent with the *mathematical* axioms of economic decision making, on which economics lays its foundations, to behave in a way that does not maximize one's narrowly defined dollar-denominated bottom line at the expense of other things. As I said earlier in the chapter, it is not irrational, according to economic theory, to leave money on the table because of your personal preference; the notion of incentives as limited to financial gain cannot otherwise explain the very existence of an economics academia that promotes the idea of self-interest.[*]

We may be better off in a narrowly defined accounting sense (in the aggregate) by exporting jobs. But that's not what people may really want. I write because that's what I am designed to do, just as a knife cuts because that's what its mission is, Aristotle's *arête*—and subcontracting my research and writing to China or Tunisia would (perhaps) increase my productivity, but deprive me of my identity.

So people might want to *do* things. Just to do things, because they feel it is part of their identity. A shoemaker in Westchester County wants to be a shoemaker, to enjoy the fruits of his labor and the pride of seeing his merchandise in the stores, even if his so-called "economic" condition might benefit from letting a Chinese factory make the shoes and converting to another profession. Even if such a new system allows him

---

[*] For a long time, some Swiss cantons—democratically—banned the sale of property to foreigners, to prevent the disruptions from rich jet-setters without skin in the game in the place who come to bid up prices, and hurt new young buyers permanently priced out of the market. Is this silly, economically? Not at all, though some real estate developers would strongly disagree.

to buy flat-screen TV sets, more cotton shirts, and cheaper bicycles, something is missing. It may be cruel to cheat people of their profession. People want to have their soul in the game.

In that sense, decentralization and fragmentation, aside from stabilizing the system, improves people's connection to their labor.

Skin in the Ruling

Let us close with a historical anecdote.

Some might well ask: law is great, but what would you do with a corrupt or incompetent judge? He could make mistakes with impunity. He could be the weak link. Not quite, or at least not historically. A friend once showed me a Dutch painting representing the Judgment of Cambyses. The scene is from the story reported by Herodotus, concerning the corrupt Persian judge Sisamnes. He was flayed alive on the order of King Cambyses as a punishment for violating the rules of justice. The scene of the painting is Sisamnes's son dispensing justice from his father's chair, upholstered with the flayed skin as a reminder that justice comes with, literally, skin in the game.

PROLOGUE, PART 3

The Ribs of the Incerto

Seven pages per sitting, seven pages annum is the perfect rate—
Rereaders need rereviewers

———

Now that we've outlined the main ideas, let us see how this discussion fits the rest of the *Incerto* project. Just as Eve came out of Adam's ribs, so does each book of the *Incerto* emerge from the penultimate one's ribs. *The Black Swan* was an occasional discussion in *Fooled by Randomness;* the concept of convexity to random events, the theme of *Antifragile,* was adumbrated in *The Black Swan;* and, finally, *Skin in the Game* was a segment of *Antifragile* under the banner: *Thou shalt not become antifragile at the expense of others.* Simply, asymmetry in risk bearing leads to imbalances and, potentially, to systemic ruin.

The Bob Rubin trade connects to my business as a trader (as we saw, when these people make money, they keep the profits; when they lose, someone else bears the costs while they do their Black Swan invocation). Its manifestations are so ubiquitous that it has been the backbone of every book of the *Incerto.* Whenever there is a mismatch between a bonus period (yearly) and the statistical occurrence of a blowup (every, say, ten years) the agent has an incentive to play the Bob Rubin risk-transfer game. Given the number of people trying to get on the money-making bus, there is a progressive accumulation of Black Swan risks in such systems. Then, boom, the systemic blowup happens.*

---

* The hidden risk transfer is not limited to bankers and corporations. Some segments of the population play it quite effectively. For instance, people who live in those coastal areas that are prone to hurricanes and floods are effectively subsidized by the state—hence taxpayers. Although they play

THE ROAD

We will be guided by what is most lively. The ethics side is straightforward, as part of the general Fat Tony–Isocrates asymmetry, and I have gone deeply into the matter thanks to a highly argumentative collaboration with the philosopher (and walking companion) Constantine Sandis. Tort law is equally straightforward, and I had thought it would occupy a large section of this volume, but it will thankfully be minimal. Why?

Tort law is insipid to those who don't have the temperament that takes one to law school. For, prompted by the fearless Ralph Nader, a coffee table in my study accumulated close to twenty volumes on contract law and torts. But I found the topic so dull that it was a Herculean task for me to read more than seven lines per sitting (which is the reason God mercifully invented social media and Twitter fights): unlike science and mathematics, law, while being very rigorous, doesn't offer surprises. Law cannot be playful. The mere sight of these books reminds me of a lunch with a former member of the Federal Reserve Board, the kind of thing to which one should never be subjected more than once per lifetime. So I will dispatch the topic of torts in a few lines.

As we intimated in the first paragraphs of the introduction, some nonsoporific topics (pagan theology, religious practices, complexity theory, ancient and medieval history, and, of course, probability and risk taking) match this author's naturalistic filter. Simply: if you can't put your soul into something, give it up and leave that stuff to someone else.

Talking about soul in the game, I had to overcome some shame as follows. In the Paris episode of Hammurabi at the Louvre, when I stood in front of the imposing basalt stele (in the room with Koreans with selfie sticks), I felt uneasy not being able to read the stuff and having to rely on experts. What experts? This would have been fine if it was a cultural journey, but here I am professionally writing a book going very deep into that stuff! It felt like cheating not knowing the ancient text the way it was read and recited at the time. In addition, one of my episodic hobbies is Semitic philology, so I had no excuse. So I have been distracted by an obsession to learn enough Akkadian in order to recite Hammurabi's law with Semitic phonetics, sort of having some soul in

---

victims on television after an event happens, they and the real estate developers are getting the benefits others pay for.

the game. It may have delayed the completion of this book, but, at least, when I mention Hammurabi, my conscience doesn't make me feel I am faking anything.

AN ENHANCED DETECTOR

This book came after a deep—nonacademic—unplanned flirtation with mathematics. For after finishing *Antifragile,* I thought of retiring my pen for a while and settling into the comfortable life of a quarter university position, enjoying squid-ink pasta in bon vivant company, lifting weights with my blue-collar friends, and playing bridge in the afternoon, the kind of tranquil, worry-free life of the nineteenth-century gentry.

What I didn't forecast is that my dream of a *tranquil* life lasted only a few weeks. For I exhibited no skills whatsoever in retirement activities such as contract bridge, chess, lotto, visits to the pyramids in Mexico, etc. I once, by happenstance, tried to solve a mathematical brain teaser, and it lead to five years of compulsive, time-invasive mathematical practice, with the obsessive bouts that plague people inhabited with problems. As usual with these things, I didn't do mathematics to solve a problem, just to satisfy a fixation. But I never expected the following effect. It made my bull***t detector so sensitive that listening to well-marketed nonsense (by verbalistic people, especially academics) had the same effect as being put in a room with instances of randomly occurring piercing and jarring sounds, the type that kill animals. I am never bothered by normal people; it is the bull***tter in the "intellectual" profession who bothers me. Seeing the psychologist Steven Pinker making pronouncements about things intellectual has a similar effect to encountering a drive-in Burger King while hiking in the middle of a national park.

It is under such an oversensitive bull***t detector that I have been writing this book.

THE BOOK REVIEWERS

And since we are talking about books, I close this introductory section with that one thing I've learned from my time in that business. Many book reviewers are intellectually honest and straightforward people, but the industry has a fundamental conflict with the public, even while appointing itself as representative of the general class of readers. For instance, when it comes to books written by risk takers, the general public (and some, but very few, book editors) can detect what is interesting to them in a certain account, something those in the fake space of word production (in other words, nondoers) chronically fail to get—and they cannot understand what it is that they don't understand because they are not really part of active and transactional life.

Nor can book reviewers—by the very definition of their function—judge books that one *rereads*. For those familiar with the idea of non-linear effects from *Antifragile,* learning is rooted in repetition and convexity, meaning that the reading of a single text twice is more profit-able than reading two different things once, provided of course that said text has some depth of content. The convexity is implanted in Semitic vocabulary: *mishnah,* which in Hebrew refers to the pre-Talmudic com-pilation of oral tradition, means "doubling"; *midrash* itself may also be related to stamping and repeated grinding, and has a counterpart in the *madrassa* of the children of Ishmael.

Books should be organized the way the reader reads, or wants to read, and according to how deep the author wants to go into a topic, not to make life easy for the critics to write reviews. Book reviewers are bad middlemen; they are currently in the process of being disintermediated just like taxi companies (what some call *Uberized*).

How? There is, here again, a skin-in-the-game problem: a conflict of interest between professional reviewers who think they ought to decide how books should be written, and genuine readers who actually read books because they like to read books. For one, reviewers command an unchecked and arbitrary power over authors: someone has to have read the book to notice that a reviewer is full of baloney, so in the absence of skin in the game, reviewers such as Michiko Kakutani of *The New York Times* (now retired) or David Runciman, who writes for *The Guardian,* can go on forever without anyone knowing they are either fabricating or drunk (or, as I am certain, in the case of Kakutani, both). Book reviews are judged according to how *plausible* and well written they are, never in how they map to the book (unless of course the author makes them accountable for misrepresentations).[*]

---

[*] It took close to three years for *Fooled by Randomness* to be understood as "there is more luck than you think," rather than the message people were getting from reviews: "it is all dumb luck." Most books don't survive three months.

Now, almost two decades after the first installment of the *Incerto*, I have established ways to interact directly with you, the reader.

ORGANIZATION OF THE BOOK

Book 1 was the introduction we just saw, with its three parts.

Book 2, "A First Look at Agency," is a deeper exposition of symmetry and agency in risk sharing, bridging commercial conflict of interest with general ethics. It also introduces us briefly to the notion of scaling and the difference between individual and collective, hence the limitations of globalism and universalism.

Book 3, "That Greatest Asymmetry," is about the minority rule by which a small segment of the population inflicts its preferences on the general population. The (short) appendix for Book 3 shows 1) how a collection of units doesn't behave like a sum of units, but something with a mind of its own, and 2) the consequences of much of something called social "science."

Book 4, "Wolves Among Dogs," deals with dependence and, let's call a spade a spade, *slavery* in modern life: why employees exist because they have much more to lose than contractors. It also shows how, even if you are independent and have *f*** you money*, you are vulnerable if people you care about can be targeted by evil corporations and groups.

Book 5, "Being Alive Means Taking Certain Risks," shows in Chapter 5 how risk taking makes you look superficially less attractive, but vastly more convincing. It clarifies the difference between life as real life and life as imagined in an experience machine, how Jesus had to be man, not quite god, and how Donaldo won the election *thanks* to his imperfections. Chapter 6, "The Intellectual Yet Idiot," presents the IYI who doesn't know that having skin in the game makes you understand the world (which includes bicycle riding) better than lectures. Chapter 7 explains the difference between inequality in risk and inequality in salary: you can be richer, but then you should be a real person and take some risk. It also presents a dynamic view of inequality, as opposed to the IYI static one. The most egregious contributor to inequality is the condition of a high-ranking civil servant or tenured academic, not that of an entrepreneur. Chapter 8 explains the Lindy effect, that expert of experts who can tell us why plumbers are experts, but not clinical psychologists, why *The New Yorker* commentators on experts are not themselves experts. The Lindy effect separates things that gain from time from those that are destroyed by it.

Book 6, "Deeper into Agency," looks for consequential hidden asymmetries. Chapter 9 shows that, viewed from the standpoint of practice, the world is simpler and solid experts don't look like actors playing the part. The chapter presents BS detection heuristics. Chapter 10 shows how rich people are suckers who fall prey to people complicating their lifestyle to sell them something. Chapter 11 explains the difference between threats and real threats and shows how you can own an enemy by not killing him. Chapter 12 presents the agency problem of journalists: they will sacrifice truth and build a wrong narrative because of the necessity to please other journalists. Chapter 13 explains why virtue requires risk taking, not the reputational risk reduction of playing white knight on the Internet or writing a check to some nongovernmental organization (NGO) who might help destroy the world. Chapter 14 explains the agency problem of people in geopolitics, and historians who tend to report on wars rather than peace, leaving us with a deformed view of the past. History is also plagued with probabilistic confusions. If we got rid of "peace" experts, the world would be safer and many problems would be solved organically.

Book 7, "Religion, Belief, and Skin in the Game," explains creeds in terms of skin in the game and revealed preferences: how atheists are functionally indistinguishable from Christians, though not Salafi Muslims. Avoid the verbalistic: "religions" are not quite religions: some are philosophies, others are just legal systems.

Book 8, "Risk and Rationality," has the two central chapters, which I elected to leave for the end. There is no rigorous definition of rationality that is not related to skin in the game; it is all about actions, not verbs, thoughts, and *tawk*. Chapter 19, "The Logic of Risk Taking," summarizes all my tenets about risk and exposes the errors concerning small-probability events. It also classifies risks in layers (from the individual to the collective) and manages to prove that courage and prudence are not in contradiction provided one is acting for the benefit of the collective. It explains ergodicity, which was left hanging. Finally, the chapter outlines what we call the precautionary principle.

Appendix:
Asymmetries in Life and Things

TABLE 2 • ASYMMETRIES IN SOCIETY

WHERE WE LEFT OFF IN *ANTIFRAGILE*

NO SKIN IN THE GAME	SKIN IN THE GAME	SKIN IN THE GAME OF OTHERS, OR SOUL IN THE GAME
(Keeps upside, transfers downside to others, owns a hidden option at someone else's expense)	*(Keeps his own downside, takes his or her own risk)*	*(Takes the downside on behalf of others, or for universal values)*
Bureaucrats, policy wonks	Citizens	Saints, knights, warriors, soldiers
Consultants, sophists	Merchants, businessmen	Prophets, philosophers (in the pre-modern sense)
Large corporations with access to the state	Artisans	Artists, some artisans
Corporate executives (with suit)	Entrepreneurs	Entrepreneurs/Innovators
Scientists who play the system, theoreticians, data miners, observational studies	Laboratory and field experimenters	Maverick scientists who take risks with conjecture at distance from common beliefs
Centralized government	Government of city-states	Municipal government
Copy editors	Writers, (some) editors	Real writers
Journalists who "analyze" and predict	Speculators	Journalists who take risks and *expose* frauds (powerful regimes, corporations), rebels

NO SKIN IN THE GAME	SKIN IN THE GAME	SKIN IN THE GAME OF OTHERS, OR SOUL IN THE GAME
Politicians	Activists	Dissidents, revolutionaries
Bankers	Hedge fund traders	(They would not engage in vulgar commerce)
Seeks awards, prizes, honors, ceremonies, medals, tea with the Queen of England, membership in academies, handshake with Obama		Highest—even only— award is death for one's ideas or positions: Socrates, Jesus, Saint Catherine, Hypatia, Joan of Arc

---

BOOK 2

A FIRST LOOK AT AGENCY

CHAPTER 1

Why Each One Should Eat His Own Turtles: Equality in Uncertainty

Taste of turtle—Where are the new customers?—Sharia and asymmetry—There are the Swiss, and other people—Rav Safra and the Swiss (but different Swiss)

———

Y ou who caught the turtles better eat them, goes the ancient adage.*
The origin of the expression is as follows. It was said that a group of fishermen caught a large number of turtles. After cooking them, they found out at the communal meal that these sea animals were much less edible than they thought: not many members of the group were willing to eat them. But Mercury happened to be passing by— Mercury was the most multitasking, sort of put-together god, as he was the boss of commerce, abundance, messengers, the underworld, as well as the patron of thieves and brigands and, not surprisingly, luck. The group invited him to join them and offered him the turtles to eat. Detecting that he was only invited to relieve them of the unwanted food, he forced them all to eat the turtles, thus establishing the principle that you need to eat what you feed others.

A CUSTOMER IS BORN EVERY DAY

I have learned a lesson from my own naive experiences:

> *Beware of the person who gives advice, telling you that a certain action on your part is "good for you" while it is also good for him, while the harm to you doesn't directly affect him.*

———

* *Ipsi testudines edite, qui cepistis.*

Of course such advice is usually unsolicited. The asymmetry is when said advice applies to you but not to him—he may be selling you something, or trying to get you to marry his daughter or hire his son-in-law.

Years ago I received a letter from a lecture agent. His letter was clear; it had about ten questions of the type "Do you have the time to field requests?," "Can you handle the organization of the trip?" The gist of it was that a lecture agent would make my life better and make room for the pursuit of knowledge or whatever else I was about (a deeper understanding of gardening, stamp collections, Mediterranean genetics, or squid-ink recipes) while the burden of the gritty would fall on someone else. And it wasn't any lecture agent: only *he* could do all these things; he reads books and can get in the mind of intellectuals (at the time I didn't feel insulted by being called an intellectual). As is typical with people who volunteer unsolicited advice, I smelled a rat: at no phase in the discussion did he refrain from letting me know that it was "good for me."

As a sucker, while I didn't buy into the argument, I ended up doing business with him, letting him handle a booking in the foreign country where he was based. Things went fine until, six years later, I received a letter from the tax authorities of that country. I immediately contacted him to wonder if similar U.S. citizens he had hired incurred such tax conflict, or if he had heard of similar situations. His reply was immediate and curt: "I am not your tax attorney"—volunteering no information as to whether other U.S. customers who hired him because it was "good for them" encountered such a problem.

Indeed, in the dozen or so cases I can pull from memory, it always turns out that what is presented as good for you is not really good for you but certainly good for the other party. As a trader, you learn to identify and deal with upright people, those who inform you that they have something to sell, by explaining that the transaction arises for their own benefit, with such questions as "Do you have an *ax*?" (meaning an inquiry whether you have a certain interest). Avoid at all costs those who call you to tout a certain product disguised with advice. In fact the story of the turtle is the archetype of the history of transactions between mortals.

I worked once for a U.S. investment bank, one of the prestigious variety, called "white shoe" because the partners were members of hard-to-join golf clubs for proto-aristocrats where they played the game wearing white footwear. As with all such firms, an image of ethics and professionalism was cultivated, emphasized, and protected. But the job of the salespeople (actually, salesmen) on days when they wore black shoes was to "unload" inventory with which traders were "stuffed," that is, securities they had in excess in their books and needed to get rid of to lower their risk profile. Selling to other dealers was out of the question as professional traders, typically non-golfers, would smell excess inventory and cause the price to drop. So they needed to sell to some client, on what is called the "buy side." Some traders paid the sales force with (percentage) "points," a variable compensation that increased with our eagerness to part with securities. Salesmen took clients out to dinner, bought them expensive wine (often, ostensibly the highest on the menu), and got a huge return on the thousands of dollars of restaurant bills by unloading the unwanted stuff on them. One expert salesman candidly explained to me: "If I buy the client, someone working for the finance department of a municipality who buys his suits at some department store in New Jersey, a bottle of $2,000 wine, I own him for the next few months. I can get at least $100,000 profits out of him. Nothing in the *mahket* gives you such return."

Salesmen hawked how a given security would be perfect for the client's portfolio, how they were certain it would rise in price and how the client would suffer great regret if he missed "such an opportunity"— that type of discourse. Salespeople are experts in the art of psychological manipulation, making the client trade, often against his own interest, all the while being happy about it and loving them and their company. One of the top salesmen at the firm, a man with huge charisma who came to work in a chauffeured Rolls Royce, was once asked whether customers didn't get upset when they got the short end of the stick. "Rip them off, don't tick them off" was his answer. He also added, "Remember that every day a new customer is born."

As the Romans were fully aware, one lauds merrily the merchandise to get rid of it.*

---

* *Plenius aequo laudat venalis qui vult extrudere merces.* —Horace

THE PRICE OF CORN IN RHODES

So, "giving advice" as a sales pitch is fundamentally unethical—selling cannot be deemed advice. We can safely settle on that. You can give advice, or you can sell (by advertising the quality of the product), and the two need to be kept separate.

But there is an associated problem in the course of the transactions: how much should the seller reveal to the buyer?

The question "Is it ethical to sell something to someone knowing the price will eventually drop?" is an ancient one—but its solution is no less straightforward. The debate goes back to a disagreement between two stoic philosophers, Diogenes of Babylon and his student Antipater of Tarsus, who took the higher moral ground on asymmetric information and seems to match the ethics endorsed by this author. Not a piece from both authors is extant, but we know quite a bit from secondary sources, or, in the case of Cicero, tertiary. The question was presented as follows, retailed by Cicero in *De Officiis*. Assume a man brought a large shipment of corn from Alexandria to Rhodes, at a time when corn was expensive in Rhodes because of shortage and famine. Suppose that he also knew that many boats had set sail from Alexandria on their way to Rhodes with similar merchandise. Does he have to inform the Rhodians? How can one act honorably or dishonorably in these circumstances?

We traders had a straightforward answer. Again, "stuffing"—selling quantities to people without informing them that there are large inventories waiting to be sold. An upright trader will not do that to other professional traders; it was a no-no. The penalty was ostracism. But it was sort of permissible to do it to the anonymous market and the faceless nontraders, or those we called "the Swiss," some random suckers far away. There were people with whom we had a *relational* rapport, others with whom we had a *transactional* one. The two were separated by an ethical wall, much like the case with domestic animals that cannot be harmed, while rules on cruelty are lifted when it comes to cockroaches.

Diogenes held that the seller ought to disclose as much as civil law requires. As for Antipater, he believed that everything ought to be disclosed—beyond the law—so that there was nothing that the seller knew that the buyer didn't know.

Clearly Antipater's position is more robust—robust being invariant to time, place, situation, and color of the eyes of the participants. Take for now that

> *The ethical is always more robust than the legal. Over time, it is the legal that should converge to the ethical, never the reverse.*

Hence:

> *Laws come and go; ethics stay.*

For the notion of "law" is ambiguous and highly jurisdiction dependent: in the U.S., civil law, thanks to consumer advocates and similar movements, integrates such disclosures, while other countries have different laws. This is particularly visible with securities laws, as there are "front running" regulations and those concerning insider information that make such disclosure mandatory in the U.S., though this wasn't so for a long time in Europe.

Indeed much of the work of investment banks in my day was to play on regulations, find loopholes in the laws. And, counterintuitively, the more regulations, the easier it was to make money.

EQUALITY IN UNCERTAINTY

Which brings us to asymmetry, the core concept behind skin in the game. The question becomes: to what extent can people in a transaction have an informational differential between them? The ancient Mediterranean and, to some extent, the modern world, seem to have converged to Antipater's position. While we have "buyer beware" (*caveat emptor*) in the Anglo-Saxon West, the idea is rather new, and never general, often mitigated by lemon laws. (A "lemon" was originally a chronically defective car, say, my convertible Mini, in love with the garage, now generalized to apply to anything that moves).

So, to the question voiced by Cicero in the debate between the two ancient stoics, *"If a man knowingly offers for sale wine that is spoiling, ought he to tell his customers?,"* the world is getting closer to the position of transparency, not necessarily via regulations as much as thanks to tort laws, and one's ability to sue for harm in the event a seller deceives him or her. Recall that tort laws put some of the seller's skin back into the game—which is why they are reviled, hated by corporations. But tort laws have side effects—they should only be used in a nonnaive way, that is, in a way that cannot be gamed. As we will see in the discussion of the visit to the doctor, they will be gamed.

Sharia, in particular the law regulating Islamic transactions and finance, is of interest to us insofar as it preserves some of the lost Mediterranean and Babylonian methods and practices—not to prop up the ego of Saudi princes. It exists at the intersection of Greco-Roman law (as reflected from people in Semitic territories' contact with the school of law of Berytus), Phoenician trading rules, Babylonian legislations, and Arab tribal commercial customs and, as such, it provides a repository of ancient Mediterranean and Semitic lore. I hence view Sharia as a museum of the history of ideas on symmetry in transactions. Sharia establishes the interdict of *gharar*, drastic enough to be totally banned in any form of transaction. It is an extremely sophisticated term in decision theory that does not exist in English; it means both uncertainty and deception—my personal take is that it means something beyond informational asymmetry between agents: *inequality of uncertainty*. Simply, as the aim is for both parties in a transaction to have the same uncertainty facing random outcomes, an asymmetry becomes equivalent to theft. Or more robustly:

> No *person in a transaction should have certainty about the outcome while the other one has uncertainty.*

Gharar, like every legalistic construct, will have its flaws; it remains weaker than Antipater's approach. If only one party in a transaction has certainty all the way through, it is a violation of Sharia. But if there is a weak form of asymmetry, say, someone has inside information which gives an edge in the markets, there is no *gharar* as there remains enough uncertainty for both parties, given that the price is in the future and only God knows the future. Selling a defective product (where there is certainty as to the defect), on the other hand, is illegal. So the knowledge by the seller of corn in Rhodes in my first example does not fall under *gharar,* while the second case, that of a defective liquid, would.

As we see, the problem of asymmetry is so complicated that different schools give different ethical solutions, so let us look at the Talmudic approach.

RAV SAFRA AND THE SWISS

Jewish ethics on the matter is closer to Antipater than Diogenes in its aims at transparency. Not only should there be transparency concerning the merchandise, but perhaps there has to be transparency concerning what the seller has in mind, what he thinks *deep down*. The medieval rabbi Shlomo Yitzhaki (aka Salomon Isaacides), known as "Rashi," relates the following story. Rav Safra, a third-century Babylonian scholar who was also an active trader, was offering some goods for sale. A buyer came as he was praying in silence, tried to purchase the merchandise at an initial price, and given that the rabbi did not reply, raised the price. But Rav Safra had no intention of selling at a higher price than the initial offer, and felt that he had to honor the initial *intention*. Now the question: Is Rav Safra obligated to sell at the initial price, or should he take the improved one?

Such total transparency is not absurd and not uncommon in what seems to be a cutthroat world of transactions, my former world of trading. I have frequently faced that problem as a trader and will side in favor of Rav Safra's action in the debate. Let us follow the logic. Recall the rapacity of salespeople earlier in the chapter. Sometimes I would offer something for sale for, say, $5, but communicated with the client through a salesperson, and the salesperson would come back with an "improvement," of $5.10. Something never felt right about the extra ten cents. It was, simply, not a sustainable way of doing business. What if the customer subsequently discovered that my initial offer was $5? No compensation is worth the feeling of shame. The overcharge falls in the same category as the act of "stuffing" people with bad merchandise. Now, to apply this to Rav Safra's story, what if he sold to one client at the marked-up price, and to another one the exact same item for the initial price, and the two buyers happened to know one another? What if they were agents for the same customer?

It may not be ethically required, but the most effective, shame-free policy is maximal transparency, even transparency of intentions.

However, the story doesn't tell us whether the purchaser was a "Swiss," those outsiders our ethical rules don't apply to. I suspect that there would be a species for which our ethical rules would be relaxed or possibly lifted. Recall our discussion of Kant: theory is too theoretical for humans. The more confined our ethics, the less abstract, the better it works. Otherwise, as we will see with Elinor Ostrom's result later in this chapter, the system cannot function properly. And, before Ostrom, our old friend Friedrich Nietzsche got the point:

Sympathy for all would be tyranny for thee, my good neighbor.

Nietzsche, by the way, is the one person Fat Tony (upon hearing his quotes) said he would never debate.

MEMBERS AND NON-MEMBERS

For the exclusion of the "Swiss" from our ethical realm is not trivial. Things don't "scale" and generalize, which is why I have trouble with intellectuals talking about abstract notions. A country is not a large city, a city is not a large family, and, sorry, the world is not a large village. There are scale transformations we will discuss here, and in the appendix of Book 3.

When Athenians treat all opinions equally and discuss "democracy," they only apply it to their citizens, not slaves or metics (the equivalent of green card or H-1B visa holders). Effectively, Theodosius's code deprived Roman citizens who married "barbarians" of their legal rights—hence ethical parity with others. They lost their club membership. As to Jewish ethics: it distinguishes between thick blood and thin blood: we are all brothers, but some are more brothers than others.

Free citizens, in ancient and post-classical societies, were traditionally part of clubs, with rules and member behavior similar to those in today's country clubs, with an inside and an outside. As club members know, the very purpose of a club is exclusion and size limitation. Spartans could hunt and kill Helots, those noncitizens with a status of slaves, *for training*, but they were otherwise equal to other Spartans and expected to die for the sake of Sparta. The large cities in the pre-Christian ancient world, particularly in the Levant and Asia Minor, were full of fraternities and clubs, open and (often) secret societies—there was even such a thing as funeral clubs, where members shared the costs, and participated in the ceremonials, of funerals.

Today's Roma people (aka Gypsies) have tons of strict rules of behavior toward Gypsies, and others toward the *unclean* non-Gypsies called *payos*. And, as the anthropologist David Graeber has observed, even the investment bank Goldman Sachs, known for its aggressive cupidity, acts like a communist community from *within*, thanks to the partnership system of governance.

So we exercise our ethical rules, but there is a limit—from scaling—beyond which the rules cease to apply. It is unfortunate, but the general kills the particular. The question we will reexamine later, after deeper discussion of complexity theory, is whether it is possible to be both ethical and universalist. In theory, yes, but, sadly, not in practice. For whenever the "we" becomes too large a club, things degrade, and each one starts fighting for his own interest. The abstract is way too abstract for us. This is the main reason I advocate political systems that start with the municipality, and work their way up (ironically, as in Switzerland, those "Swiss"), rather than the reverse, which has failed with larger states. Being somewhat tribal is not a bad thing—and we have to work in a fractal way in the organized harmonious relations between tribes, rather than merge all tribes in one large soup. In that sense, an American-style federalism is the ideal system.

This scale transformation from the particular to the general is behind my skepticism about unfettered globalization and large centralized multiethnic states. The physicist and complexity researcher Yaneer Bar-Yam showed quite convincingly that "better fences make better neighbors"—something both "policymakers" and local governments fail to get about the Near East. Scaling matters, I will keep repeating until I get hoarse. Putting Shiites, Christians, and Sunnis in one pot and asking them to sing "Kumbaya" around the campfire while holding hands in the name of unity and fraternity of mankind has failed. (Interventionistas aren't yet aware that "should" is not a sufficiently empirically valid statement to "build nations.") Blaming people for being "sectarian"—instead of making the best of such a natural tendency—is one of the stupidities of interventionistas. Separate tribes for administrative purposes (as the Ottomans did), or just put some markers somewhere, and they suddenly become friendly to one another.* The Levant has suffered (and keeps suffering) from Western (usually Anglo-Saxon) Arabists enamored with their subject, with no skin in the game in the place, who somehow have a vicious mission to destroy local indigenous

---

* Even then, the Ottomans did not go far enough in granting autonomy. Some argue that had Armenians heeded the call by the novelist Raffi for additional autonomy, the tragedies of the 1890s and 1915 would have been mitigated.

cultures and languages, and separate the Levant from its Mediterranean roots.*

But we don't have to go very far to get the importance of scaling. You know instinctively that people get along better as neighbors than roommates.

When you think about this, it is obvious, even trite, from the well-known behavior of crowds in the "anonymity" of big cities compared to groups in small villages. I spend some time in my ancestral village, where it feels like a family. People attend others' funerals (funeral clubs were mostly for large cities), help out, and care about the neighbor, even if they hate his dog. There is no way you can get the same cohesion in a larger city when the "other" is a theoretical entity, and our behavior toward him or her is governed by some general ethical rule, not someone in flesh and blood. We get it easily when seen that way, but fail to generalize that ethics is something fundamentally local.

Now what's the reason? Modernity put it in our heads that there are two units: the individual and the universal collective—in that sense, skin in the game for you would be just for *you*, as a unit. In reality, my skin lies in a broader set of people, one that includes a family, a community, a tribe, a fraternity. But it cannot possibly be the universal.

NON MIHI NON TIBI, SED NOBIS (NEITHER MINE NOR YOURS, BUT OURS)

Let us get into the gut of Ostrom's idea. The "tragedy of the commons," as exposed by economists, is as follows—the commons being a collective property, say, a forest or fishing waters or your local public park. Collectively, farmers as a community prefer to avoid overgrazing, and fishermen overfishing—the entire resource becomes thus degraded. But every single individual farmer would personally gain from his own overgrazing or overfishing under, of course, the condition that others don't. And that is what plagues socialism: people's individual interests do not

---

* The head of the Arab League, one Amr Moussa, was horrified at a lecture I gave outlining the notion that "good fences make better neighbors." He was offended by my message "promoting sectarianism." The common strategy by the Sunni-dominant majority in Arabic-speaking countries has been to call any attempt by a group to establish some autonomy "sectarianism" (ironically, these people, when rich, often have houses in Switzerland). It is always convenient to invoke universalism when you are in the majority. Since they are good at labels, they also accuse you of "racism" if, like the Kurds, Maronites, and Copts, you make any remote claim about self-rule. The term "racism" has undergone some devaluation, as it can be funny to observe Iraqis and Kurds calling one another racist for both wanting and opposing Kurdish self-determination.

quite work well under collectivism. But it is a critical mistake to think that people can function only under a private property system.

What Ostrom found empirically is that there exists a certain community size below which people act as collectivists, protecting the commons, as if the entire unit became rational. Such a commons cannot be too large. It is like a club. Groups behave differently at a different scale. This explains why the municipal is different from the national. It also explains how tribes operate: you are part of a specific group that is larger than the narrow *you,* but narrower than humanity in general. Critically, people share some things *but not others* within a specified group. And there is a protocol for dealing with the outside. Arab pastoral tribes have firm rules of hospitality toward nonhostile strangers who don't threaten their commons, but get violent when the stranger is a threat.

> *The skin-in-the-game definition of a commons: a space in which you are treated by others the way you treat them, where everyone exercises the Silver Rule.*

The "public good" is something abstract, taken out of a textbook. We will see further in Chapter 19 that the "individual" is an ill-defined entity. "Me" is more likely to be a group than a single person.

ARE YOU ON THE DIAGONAL?

A saying by the brothers Geoff and Vince Graham summarizes the ludicrousness of scale-free political universalism.

> I am, at the Fed level, libertarian;
> at the state level, Republican;
> at the local level, Democrat;
> and at the family and friends level, a socialist.

If that saying doesn't convince you the fatuousness of left vs. right labels, nothing will.

The Swiss are obsessive about governance—and indeed their political system is neither "left" nor "right," but governance-based. The thoughtful mathematician Hans Gersbach once organized a workshop on skin in the game in Zurich on how to properly reward (and punish) politicians whose interests are not lined up with those of the people they represent. It struck me that if things worked well in Switzerland and other Germanic countries, it is not because of accountability so much as scaling, which makes them very prone to accountability: Germany is a federation.

Let us next generalize to risk sharing.

ALL (LITERALLY) IN THE SAME BOAT

Greek is a language of precision; it has a word describing the opposite of risk transfer: risk sharing. *Synkyndineo* means "taking risks together," which was a requirement in maritime transactions.*

The *Acts of the Apostles* describes a voyage of St. Paul on a cargo ship from Sidon to Crete to Malta. As they hit a storm: *"When they had eaten what they wanted they lightened the ship by throwing the corn overboard into the sea."*

Now while they jettisoned *particular* goods, all owners were to be proportioned the costs of the lost merchandise, not just the specific owners of the lost merchandise. For it turned out that they were following a practice that dates to at least 800 B.C., codified in Lex Rhodia, Rhodian Law, after the mercantile Aegean island of Rhodes; the code is no longer extant but has been cited since antiquity. It stipulates that the risks and costs for contingencies are to be incurred equally, with no concern for responsibility. Justinian's code summarizes it:

> It is provided by the Rhodian Law that where merchandise is thrown overboard for the purpose of lightening a ship, what has been lost for the benefit of all must be made up by the contribution of all.

And the same mechanism for risk sharing took place with caravans along desert routes. If merchandise was stolen or lost, all merchants had to split the costs, not just its owner.

Synkyndineo has been translated into Latin by maestro classicist Armand D'Angour as *compericlitor*, hence, if it ever makes it into English, it should be *compericlity*, and its opposite, the Bob Rubin risk transfer, will be *incompericlity*. But I guess *risk sharing* will do in the meanwhile.

---

* "For he to-day that sheds his blood with me shall be my brother." (Shakespeare, *Henry V*)

Next, we discuss some distortions from the introduction of skin in the game.

TALKING ONE'S BOOK

I went on television once to announce a newly published book and got stuck in the studio, drafted to become part of a roundtable with two journalists plus the anchor. The topic of the day was Microsoft, a company that was in existence at the time. Everyone, including the anchor, chipped in. My turn came: "I own no Microsoft stock, I am short no Microsoft stock [i.e., would benefit from its decline], hence I can't talk about it." I repeated my dictum of Prologue 1: *Don't tell me what you think, tell me what you have in your portfolio.* There was immeasurable confusion in the faces: a journalist is typically not supposed to talk about stocks he owns—and, what is worse, is supposed to always, always make pronouncements about stuff he can barely find on a map. A journalist is meant to be an impartial "judge," yet, unlike Sisamnes in the Judgment of Cambyses, there is no threat of a secondary use of his skin.

There are two types of "talking one's book." One consists of buying a stock because you like it, *then* commenting on it (and disclosing such ownership)—the most reliable advocate for a product is its user.* Another is buying a stock so you can advertise the qualities of the company, *then* selling it, benefiting from the trumpeting—this is called market manipulation, and it is certainly a conflict of interest. We removed the skin in the game of journalists in order to prevent market manipulation, thinking that it would be a net gain to society. The arguments in this book are that the former (market manipulation) and conflicts of interest are more benign than impunity for bad advice. The main reason, we will see, is that in the absence of skin in the game, journalists will imitate, to be safe, the opinion of other journalists, thus creating monoculture and collective mirages.†

In general, skin in the game comes with conflict of interest. What I

---

* Users of products are more reliable because of a natural filtering. I bought an electric car— a Tesla—because my neighbor was enthusiastic about his (skin in the game), and I watched him remain so for a few years. No amount of advertising will match the credibility of a genuine user.

† *The Black Swan* discusses the clustering of security analysts who are not only random, but random together. The variance between analysts is smaller than that of the difference between forecasts and realizations.

hope this book will do is show that the former is more important than the latter. There is no problem if people have a conflict of interest if it is congruous with downside risk for themselves.

A SHORT VISIT TO THE DOCTOR'S OFFICE

The doctor doesn't have the Antaeus problem: medicine, while wrapping the garment of science around it, is fundamentally apprenticeship-based and, like engineering, grounded in experience, not just experimentation and theories. While economists say "assume that . . ." and produce some weird theory, doctors have none of that. So there is skin in the game at many degrees, except perhaps not fully in the agency effect separating customer from provider. And attempts at putting skin in the game there have brought a certain class of adverse effects, in shifting uncertainty from the doctor to the patient.

The legal system and regulatory measures are likely to put the skin of the doctor in the wrong game.

How? The problem resides in the reliance on metrics. Every metric is gameable—the cholesterol lowering we mentioned in Prologue 1 is a metric-gaming technique taken to its limit. More realistically, say a cancer doctor or hospital is judged by the five-year survival rates of patients, and needs to face a variety of modalities for a new patient: what choice of treatment would they elect to do? There is a tradeoff between laser surgery (a precise surgical procedure) and radiation therapy, which is toxic to both patient and cancer. Statistically, laser surgery may have worse five-year outcomes than radiation therapy, but the latter tends to create second tumors in the longer run and offers comparatively reduced twenty-year disease-specific survival. Given that the window used for the calculation of patient survival is five years, not twenty, the incentive is to shoot for radiation.

So the doctor is likely to be in the process of shifting uncertainty away from him or her by electing the second-best option.

A doctor is pushed by the system to transfer risk from himself to you, and from the present into the future, or from the immediate future into a more distant future.

You need to remember that, when you visit a medical office, you will be facing someone who, in spite of his authoritative demeanor, is in a fragile situation. He is not you, not a member of your family, so he has no direct emotional loss should your health experience a degradation. His objective is, naturally, to avoid a lawsuit, something that can prove disastrous to his career.

Some metrics can actually kill you. Now, say you happen to visit a cardiologist and turn out to be in the mild risk category, something that doesn't really raise your risk of a cardiovascular event, but precedes the stage of a possibly worrisome condition. (There is a strong nonlinearity: a person classified as prediabetic or prehypertensive is, in probability space, 90 percent closer to a normal person than to one with the condition.) But the doctor is pressured to treat you to protect himself. Should you drop dead a few weeks after the visit, a low probability event, the doctor can be sued for negligence, for not having prescribed the right medicine that is temporarily believed to be useful (as in the case of statins), but that we now know has been backed up by suspicious or incomplete studies. Deep down, he may know that statins are harmful, as they will lead to long-term side effects. But the pharmaceutical companies have managed to convince everyone that these unseen consequences are harmless, when the right precautionary approach is to consider the unseen as potentially harmful. In fact for most people except those that are very ill, the risks outweigh the benefits. Except that the long-term medical risks are hidden; they will play out in the long run, whereas the legal risk is immediate. This is no different from the Bob Rubin risk-transfer trade, of delaying risks and making them look invisible.

Now can one make medicine less asymmetric? Not directly; the solution, as I have argued in *Antifragile* and more technically elsewhere, is for the patient to avoid treatment when he or she is mildly ill, but use medicine for the "tail events," that is, for rarely encountered severe conditions. The problem is that the mildly ill represent a much larger pool of people than the severely ill—and are people who are expected to live longer and consume drugs for longer—hence pharmaceutical companies have an incentive to focus on them. (Dead people, I am told, stop taking drugs.)

In sum, both the doctor and the patient have skin in the game, though not perfectly, but administrators don't—and they seem to be the cause of the troubling malfunctioning of the system. Administrators everywhere on the planet, in all businesses and pursuits, and at all times in history, have been the plague.

NEXT

This chapter introduced us to the agency problem and risk sharing, seen from both a commercial and an ethical viewpoint, assuming the two can be disentangled. We also introduced the problem of scale. Next, we will try to get deeper into the hidden asymmetries that make aggregates strange animals.

———

BOOK 3

THAT GREATEST ASYMMETRY

CHAPTER 2

The Most Intolerant Wins:
The Dominance
of the Stubborn Minority

*Why you don't have to smoke in the smoking section—Your food
choices on the fall of the Saudi king—How to prevent a friend from
working too hard—Omar Sharif's conversion—How to make a
market collapse*

———

The main idea behind complex systems is that the ensemble behaves
in ways not predicted by its components. The interactions matter
more than the nature of the units. Studying individual ants will almost
never give us a clear indication of how the ant colony operates. For that,
one needs to understand an ant colony as an ant colony, no less, no
more, not a collection of ants. This is called an "emergent" property of
the whole, by which *parts* and *whole* differ because what matters are the
interactions between such parts. And interactions can obey very simple
rules.

The rule we discuss in this chapter is the *minority* rule, the mother
of all asymmetries. It suffices for an intransigent minority—a certain
type of intransigent minority—with significant skin in the game (or,
better, soul in the game) to reach a minutely small level, say 3 or 4 percent of the total population, for the entire population to have to submit
to their preferences. Further, an optical illusion comes with the dominance of the minority: a naive observer (who looks at the standard average) would be under the impression that the choices and preferences are
those of the majority. If it seems absurd, it is because our scientific intuitions aren't calibrated for this. (Fughedabout scientific and academic
intuitions and snap judgments; they don't work, and your standard in-

tellectualization fails with complex systems, though your grandmothers' wisdom doesn't.)

Among other things, many other things, the minority rule will show
us how all it takes is a small number of intolerant, virtuous people with
skin in the game, in the form of courage, for society to function properly.

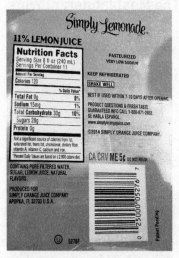

FIGURE 1. The lemonade container with the
circled U indicating it is (literally) kosher.

This example of complexity hit me, ironically, as I was helping with
the New England Complex Systems Institute summer barbecue. As the
hosts were setting up the table and unpacking the drinks, a friend who
was observant and ate only kosher dropped by to say hello. I offered him
a glass of that type of yellow sugared water with citric acid people
sometimes call lemonade, almost certain that he would reject it owing
to his dietary laws. He didn't. He drank the liquid, and another kosher
person commented, "Around here, drinks are kosher." We looked at the
carton container. There was a fine print: a tiny symbol, a *U* inside a
circle, indicating that it was kosher. The symbol will be detected by
those who need to know and look for the minuscule print. As for myself,
like the character in Molière's play *Le Bourgeois Gentilhomme* who
suddenly discovers that he has been speaking in prose all these years
without knowing it, I realized that I had been drinking kosher liquids
without knowing it.

CRIMINALS WITH PEANUT ALLERGIES

A strange idea hit me. The kosher population represents less than three tenths of a percent of the residents of the United States. Yet, it appears that almost all drinks are kosher. Why? Simply because going full kosher allows the producers, grocers, and restaurants to not have to distinguish between kosher and nonkosher for liquids, with special markers, separate aisles, separate inventories, different stocking sub-facilities. And the simple rule that changes the total is as follows:

> *A kosher (or halal) eater will never eat nonkosher (or nonhalal) food, but a nonkosher eater isn't banned from eating kosher.*

Or, rephrased in another domain:

> *A disabled person will not use the regular bathroom, but a nondisabled person will use the bathroom for disabled people.*

Granted, sometimes in practice we hesitate to use a bathroom with a disabled sign on it owing to some confusion—mistaking the rule for the one for parking cars, believing that the bathroom is reserved for exclusive use by the handicapped.

> *Someone with a peanut allergy will not eat products that touch peanuts, but a person without such an allergy can eat items with no peanut traces in them.*

Which explains why it is so hard to find peanuts on U.S. airplanes and why schools are often peanut-free (which, in a way, increases the number of persons with peanut allergies, as reduced exposure is one of the causes behind such allergies).

Let us apply the rule to domains where it can get entertaining:

> *An honest person will never commit criminal acts, but a criminal will readily engage in legal acts.*

Let us call such minority an *intransigent* group, and the majority a *flexible* one. And their relationship rests on an asymmetry in choices.

I once pulled a prank on a friend. Years ago, when Big Tobacco was hiding and repressing the evidence of harm from secondary smoke, New York had smoking and nonsmoking sections in restaurants (even airplanes had, absurdly, a smoking section). I once went to lunch with a fellow visiting from Europe: the restaurant only had availability in the smoking section. I convinced my visitor that we needed to buy cigarettes, as we *had to* smoke in the smoking section. He complied.

Two more things. First, the geography of the terrain, that is, the spatial structure, matters a bit; it makes a big difference whether the intransigents are in their own district or are mixed with the rest of the population. If people following the minority rule lived in ghettos with a separate small economy, then the minority rule would not apply. But when a population has an even spatial distribution, say, when the ratio of such a minority in a neighborhood is the same as that in the entire village, that in the village is the same as in the county, that in the county is the same as in the state, and that in the state is the same as nationwide, then the (flexible) majority will have to submit to the minority rule. Second, the cost structure matters quite a bit. It happens in our first example that making lemonade compliant with kosher laws doesn't change the price by much—it is a matter of avoiding some standard additives. But if the manufacturing of kosher lemonade costs substantially more, then the rule will be weakened in some nonlinear proportion to the difference in costs. If it costs ten times as much to make kosher food, then the minority rule will not apply, except perhaps in some very rich neighborhoods.

Muslims have kosher laws, so to speak, but these are much narrower and apply only to meat. Muslims and Jews have near-identical slaughter rules (all kosher is halal for most Sunni Muslims, or was so in past centuries, but the reverse is not true). Note that these slaughter rules are skin-in-the-game driven, inherited from the ancient Eastern Mediterranean Greek and Levantine practice of economically burdensome animal sacrifice, to only worship the Gods if one has skin in the game. The Gods do not like cheap signaling.

Now consider this manifestation of the dictatorship of the minority. In the United Kingdom, where the (practicing) Muslim population is only 3 to 4 percent, a very high proportion of the meat we find is halal. Close to 70 percent of lamb imports from New Zealand are halal. Close to 10 percent of Subway stores carry halal-only meat (meaning no pork), in spite of the high costs of losing the business of ham eaters (like myself). The same holds in South Africa, which has about the same proportion of Muslims. There, a disproportionately high share of chicken is halal certified. But in the U.K. and other nominally Christian countries, halal is not neutral enough to reach a high level, as people may rebel against being forced to abide by others' sacred values—accepting and respecting the sacred values of other religions might signal some type of violation of yours, if you are a true monotheist. For instance, the seventh century Christian Arab poet Al-Akhtal made a point to never eat halal meat in his famous defiant poem boasting his Christianity: "I do not eat sacrificial flesh": *Wa lastu bi'akuli lahmal adahi.*

Al-Akhtal was reflecting a standard Christian reaction from three or four centuries earlier—Christians were tortured in pagan times by being forced to eat sacrificial meat, which they found sacrilegious. Many Christian martyrs took the heroic stance of starving to death rather than ingest impure food.

One can expect the same rejection of others' religious norms to take place in the West as the Muslim populations in Europe grow.

So the minority rule may produce a larger share of halal food in the stores than warranted by the proportion of halal eaters in the population, but with a headwind somewhere because some people may have a taboo against the custom. But with some non-religious kashrut rules, so to speak, the share can be expected to converge closer to a 100 percent (or some high number). In the U.S. and Europe, "organic" food companies are selling more and more products precisely because of the minority rule, and because ordinary and unlabeled food may be seen by some to contain pesticides, herbicides, and transgenic genetically modified organisms, or GMOs, with, according to them, unknown risks. (What we call GMOs in this context means transgenic food, entailing the transfer of genes from a foreign organism or species that would not have occurred in nature). Or it could be for some existential reasons, cautious behavior, or Burkean conservatism (that is, following the precautionary ideas of Edmund Burke)—some may not want to venture too far too fast from what their grandparents ate. Labeling something "organic" is a way to say that it contains no transgenic GMOs.

In promoting genetically modified food via all manner of lobbying, purchasing of congressmen, and overt scientific propaganda (with smear campaigns against such persons as yours truly, much about which later), big agricultural companies foolishly believed that all they needed was to win the majority. No, you idiots. Your snap "scientific" judgment is too naive for these types of decisions. Consider that transgenic-GMO eaters will eat non-GMOs, but not the reverse. So it may suffice to have a tiny percentage—say, no more than 5 percent—of an evenly spatially distributed population of non-genetically modified eaters for the *entire* population to have to eat non-GMO food. How? Say you have a corporate event, a wedding, or a lavish party to celebrate the fall of the Saudi Arabian regime, the bankruptcy of the rent-seeking investment bank Goldman Sachs, or the public reviling of Ray Kotcher, chairman of Ketchum the contemptible public relations firm, the enemy of scientists and scientific whistleblowers. Do you need to send a questionnaire asking people if they eat or don't eat transgenic GMOs and reserve special meals accordingly? No. You just select everything non-GMO, provided the price difference is not consequential. And the price difference appears to be small enough to be negligible, as (perishable) food costs in America are largely, up to about 80 or 90 percent, determined by distribution and storage, not the cost at the agricultural level. And as organic food is in higher demand, thanks to the minority rule, distribution costs decrease and the minority rule ends up accelerating in its effect.

"Big Ag" (the large agricultural firms) does not realize that this is the equivalent of entering a game in which one needed to not just win more points than the adversary, but win 97 percent of the total points just to be safe. It is strange to see an industry that spends hundreds of millions of dollars on research-cum-smear-campaigns, with hundreds of these scientists who think of themselves as more intelligent than the rest of us, miss such an elementary point about asymmetric choices.

Another example: do not think that the spread of automatic shifting cars is necessarily due to a majority preference; it could just be because those who can drive manual shifts can always drive automatic, but the reverse is not true.

The method of analysis employed here is called a "renormalization group," a powerful apparatus in mathematical physics that allows us to see how things scale up (or down). Let us examine it next—without mathematics.

FIGURE 2. Renormalization group, steps one through three (start from the top): Four boxes containing four boxes, with one of the boxes dark at step one, with successive applications of the minority rule.

RENORMALIZATION GROUP

Figure 2 shows four boxes exhibiting what is called fractal self-similarity. Each box contains four smaller boxes. Each one of the four boxes will contain four boxes, and so all the way down, and all the way up until we reach a certain level. There are two shades: light for the majority choice, and dark for the minority one.

Assume the smaller unit contains four people, a family of four. One of them is in the intransigent minority and eats only non-GMO food (which includes organic). The color of this box is dark, and the others light. We "renormalize once" as we move up: the stubborn daughter manages to impose her rule on the four and the unit is now all dark, i.e., will opt for non-GMO. Now, step three, you have the family going to a barbecue party attended by three other families. As they are known to only eat non-GMO, the guests will cook only organic. The local grocery store, realizing the neighborhood is only non-GMO, switches to non-GMO to simplify life, which impacts the local wholesaler, and the system continues to "renormalize."

By some coincidence, the day before the Boston barbecue, I was flaneuring in New York, and I dropped by the office of Raphael Douady, a friend I wanted to prevent from working, that is, engaging in an activity that, when abused, causes the loss of mental clarity, in addition to bad posture and loss of definition in facial features. The French physicist Serge Galam happened to be visiting, and chose the friend's office to kill time and taste Raphael's bad espresso. Galam was first to apply these renormalization techniques to social matters and political science; his name was familiar, as he is the author of the main book on the subject, which had then been sitting for months in an unopened Amazon box in my basement. He elaborated on his research and showed me a computer model of elections by which it suffices for some minority to exceed a certain level for its choices to prevail.

So the same illusion exists in political discussions, spread by political "scientists": you think that because some extreme right- or left-wing party has, say, the support of ten percent of the population, their candidate will get ten percent of the votes. No: these baseline voters should be classified as "inflexible" and will always vote for their faction. But some of the flexible voters *can* also vote for that extreme faction, just as non-kosher people can eat kosher. These people are the ones to watch out for, as they may swell the number of votes for the extreme party. Galam's models produced a bevy of counterintuitive effects in political science—and his predictions have turned out to be way closer to real outcomes than the naive consensus.

THE VETO

What we saw in the renormalization group was the "veto" effect, as a person in a group can steer choices. The advertising executive (and extremely bon vivant) Rory Sutherland suggested to me that this explains why some fast-food chains, such as McDonald's, thrive. It's not because they offer a great product, but because they are not vetoed in a certain socio-economic group—and by a small proportion of people in that group at that.*

When there are few choices, McDonald's appears to be a safe bet. It is also a safe bet in shady places with few regulars where the food variance from expectation can be consequential—I am writing these lines in the Milan train station and, as offensive as it can be to someone who spent all this money to go to Italy, McDonald's is one of the few restaurants there. And it is packed. Shockingly, Italians are seeking refuge there from a risky meal. They may hate McDonald's, but they certainly hate uncertainty even more.

Pizza is the same story: it is a commonly accepted food, and, outside a gathering of pseudo-leftist caviar eaters, nobody will be blamed for ordering it.

Rory wrote to me about the beer-wine asymmetry and the choices made for parties: "Once you have 10 percent or more women at a party, you cannot serve only beer. But most men will drink wine. So you only need one set of glasses if you serve only wine—the universal donor, to use the language of blood groups."

This strategy of seeking the optimal among not necessarily great options might have been played by the Khazars when they were looking to choose between Islam, Judaism, and Christianity. Legend has it that three high-ranking delegations (bishops, rabbis, and sheikhs) came to make the sales pitch. The Khazar lords asked the Christians: if you were forced to choose between Judaism and Islam, which one would you pick? Judaism, they replied. Then the lords asked the Muslims: which of the two, Christianity or Judaism? Judaism, the Muslims said. Judaism it was; and the tribe converted.

LINGUA FRANCA

If a meeting is taking place in Germany in the Teutonic-looking conference room of a corporation that is sufficiently international or Euro-

---

* To put it in technical terms, it was a best worse-case divergence from expectations: a lower variance and lower mean.

pean, and one of the persons in the room doesn't speak German, the entire meeting will be run in . . . English, the brand of inelegant English used in corporations across the world. That way they can equally offend their Teutonic ancestors and the English language. It all started with the asymmetric rule that those who are nonnative in English know (bad) English, but the reverse—English speakers knowing other languages—is less likely. French was supposed to be the language of diplomacy, as civil servants coming from aristocratic backgrounds used it, while their more vulgar compatriots involved in commerce relied on English. In the rivalry between the two languages, English won as commerce grew to dominate modern life; the victory has nothing to do with the prestige of France or the efforts of their civil servants in promoting their more or less beautiful Latinized and logically spelled language over the orthographically confusing one of trans-Channel meat-pie eaters.

We can thus get some inkling of how the emergence of lingua francas can come from minority rules—and that is a point that is not visible to linguists. Aramaic is a Semitic language that succeeded the Canaanite language (that is, Phoenician-Hebrew) in the Levant and resembles Arabic; it was the language Jesus Christ spoke. The reason it came to dominate the Levant and Egypt isn't because of any particular imperial Semitic power or the fact that they have interesting noses. It was the Persians—who speak an Indo-European language—who spread Aramaic, the language of Assyria, Syria, and Babylon. Persians taught Egyptians a language that was not their own. Simply, when the Persians invaded Babylon they found an administration with scribes who could only use Aramaic and didn't know Persian, so Aramaic became the state language. If your secretary can only take dictation in Aramaic, Aramaic is what you will use. This led to the oddity of Aramaic being used in Mongolia, as records were maintained in the Syriac alphabet (Syriac is the Eastern dialect of Aramaic). And centuries later, the story would repeat itself in reverse, with the Arabs using Greek in their early administration in the seventh and eighth centuries. For during the Hellenistic era, Greek replaced Aramaic as the lingua franca in the Levant, and the scribes of Damascus maintained their records in Greek. But it was not the Greeks who spread Greek around the Mediterranean, but the Romans who accelerated the spreading of Greek, as they used it in their administration across the Eastern empire, as well as the coastal Levantines—the New Testament was written in the Greek of Syria.

A French Canadian friend from Montreal, Jean-Louis Rheault, bemoaning the loss of the French language among French Canadians outside narrowly provincial areas, commented as follows: "In Canada, when we say bilingual, it is English-speaking, and when we say French-speaking it becomes bilingual."

GENES VS. LANGUAGES

Looking at genetic data in the Eastern Mediterranean with my collaborator the geneticist Pierre Zalloua, we noticed that both invaders, Turks and Arabs, left few genes, and in the case of Turkey, the tribes from East and Central Asia brought an entirely new language. Turkey, shockingly, is still inhabited by the populations of Asia Minor you read about in history books, but with new names. Further, Zalloua and his colleagues claim that Canaanites from 3,700 years ago represent more than nine-tenths of the genes of current residents of the state of Lebanon, with only a tiny amount of new genes added, in spite of about every possible army having dropped by for sightseeing and some pillaging.[*] While Turks are Mediterraneans who speak an East Asian language, the French (North of Avignon) are largely of Northern European stock, yet they speak a Mediterranean language.

So:

Genes follow majority rule; languages minority rule.

Languages travel; genes less so.

This shows us the recent mistake of building racial theories on language, dividing people into "Aryans" and "Semites," based on linguistic considerations. While the subject was central to the German Nazis, the practice continues today in one form or another, often benign. For the great irony is that Northern European supremacists ("Aryan"), while anti-Semitic, used the classical Greeks to give themselves a pedigree and a link to a glorious civilization, but didn't realize that the Greeks and their Mediterranean "Semitic" neighbors were actually genetically close

---

[*] There is a also current controversy in the United Kingdom as the Normans left more texts and pictures in history books than genes there.

to one another. It has been recently shown that both ancient Greeks and Bronze Age Levantines share an Anatolian origin. It just happened that the languages diverged.

THE ONE-WAY STREET OF RELIGIONS

In the same manner, the spread of Islam in the Near East, where Christianity was heavily entrenched (remember that it was born there), can be attributed to two simple asymmetries. The original Islamic rulers weren't particularly interested in converting Christians, as these provided them with tax revenues—the proselytism of Islam did not initially address those called "people of the book," i.e. individuals of Abrahamic faith. In fact, my ancestors who survived thirteen centuries under Muslim rule saw clear advantages in not being Muslim: mostly in the avoidance of military conscription.

The two asymmetric rules are as follows. First, under Islamic law, if a non-Muslim man marries a Muslim woman, he needs to convert to Islam—and if *either* parent of a child happens to be Muslim, the child will be Muslim.* Second, becoming Muslim is irreversible, as apostasy is the heaviest crime under the religion, sanctioned by the death penalty. The famous Egyptian actor Omar Sharif, born Mikhael Demetri Shalhoub, came from a Lebanese Christian family. He converted to Islam to marry a famous Egyptian actress and had to change his name to an Arabic one. He later divorced, but did not revert to the faith of his ancestors.

Under these two asymmetric rules, one can do simple simulations and see how a small Islamic group occupying Christian (Coptic) Egypt can lead, over the centuries, to the Copts becoming a tiny minority. All one needs is a small rate of interfaith marriages. Likewise, one can see how Judaism doesn't spread and tends to stay in the minority, as the religion has weaker rules: the mother is required to be Jewish. An even stronger asymmetry than that of Judaism explains the depletion in the Near East of three Gnostic faiths: the Druze, the Ezidi, and the Mandeans (Gnostic religions are those with *mysteries* and *knowledge* that are typically accessible to only a minority of elders, with the rest of the

---

* There are some minor variations across regions and Islamic sects. The original rule is that if a Muslim woman marries a non-Muslim man, he needs to convert. But in practice, in many countries, both need to do so.

members kept in the dark about the details of the faith). Unlike Islam, which requires either parent to be Muslim, and Judaism, which asks for at least the mother to have the faith, these three religions require *both* parents to be of the faith, otherwise the child and the parents say *toodaloo* to the community.

In places such as Lebanon, Galilee, and Northern Syria, with mountainous terrain, Christians and other non-Sunni Muslims remained concentrated. Christians, not being exposed to Muslims, experienced no intermarriage. By contrast, Egypt has a flat terrain. The distribution of the population presents homogeneous mixtures there, which permits renormalization (i.e. allows the asymmetric rule to prevail).

Egypt's Copts suffered from an additional problem: the irreversibility of Islamic conversions. Many Copts during Islamic rule converted to the dominant religion when it was merely an administrative procedure, something that helps one land a job or handle a problem that requires Islamic jurisprudence. One did not have to really believe in it, since Islam doesn't conflict markedly with Orthodox Christianity. Little by little a Christian or Jewish family engaging in a Marrano-style conversion becomes truly converted, as, a couple of generations later, the descendants forget the arrangement of their ancestors.

So all Islam did was out-stubborn Christianity, which itself won thanks to its own stubbornness. For before Islam, the original spread of Christianity in the Roman empire was largely due to . . . the blinding intolerance of Christians; their unconditional, aggressive, and recalcitrant proselytizing. Roman pagans were initially tolerant of Christians, as the tradition was to share gods with other members of the empire. But they wondered why these Nazarenes didn't want to give and take gods and offer that Jesus fellow to the Roman pantheon in exchange for some other gods. What, our gods aren't good enough for them? But Christians were intolerant of Roman paganism. The "persecution" of the Christians had vastly more to do with the intolerance of the Christians for the pantheon of local gods than the reverse. What we read is history written by the Christian side, not the Greco-Roman one.

We know too little about the Roman perspective during the rise of Christianity, as hagiographies have dominated the discourse: we have for instance the narrative of the martyr Saint Catherine, who kept converting her jailors until she was beheaded, except that . . . she may have never existed. But the beheading of Saint Cyprian, bishop of Carthage, under Valerian, was real. So there are endless histories of Christian martyrs and saints—but very little is known of pagan heroes. Even the early Christians of the Gnostic tradition have been expurgated from the record. When Julian the Apostate tried to go back to ancient paganism, it was like trying to sell French food in South Jersey: it simply had no market. It was like trying to keep a balloon under water. And it was not because pagans had an intellectual deficit: in fact, my heuristic is that the more pagan, the more brilliant one's mind, and the higher one's ability to handle nuances and ambiguity. Purely monotheistic religions such as Protestant Christianity, Salafi Islam, or fundamentalist atheism accommodate literalist and mediocre minds that cannot handle ambiguity.*

In fact, we can observe in the history of Mediterranean "religions" or, rather, rituals and systems of behavior and belief, a drift dictated by the intolerant, actually bringing the system closer to what we can call a religion. Judaism might have almost lost because of the mother rule and its confinement to a tribal base, but Christianity ruled, and for the very same reasons, Islam did. Islam? There have been many *Islams,* the final accretion quite different from the earlier ones. For Islam itself is ending up being taken over (in the Sunni branch) by purists simply because they are more intolerant than the rest: the Wahhabis (aka Salafis), founders of Saudi Arabia, destroyed the shrines in most parts of what is now their country during the nineteenth century. They went on to impose the maximally intolerant rule in a manner that was later imitated by ISIS. Every single accretion of Salafism seems to exist to accommodate the most intolerant of its branches.

DECENTRALIZE, AGAIN

Another attribute of decentralization, and one that the "intellectuals" opposing an exit of Britain from the European Union (Brexit) don't get: if one needs, say, a 3 percent threshold in a political unit for the minority rule to take its effect, and *on average* the stubborn minority represents 3

---

* It is a fact that while Christianity eradicated previous records, it may also have eradicated . . . its own history. For we are discovering that branches such as the Gnostics had a quite different record of the early religion. But the Gnostics were largely a secret religion—closed to outsiders and secret about their own records. And secret religions, well, bury their secrets.

percent of the population, with variations around the average, then some states will be subject to the rule, but not others. If, on the other hand, we merge all states in one, then the minority rule will prevail all across. This is the reason the U.S.A. works so well. As I have been repeating to everyone who listens, we are a federation, not a republic. To use the language of *Antifragile*, decentralization is *convex* to variations.

IMPOSING VIRTUE ON OTHERS

This idea of one-sidedness can help us debunk a few more misconceptions. How do books get banned? Certainly not because they offend the average person—most persons are passive and don't really care, or don't care enough to request the banning. From past episodes, it looks like all it takes is a few (motivated) activists for the banning of some books, or the blacklisting of some people. The great philosopher and logician Bertrand Russell lost his job at the City University of New York owing to a letter by an angry—and stubborn—mother who did not wish to have her daughter in the same room as the fellow with a dissolute lifestyle and unruly ideas.

The same seems to apply to prohibitions—at least to the prohibition of alcohol in the United States, which led to interesting mafia stories.

Let us conjecture that the formation of moral values in society doesn't come from the evolution of the consensus. No, it is the most intolerant person who imposes virtue on others precisely because of that intolerance. The same can apply to civil rights.

An insight into how the mechanisms of religion and the transmission of morals obey the same renormalization dynamics as dietary laws—and how we can show that morality is more likely to be something enforced by a minority. We saw earlier in the chapter the asymmetry between obeying and breaking rules: a law-abiding (or rule-abiding) fellow always follows the rules, but a felon or someone with looser sets of principles will not *always* break the rules. Likewise we discussed the strong asymmetric effects of *halal* dietary laws. Let us merge the two. It turns out that, in classical Arabic, the term *halal* has one opposite: *haram*. Violating legal and moral rules—any rule—is called *haram*. It is the exact same interdict that governs food intake and *all* other human behaviors, like sleeping with the wife of your neighbor, lending with interest (without partaking of downside of the borrower), or killing one's landlord for pleasure. *Haram* is *haram* and is asymmetric.

Once a moral rule is established, it will suffice to have a small, intransigent minority of geographically distributed followers to dictate a norm in society. The sad news is that one person looking at mankind as an aggregate may mistakenly believe that humans are spontaneously becoming more moral, better, and more gentle, with better breath, when this applies to only a small proportion of mankind.

But things work both ways, the good and the bad. While some believe that the average Pole was complicit in the liquidation of Jews, the historian Peter Fritzsche, when asked, "Why didn't the Poles in Warsaw help their Jewish neighbors more?," responded that they generally did. But it took seven or eight Poles to help one Jew. It took only one Pole, acting as an informer, to turn in a dozen Jews. Even if such select anti-Semitism is contestable, we can easily imagine bad outcomes stemming from a minority of bad agents.

STABILITY OF THE MINORITY RULE, A PROBABILISTIC ARGUMENT

Wherever you look across societies and histories, you tend to find the same general moral laws prevailing, with some, but not significant, variations: *do not steal* (at least not from within the tribe); *do not hunt orphans for entertainment; do not gratuitously beat up Spanish grammar specialists for training, instead use boxing bags* (unless you are Spartan and even then you can only kill a limited number of helots for training purposes), and similar interdicts. And we can see these rules evolved over time to become more universal, expanding to a broader set, to progressively include slaves, other tribes, other species (animals, economists), etc. And one property of these laws: they are black-and-white, binary, discrete, and allow no shadow. You cannot steal "a little bit" or murder "moderately"—just as you cannot keep kosher and eat "just a little bit" of pork at Sunday barbecues.

I don't think that if you fondled the breast of the wife or girlfriend of some random weight lifter in front of him, you would do well in the intervening noisy episode, nor would you be able to convince him that it was "just a little bit."

Now, it would be vastly more likely that these values emerged from a minority than a majority. Why? Take the following two theses:

Outcomes are paradoxically more stable under the minority rule—
the variance of the results is lower and the rule is more likely to
emerge independently across separate populations.

What emerges from the minority rule is more likely to be black-
and-white, binary rules.

An example. Consider that an evil person, say an economics professor, decides to poison the collective by putting some product into soda cans. He has two options. The first is cyanide, which obeys a minority rule: a drop of poison (higher than a small threshold) makes the *entire* liquid poisonous. The second is a "majority-style" poison; it requires more than half the ingested liquid to be poisonous in order to kill. Now look at the inverse problem, a collection of dead people after a dinner party. The local Sherlock Holmes would assert that, conditional on the outcome that *all people drinking the soda having been killed,* the evil man opted for the first, not the second option. Simply, the majority rule leads to fluctuations around the average, with a high rate of survival. Not the minority rule. The minority rule produces low-variance in outcomes.

POPPER-GOEDEL'S PARADOX

I was at a large, multi-table dinner party, the kind where you have to choose between the vegetarian risotto and the non-vegetarian option, when I noticed that my neighbor had his food catered (including silverware) on a tray reminiscent of airplane fare. The dishes were sealed with aluminum foil. He was evidently ultra-kosher. It did not bother him to be seated with prosciutto eaters, who, in addition, mix butter and meat in the same dishes. He just wanted to be left alone to follow his own preferences.

For Jews and Muslim minorities such as Shiites, Sufis, and (vaguely) associated religions such as Druze and Alawis, the aim is to be left alone—with historical exceptions here and there. But had my neighbor been a Sunni Salafi, he would have required the entire room to be eating halal. Perhaps the entire building. Perhaps the entire town. Hopefully the entire country. Ideally, the entire planet. Indeed, given the total lack of separation between church and state in his creed, and between the holy and the profane, to him *haram* (the opposite of halal) means literally illegal. The entire room was committing a legal violation.

As I am writing these lines, people are disputing whether the freedom of the enlightened West can be undermined by the intrusive policies that would be needed to fight fundamentalists.

Can democracy—by definition the majority—tolerate enemies? The question is as follows: "Would you agree to deny the freedom of speech to every political party that has in its charter the banning of freedom of speech?" Let's go one step further: "Should a society that has elected to be tolerant be intolerant about intolerance?"

This is in fact the incoherence that Kurt Gödel (the grandmaster of logical rigor) detected in the United States Constitution while taking the naturalization exam. Legend has it that Gödel started arguing with the judge, and Einstein, who was his witness during the process, saved him. The philosopher of science Karl Popper independently discovered the same inconsistency in democratic systems.

I wrote about people with logical flaws asking me if one should be "skeptical about skepticism"; I used a similar answer as Popper when I was asked if "one could falsify falsification." I just walked away.

We can answer these points using the minority rule. Yes, an intolerant minority can control and destroy democracy. Actually, it *will* eventually destroy our world.

So, we need to be more than intolerant with *some* intolerant minorities. Simply, they violate the Silver Rule. It is not permissible to use "American values" or "Western principles" in treating intolerant Salafism (which denies other peoples' right to have their own religion). The West is currently in the process of committing suicide.

IRREVERENCE OF MARKETS AND SCIENCE

Now consider markets. We can say that markets aren't the sum of market participants, but price changes reflect the activities of the most *motivated* buyer and seller. Yes, the most motivated rules. Indeed this is something that only traders seem to understand: why a price can drop by ten percent because of a single seller. All you need is a stubborn seller. Markets react in a way that is disproportional to the impetus. The overall stock markets currently represent more than thirty trillion dollars, but a single order in 2008, only fifty billion, that is, less than two-tenths of a percent of the total, triggered a drop of close to 10 percent, causing losses of around three trillion dollars. As retold in *Antifragile,* it was an order activated by the Parisian bank Société Générale, which discovered a hidden acquisition by a rogue trader and wanted to reverse the purchase. Why did the market react so disproportionately? Because the order was one-way—stubborn: they had to sell and there was no way to convince the management otherwise. My personal adage is:

> *The market is like a large movie theater with a small door.*

And the best way to detect a sucker is to see if his focus is on the size of the theater rather than that of the door. Stampedes happen in cinemas— say, when someone shouts "fire"—because those who want to be out do not want to stay in, exactly the same unconditionality we saw with kosher observance or panic selling.

Science acts similarly. As we saw earlier, the minority rule is behind Karl Popper's thinking. But Popper is too stern, so let us leave him for later and, for now, discuss the more entertaining and jovial Richard Feynman, the most irreverent and playful scientist of his day. His book of anecdotes, *What Do You Care What Other People Think?,* conveys the idea of the fundamental irreverence of science, which proceeds through a similar mechanism as the kosher asymmetry. How? Science isn't the sum of what scientists think, but exactly as with markets, it is a procedure that is highly skewed. Once you debunk something, it is now wrong. Had science operated by majority consensus, we would be still stuck in the Middle Ages, and Einstein would have ended as he started, a patent clerk with fruitless side hobbies.

UNUS SED LEO: ONLY ONE BUT A LION

Alexander said that it was preferable to have an army of sheep led by a lion than an army of lions led by a sheep. Alexander (or whoever produced this probably apocryphal saying) understood the value of the active, intolerant, and courageous minority. Hannibal terrorized Rome for a decade and a half with a tiny army of mercenaries, winning twenty-two battles against the Romans, battles in which he was outnumbered each time. He was inspired by a version of this maxim. For, at the battle of Cannae, he remarked to Gisco, who was concerned that the Carthaginians were outnumbered by the Romans: "There is one thing that's more wonderful than their numbers . . . in all that vast number there is not one man called Gisgo."*

This large payoff from stubborn courage is not limited to the military. "Never doubt that a small group of thoughtful citizens can change the world. Indeed, it is the only thing that ever has," wrote Margaret Mead. Revolutions are unarguably driven by an obsessive minority. And the entire growth of society, whether economic or moral, comes from a small number of people.

SUMMARY AND NEXT

So we summarize this chapter and link it to hidden asymmetries, the subtitle of the book. Society doesn't evolve by consensus, voting, majority, committees, verbose meetings, academic conferences, tea and cucumber sandwiches, or polling; only a few people suffice to disproportionately move the needle. All one needs is an asymmetric rule somewhere—and someone with soul in the game. And asymmetry is present in about everything.†

We promised in the Prologue to explain that slavery is more widespread than anticipated—actually, quite a bit more. Let us see next, after the Appendix.

---

* The Carthaginians seem to be short in name variety: there are plenty of Hamilcars and Hasdrupals confusing historians. Likewise there appear to be many Giscos, including the character in Flaubert's *Salambo*.

† All it takes is, say, a 3 percent minority, for "Merry Christmas" to become "Happy Holidays." But I suspect that should the minority rise in numbers, the effect would go away, as diverse societies are more syncretic. I grew up in Lebanon at the time when the population was about half Christian: people greeted one another in the Roman pagan way of sharing one another's holidays. Today Shiites (and some Sunnis not yet brainwashed by Saudi Arabia) would wish a Christian "Merry Christmas."

A Few More Counterintuitive Things About the Collective

*A*ntifragile has been about the failure of the average to represent anything in the presence of nonlinearities and asymmetries similar to the minority rule. So let us go beyond:

> *The* average *behavior of the market participant will not allow us to understand the general behavior of the market.*

You can examine markets as markets and individuals as individuals, but markets are not sums of average individuals (a sum is an average multiplied by a constant so they are both equally affected). These points now appear clear thanks to our discussion about renormalization. But to show how claims by the entire field of social science may fall apart, take one step further:

> *The psychological experiments on individuals showing "biases" do not allow us to automatically understand aggregates or collective behavior, nor do they enlighten us about the behavior of groups.*

Human nature is not defined outside of transactions involving other humans. Remember that we do not live alone, but in packs, and almost nothing of relevance concerns a person in isolation—which is what is typically done in laboratory-style works.*

Groups are units on their own. There are qualitative differences between a group of ten and a group of, say, 395,435. Each is a different

---

* What I just said explains the failure of the so-called field of behavioral economics to give us any more information than orthodox economics (itself rather poor) on how to play the market or understand the economy, or generate policy.

animal, in the literal sense, as different as a book is from an office build-ing. When we focus on commonalities, we get confused, but, at a certain scale, things become different. Mathematically different. The higher the dimension, in other words, the higher the number of possible interac-tions, and the more disproportionally difficult it is to understand the macro from the micro, the general from the simple units. This dispro-portionate increase of computational demands is called the *curse of dimensionality*. (I have actually found situations where, in the presence of small random errors, a single additional dimension may more than double some aspect of the complexity. Going from 1,000 to 1,001 may cause complexity to be multiplied by a billion times.)

Or, in spite of the huge excitement about our ability to see into the brain using the so-called field of neuroscience:

Understanding how the subparts of the brain (say, neurons) work will never allow us to understand how the brain works.

A group of neurons or genes, like a group of people, differs from the individual components—because the interactions are not necessarily linear. So far we have no f***ing idea how the brain of the worm *C. el-egans* works, which has around three hundred neurons. *C. elegans* was the first (multicellular) living unit to have its genes sequenced. Now con-sider that the human brain has about one hundred billion neurons, and that going from 300 to 301 neurons, because of the curse of dimension-ality, may double the complexity. So the use of *never* here is appropri-ate. And if you also want to understand why, in spite of the trumpeted "advances" in sequencing the DNA, we are largely unable to get infor-mation except in small isolated pockets for some diseases, same story. Monogenic diseases, those for which a single gene plays a role, are quite tractable, but anything entailing higher dimensionality falls apart.

Understanding the genetic makeup of a unit will never allow us to understand the behavior of the unit itself.

A reminder that what I am writing here isn't an opinion. It is a straightforward mathematical property.

The mean-field approach is when one uses the average interaction between, say, two people, and generalizes to the group—it is only possible if there are no asymmetries. For instance, Yaneer Bar-Yam has applied the failure of mean-field to evolutionary theory of the *selfish-gene* narrative trumpeted by such aggressive journalistic minds as Richard Dawkins and Steven Pinker, with more mastery of English than probability theory. He shows that local properties fail and the so-called mathematics used to prove the selfish gene are woefully naive and misplaced. There has been a storm around work by Martin Nowack and his colleagues (which include the biologist E. O. Wilson) about the terminal flaws in the selfish gene theory.*

The question is: could it be that much of what we have read about the advances in behavioral sciences is nonsense? Odds are it is. Many people have been accused of racism, segregationism, and somethingism without merit. Using cellular automata, a technique similar to renormalization, the late Thomas Schelling showed a few decades ago how a neighborhood can be segregated without a single segregationist among its inhabitants.

ZERO-INTELLIGENCE MARKETS

The underlying structure of reality matters much more than the participants, something policymakers fail to understand.

> *Under the right market structure, a collection of idiots produces a well-functioning market.*

The researchers Dhananjay Gode and Shyam Sunder came to a surprising result in 1993. You populate markets with *zero* intelligence agents, that is buying and selling randomly, under some structure such that a proper auction process matches bids and offers in a regular way. And guess what? We get the same allocative efficiency as if market participants were intelligent. Friedrich Hayek has been, once again, vindicated. Yet one of the most cited ideas in history, that of the invisible hand, appears to be the least integrated into modern psyche.

---

* It is worth mentioning names here as these people acted as attack dogs against those who discounted the selfish-gene theory, without addressing the mathematics provided (they can't), yet kept barking.

Furthermore:

It may be that some idiosyncratic behavior on the part of the individual (deemed at first glance "irrational") may be necessary for efficient functioning at the collective level.

More critically for the "rationalist" crowd,

Individuals don't need to know where they are going; markets do.

Leave people alone under a good structure and they will take care of things.

BOOK 4

WOLVES AMONG DOGS

CHAPTER 3

How to Legally Own
Another Person

*Even the church had its hippies—Coase does not need math—Avoid
lawyers during Oktoberfest—The expat life ends one day—People who
have been employees are signaling domestication*

————

n its early phase, as the church was starting to get established in Europe, there was a group of itinerant people called the gyrovagues. They were gyrating and roaming monks without any affiliation to any institution. Theirs was a freelance (and ambulatory) variety of monasticism, and their order was sustainable, as the members lived off begging and from the good graces of townsmen who took interest in them. It was a weak form of sustainability, as one can hardly call sustainable a group of a people with vows of celibacy: they cannot grow organically, and would need continuous enrollment. But they managed to survive thanks to help from the population, who provided them with food and temporary shelter.

Until sometime around the fifth century, when they started disappearing—they are now extinct. The gyrovagues were unpopular with the church, banned by the Council of Chalcedon in the fifth century, then banned again by the second Council of Nicaea about three hundred years later. In the West, Saint Benedict of Nursia, their greatest detractor, favored a more institutional brand of monasticism, and ended up prevailing with his rules that codified the activity, with a hierarchy and strong supervision by an abbot. For instance, Benedict's rules, put together in a sort of instruction manual, stipulate that a monk's possessions should be in the hands of the abbot (Rule 33), and Rule 70 bans angry monks from hitting other monks.

Why were they banned? They were, simply, totally free. They were financially free, and secure, not because of their means but because of their lack of wants. Ironically, by being beggars, they had the equivalent of *f*** you money,* which we can more easily get by being at the lowest rung than by joining the income-dependent classes.

Complete freedom is the last thing you want if you have an organized religion to run. Total freedom for your employees is also a very, very bad thing if you have a firm to run, so this chapter is about the question of employees and the nature of the firm and other institutions.

Benedict's instruction manual aims explicitly at removing any hint of freedom from the monks under the principles of *stabilitate sua et conversatione morum suorum et oboedientia*—"stability, conversion of manners, and obedience." And of course monks are put through a probation period of one year to see if they are sufficiently obedient.

In short, every organization wants a certain number of people associated with it to be deprived of a certain share of their freedom. How do you own these people? First, by conditioning and psychological manipulation; second, by tweaking them to have some skin in the game, forcing them to have something significant to lose if they disobey authority—something hard to do with gyrovague beggars who flout their scorn for material possessions. In the orders of the mafia, things are simple: *made men* (that is, ordained) can be *whacked* if the capo suspects a lack of allegiance, with a transitory stay in the trunk of a car—and a guaranteed presence of the boss at their funerals. For other professions, skin in the game comes in more subtle forms.

TO OWN A PILOT

Let us say that you own a small airline company. You are a very modern person; having attended many conferences and spoken to consultants, you believe that the traditional company is a thing of the past: everything can be organized through a web of contractors. It is more *efficient* to do so, you are certain.

Bob is a pilot with whom you have entered into a specific contract, in a well-defined drawn-out legal agreement, for precise flights, commitments made a long time in advance, which includes a penalty for non-performance. Bob supplies the co-pilot and an alternative pilot in case someone is sick. Tomorrow evening you will be operating a scheduled flight to Munich as part of an Oktoberfest special. The flight is full with motivated budget passengers, some of whom went on a preparatory diet; they have been waiting a whole year for this Gargantuan episode of beer, pretzels, and sausage in laughter-filled hangars.

Bob calls you at five P.M. to let you know that he and the copilot, well, they love you . . . but, *you know,* they will not fly the plane tomorrow. *You know,* they had an offer from a Saudi Arabian Sheikh, a devout man who wants to take a special party to Las Vegas, and needs Bob *and* his team to run the flight. The Sheikh and his retinue were impressed with Bob's manners, the fact that Bob had never had a drop of alcohol in his life, his expertise in fermented yoghurt drinks, and told him that money was no object. The offer is so generous that it covers whatever penalty there is for a breach of a competing contract by Bob.

You kick yourself. There are plenty of lawyers on these Oktoberfest flights, and, worse, retired lawyers without hobbies who love to sue as a way to kill time, regardless of outcome. Consider the chain reaction: if your plane doesn't take off, you will not have the equipment to bring the beer-fattened passengers back from Munich—and you will most certainly miss many round trips. Rerouting passengers is costly and not guaranteed.

You make a few phone calls and it turns out that it is easier to find an academic economist with common sense than find another pilot— that is, an event of probability zero. You have all this equity in a firm that is now under severe financial threat. You are certain that you will go bust.

You start thinking: well, *you know,* if Bob were a slave, someone you own, *you know,* these kind of things would not be possible. Slave? But wait . . . what Bob just did isn't something that employees who are in the business of being employees do! People who are employees for a living don't behave so opportunistically. Contractors are exceedingly free; as risk-takers, they fear mostly the law. But employees have a reputation to protect. And they can be fired.

People you find in employment love the regularity of the payroll, with that special envelop on their desk the last day of the month, and without which they would act as a baby deprived of mother's milk. You realize that had Bob been an employee rather than something that appeared to be cheaper, that contractor thing, then you wouldn't be having so much trouble.

But employees are expensive. You have to pay them even when you've got nothing for them to do. You lose your flexibility. Talent for talent, they cost a lot more. Lovers of paychecks are lazy . . . but they would never let you down at times like these.

So employees exist because they have significant skin in the game—and the risk is shared with them, enough risk for it to be a deterrent and a penalty for acts of undependability, such as failing to show up on time. You are buying dependability.

And dependability is a driver behind many transactions. People of some means have a country house—which is inefficient compared to hotels or rentals—because they want to make sure it is available if they decide they want to use it on a whim. There is a trader's expression: "Never buy when you can rent the three *F*s: what you Float, what you Fly, and what you . . . (*that something else*)." Yet many people own boats and planes, and end up stuck with that something else.

True, a contractor has downside, a financial penalty that can be built into the contract, in addition to reputational costs. But consider that an employee will always have more risk. And conditional on someone being an employee, such a person will be risk averse. By being employees they signal a certain type of domestication.

Someone who has been employed for a while is giving you strong evidence of submission.

Evidence of submission is displayed by the employee's going through years depriving himself of his personal freedom for nine hours every day, his ritualistic and punctual arrival at an office, his denying himself his own schedule, and his not having beaten up anyone on the way back home after a bad day. He is an obedient, housebroken dog.

FROM THE COMPANY MAN TO THE COMPANIES PERSON

Even when an employee ceases to be an employee, he will remain diligent. The longer the person stays with a company, the more emotional investment they will have in staying, and, when leaving, are guaranteed in making an "honorable exit."*

If employees lower your tail risk, you lower theirs as well. Or at least, that's what they think you do.

At the time of writing, firms stay in the top league by size (the so-called S&P 500) for only about between ten and fifteen years. Companies exit the S&P 500 through mergers or by shrinking their business, both conditions leading to layoffs. Throughout the twentieth century, however, expected duration was more than sixty years. Longevity for large firms was greater; people stayed with large firms for their entire lives. There was such a thing as a company man (restricting the gender here is appropriate, as company men were almost all men).

The company man is best defined as someone whose identity is impregnated with the stamp his firm wants to give him. He dresses the part, even uses the language the company expects. His social life is so invested in the company that leaving it inflicts a huge penalty, like banishment from Athens under the Ostrakon. Saturday nights, he goes out with other company men and spouses, sharing company jokes. IBM required its employees to wear white shirts—not light blue, not with discreet stripes, but plain white. And a dark blue suit. Nothing was allowed to be fancy, or invested with the tiniest amount of idiosyncratic attribute. You were a part of IBM.

Our definition:

> *A company man is someone who feels that he has something huge to lose if he doesn't behave as a company man—that is, he has skin in the game.*

In return, the firm is bound by a pact to keep the company man on the books as long as feasible, that is, until mandatory retirement, after which he would go play golf with a comfortable pension, with former coworkers as partners. The system worked when large corporations survived a long time and were perceived to be longer lasting than nation-states.

---

* The academic tenure system is meant to give people the security to express their opinions freely. However, tenure is given (in the ideological disciplines, such as the "humanities" and social science) to the submissive ones who play the game and have shown proofs of such domestication. It's not working.

By the 1990s, however, people started to realize that working as a company man was safe . . . provided the company stayed around. But the technological revolution that took place in Silicon valley put traditional companies under financial threat. For instance, after the rise of Microsoft and the personal computer, IBM, which was the main farm for company men, had to lay off a proportion of its "lifers," who then realized that the low-risk profile of their position wasn't so low risk. These people couldn't find a job elsewhere; they were of no use to anyone outside IBM. Even their sense of humor failed outside of the corporate culture.

If the company man is, sort of, gone, he has been replaced by the companies person. For people are no longer owned by a company but by something worse: the idea that they need to be *employable*. The employable person is embedded in an industry, with fear of upsetting not just their employer, but *other* potential employers.*

COASE'S THEORY OF THE FIRM

Perhaps, by definition, an employable person is the one you will never find in a history book, because these people are designed to never leave their mark on the course of events. They are, by design, uninteresting to historians. But let us now see how this fits the theory of the firm and the ideas of Ronald Coase.

> *An employee is—by design—more valuable inside a firm than outside of it; that is, more valuable to the employer than the marketplace.*

Coase was a remarkable modern economist in that he was independent thinking, rigorous, and creative, with ideas that are applicable and explain the world around us—in other words, the real thing. His style is so rigorous that he is known for the Coase Theorem (about how markets are very smart about allocating resources and nuisances such as pollution), an idea that he posited without a single word of mathematics, but which is as fundamental as many things written in mathematics. Aside from his theorem, Coase was the first to shed light on why

---

* In some countries, executives and mid-level managers are given perks such as a car (in the disguise of a tax subsidy), which are things on which the employee would not spend his money had he been given cash (odds are he may save the funds); they make the employee even more dependent.

firms exist. For him, contracts can be too costly to negotiate due to transaction costs; the solution is to incorporate your business and hire employees with clear job descriptions because you can't afford legal and organizational bills for every transaction. A free market is a place where forces act to determine specialization, and information travels via price point; but *within* a firm these market forces are lifted because they cost more to run than the benefits they bring. So market forces will cause the firm to aim for the optimal ratio of employees and outside contractors.

As we can see, Coase stopped one or two inches short of the notion of skin in the game. He never thought in risk terms to realize that an employee is also a risk-management strategy.

Had economists, Coase or Shmoase, had any interest in the ancients, they would have discovered the risk-management strategy relied upon by Roman families who customarily had a slave for treasurer, the person responsible for the finances of the household and the estate. Why? Because you can inflict a much higher punishment on a slave than a free person or a freedman—and you do not need to rely on the mechanism of the law for that. You can be bankrupted by an irresponsible or dishonest steward who can divert your estate's funds to Bithynia. A slave has more downside.

COMPLEXITY

Welcome to the modern world. In a world in which products are increasingly made by subcontractors with increasing degrees of specialization, employees are even more necessary than before for some specific, delicate tasks. If you miss one step in a process, often the entire business shuts down—which explains why today, in a supposedly more efficient world with lower inventories and more subcontractors, things appear to run smoothly and efficiently, but errors are costlier and delays are considerably longer than in the past. One single delay in the chain can stop the entire process.

A CURIOUS FORM OF SLAVE OWNERSHIP

Slave ownership by companies has traditionally taken very curious forms. The best slave is someone you overpay and who knows it, terrified of losing his status. Multinational companies created the *expat* category, a sort of diplomat with a higher standard of living who represents the firm far away and runs its business there. All large corporations had (and some still have) employees with *expat* status and, in spite of its costs, it is an extremely effective strategy. Why? Because the further from headquarters an employee is located, the more autonomous his unit, the more you want him to be a slave so he does nothing strange on his own.

A bank in New York sends a married employee with his family to a foreign location, say, a tropical country with cheap labor, with perks and privileges such as country club membership, a driver, a nice company villa with a gardener, a yearly trip back home with the family in first class, and keeps him there for a few years, enough to be addicted. He earns much more than the "locals," in a hierarchy reminiscent of colonial days. He builds a social life with other expats. He progressively wants to stay in the location longer, but he is far from headquarters and has no idea of his minute-to-minute standing in the firm except through signals. Eventually, like a diplomat, he begs for another location when time comes for a reshuffle. Returning to the home office means loss of perks, having to revert to his base salary—a return to lower-middle-class life in the suburbs of New York City, taking the commuter train, perhaps, or, God forbid, a bus, and eating a sandwich for lunch! The person is terrified when the big boss snubs him. Ninety-five percent of the employee's mind will be on company politics . . . which is exactly what the company wants. The big boss in the board room will have a supporter in the event of some intrigue.

FREEDOM IS NEVER FREE

In the famous tale by Ahiqar, later picked up by Aesop (then again by La Fontaine), the dog boasts to the wolf all the contraptions of comfort and luxury he has, almost prompting the wolf to enlist. Until the wolf asks the dog about his collar and is terrified when he understands its use. "*Of all your meals, I want nothing.*" *He ran away and is still running.*[*]

The question is: what would you like to be, a dog or a wolf?

The original Aramaic version had a wild ass, instead of a wolf, showing off his freedom. But the wild ass ends up eaten by the lion. Freedom entails risks—real skin in the game. Freedom is never free.

---

[*] La Fontaine: *Il importe si bien, que de tous vos repas / Je ne veux en aucune sorte, / Et ne voudrais pas même à ce prix un trésor. / Cela dit, maître Loup s'enfuit, et court encor.*

Whatever you do, just don't be a dog claiming to be a wolf. In Harris's sparrows, males develop secondary traits that correlate with their fighting ability. Darker color is associated with dominance. However, experimental darkening of lighter males does not raise their status, because their behavior is not altered. In fact these darker birds get killed—as the researcher Terry Burnham once told me: "birds know that you need to walk the walk."

Another aspect of the dog vs. wolf dilemma: the feeling of false stability. A dog's life may appear smooth and secure, but in the absence of an owner, a dog does not survive. Most people prefer to adopt puppies, not grown-up dogs; in many countries, unwanted dogs are euthanized. A wolf is trained to survive. Employees abandoned by their employers, as we saw in the IBM story, cannot bounce back.

WOLVES AMONG THE DOGS

There is a category of employees who aren't slaves, but these represent a very small proportion of the pool. You can identify them as follows: they don't give a *f**** about their reputation, at least not their corporate reputation.

After business school, I spent a year in a banking training program—by some accident, as the bank was confused about my background and aims and wanted me to become an international banker. There, I was surrounded by highly employable persons (my most unpleasant experience in life), until I switched to trading (with another firm) and discovered that there were some wolves among the dogs.

One type was the salesperson whose resignation could cause a loss of business, or, what's worse, could benefit a competitor by bringing clients there. Salespeople had tension with the firm as the firm tried to dissociate accounts from them by depersonalizing the relationships with clients, usually unsuccessfully: people like people, and they drop business when they get some generic and polite person on the phone in place of their warm and often exuberant salesperson-friend. The other type was the trader about whom only one thing mattered: the profits and losses, or P and L. Firms had a love-hate relationship with these two types as they were unruly—traders and salespeople were only manageable when they were unprofitable, in which case they weren't wanted.

Traders who made money, I realized, could get so disruptive that they needed to be kept away from the rest of the employees. That's the price you pay for turning individuals into profit centers, meaning no other criterion mattered. I recall once threatening a trader who was abusing the terrified accountant with impunity, telling him such things as "I am busy earning money to pay your salary" (intimating that accounting did not add to the bottom line of the firm). But no problem; the people you meet when riding high are also those you meet when riding low, and I saw the fellow getting some (more subtle) abuse from the same accountant before he got fired, as he eventually ran out of luck. You are free—but only as free as your last trade. As we saw with Ahiqar's wild ass, freedom is never free.

When I switched firms away from the proto-company man, I was explicitly told that my employment would terminate the minute I ceased to meet the P and L target. I had my back to the wall, but I took the gamble, which forced me to engage in arbitrage, low-risk transactions with small downsides that were possible at the time because the sophistication of operators in the financial markets was very low.

I recall being asked why I didn't wear a tie, which at the time was the equivalent of walking down Fifth Avenue naked. "One part arrogance, one part aesthetics, one part convenience," was my usual answer. If you were profitable you could give managers all the crap you wanted and they ate it because they needed you and were afraid of losing their own jobs. Risk takers can be socially unpredictable people. Freedom is always associated with risk taking, whether it leads to it or comes from it. You take risks, you feel part of history. And risk takers take risks because it is in their nature to be wild animals.

Note the linguistic dimension—and why, in addition to sartorial considerations, traders needed to be kept away from the rest of nonfree, non-risk-taking people. In my day, nobody cursed in public except for gang members and those who wanted to signal that they were not slaves: traders cursed like sailors, and I have kept the habit of strategic foul language, used only outside of my writings and family life.* Those who use foul language on social networks (such as Twitter) are sending an expensive signal that they are free—and, ironically, competent. You

---

* I can't resist this story. I once received a letter from a person from the finance industry with the following request: "Dear Mr. Taleb, I am a close follower of your work, but I feel compelled to give you a piece of advice. An intellectual like you would greatly gain in influence if he avoided using foul language." My answer was very short: "f*** off."

don't signal competence if you don't take risks for it—there are few such low-risk strategies. So cursing today is a status symbol, just as oligarchs in Moscow wear blue jeans at special events to signal their power. Even in banks, traders were shown to customers on tours of the firm as if they were animals in a zoo, and the sight of a trader cursing on a phone while in a shouting match with a broker was part of the scenery.

So while cursing and bad language can be a sign of doglike status and total ignorance—the "canaille," which etymologically relates these people to dogs—ironically the highest status, that of a free man, is usually indicated by voluntarily adopting the mores of the lowest class.* It is no different from Diogenes (the one with the barrel) insulting Alexander the Great by asking him to stand out of his sun, just for signaling (legend, of course). Consider that English "manners" were imposed on the middle class as a way of domesticating them, along with instilling in them the fear of breaking rules and violating social norms.

LOSS AVERSION

Take for now the following:

> *What matters isn't what a person has or doesn't have; it is what he or she is afraid of losing.*

The more you have to lose, the more fragile you are. Ironically, in my debates, I've seen numerous winners of the so-called Nobel in Economics (the Riksbank Prize in Honor of Alfred Nobel) concerned about losing an argument. I noticed years ago that four of them were actually concerned that I, a nonperson and trader, publicly called them frauds. Why did they care? Well, the higher you go in that business, the more insecure you get, as losing an argument to a lesser person exposes you more than if you lose to some hotshot.

Being higher up in life only works under some conditions. You would think that the head of the CIA would be the most powerful person in America, but it turned out that the venerated David Petraeus was more vulnerable than a truck driver. The fellow couldn't even have an extra-

---

* My friend Rory Sutherland (the same Rory) explained that some more intelligent corporate representatives had the strategy of cursing while talking to journalists in a way to signal that they were conveying the truth, not reciting some company mantra.

marital relationship. You can risk people's lives, but you remain a slave. The entire structure of the civil service is organized that way.

WAITING FOR CONSTANTINOPLE

The exact obverse of the public-hotshot as slave is the autocrat.

As I am writing these lines, we are witnessing a nascent confrontation between several parties, which includes the current "heads" of state of members of the North Atlantic Treaty Organization (modern states don't quite have *heads,* just people who talk big) and the Russian Vladimir Putin. Clearly, except for Putin, all the others need to be elected, can come under fire by their party, and have to calibrate every single statement with how it could be misinterpreted the least by the press. On the other hand, Putin has the equivalent of *f***you money,* projecting a visible "I don't care," which in turn brings him more followers and more support. In such a confrontation Putin looks and acts as a free citizen confronting slaves who need committees, approval, and who of course feel like they have to fit their decisions to an immediate rating.

Putin's attitude mesmerizes his followers, particularly the Christians in the Levant—especially those Orthodox Christians who remember when Catherine the Great's fleet came to allow the tolling of the bells of the Saint George Cathedral in Beirut. Catherine the Great was "the last czar with balls," and she is the one who took the Crimea from the Ottomans. Before that, the Sunni Ottomans had banned Christians in the coastal cities under their control from ringing church bells—only inaccessible mountain villages allowed themselves such freedom. These Christians lost the active protection of the Russian czar in 1917 and now are hoping that Byzantium is coming back about a hundred years later. It is much easier to do business with the owner of the business than some employee who is likely to lose his job next year; likewise it is easier to trust the word of an autocrat than a fragile elected official.

Watching Putin made me realize that domesticated (and sterilized) animals don't stand a chance against a wild predator. Not a single one. Fughedabout military capabilities: it is the trigger that counts.*

---

* Universal suffrage did not change the story by much: until recently, the pool of elected people in so-called democracies was limited to a club of upper class people who cared much, much less about the press. But with more social mobility, ironically, more people could access the pool of politicians—and lose their jobs. And progressively, as with corporations, you start gathering peo-

Historically, the autocrat was both freer and—as in the special case of traditional monarchs in small principalities—in some cases had skin in the game in improving the place, more so than an elected official whose objective function is to show paper gains. This is not the case in modern times, as dictators, aware that their time might be limited, indulge in pillaging the place and transferring assets to their Swiss bank accounts—as in the case of the Saudi Royal family.

DO NOT ROCK BUREAUCRISTAN

More generally:

> *People whose survival depends on qualitative "job assessments"*
> *by someone of higher rank in an organization cannot be trusted*
> *for critical decisions.*

Although employees are reliable *by design,* it remains the case that they cannot be trusted in making decisions, hard decisions, anything that entails serious tradeoffs. Nor can they face emergencies unless they are in the emergency business, say, firefighters. The employee has a very simple objective function: fulfill the tasks that his or her supervisor deems necessary, or satisfy some gameable metric. If the employee when coming to work in the morning discovers the potential for huge opportunities, say selling anti-diabetes products to prediabetic Saudi Arabian visitors, he cannot stop and start exploiting it if he is officially in the light fixtures business, selling chandeliers to old-fashioned Park Avenue widows.

So although an employee is here to prevent an emergency, should there be a change of plan, the employee is stuck. While this paralysis can arise because the distribution of responsibilities causes a serious dilution, there is another problem of scale.

We saw the effect with the Vietnam War. Most people (sort of) believed that certain courses of action were absurd, but it was easier to continue than to stop—particularly since one can always spin a story explaining why continuing is better than stopping (the backfitting story

---

ple with minimal courage—and selected because they don't have courage, as with a regular corporation.

of sour grapes now known as cognitive dissonance). We have been witnessing the same problem in the U.S. attitude toward Saudi Arabia. It is clear since the attack on the World Trade Center (in which most of the attackers were Saudi citizens) that someone in that nonpartying kingdom had a hand—somehow—in the matter. But no bureaucrat, fearful of oil disruptions, made the right decision—instead, the absurd invasion of Iraq was endorsed because it appeared to be simpler.

Since 2001 the policy for fighting Islamic terrorists has been, to put it politely, missing the elephant in the room, sort of like treating symptoms and completely missing the disease. Policymakers and slow-thinking bureaucrats stupidly let terrorism grow by ignoring its roots—because that was not a course that was optimal for their jobs, even if optimal for the country. So we lost a generation: someone who went to grammar school in Saudi Arabia (our "ally") after September 11 is now an adult, indoctrinated into believing and supporting Salafi violence, hence encouraged to finance it. Even worse, the Wahhabis have accelerated their brainwashing of East and West Asians with their madrassas, thanks to high oil revenues. Instead of invading Iraq or blowing up "Jihadi John" and other individual terrorists, thus causing a multiplication of these agents, it would have been better to focus on the source of the problems: Wahhabi/Salafi education and the promotion of intolerant beliefs according to which a Shiite or an Ezidi or a Christian are deviant people. But, to repeat, this is not a decision that can be made by a collection of bureaucrats with a job description.

The same thing happened in 2009 with the banks. I said in Prologue 1 that the Obama administration was complicit with the Bob Rubin trade. We have plenty of evidence that they were afraid of rocking the boat and contradicting the cronies.

Now compare these policies to ones in which decision makers have skin in the game as a substitute for their annual "job assessment," and you will picture a different world.

NEXT

Next, let's talk about the Achilles' heel of the free who is not so free.

CHAPTER 4

The Skin of Others in Your Game

How to be a whistleblower—James Bond isn't a Jesuit priest, but he is a bachelor—So are both Professor Moriarty and Sherlock Holmes—Total intelligence in the P.R. firm Ketchum—Putting the skin on terrorists

———

A MORTGAGE AND TWO CATS

Imagine working for a corporation that produces a (so far) hidden harm to the community, in concealing a cancer-causing property that kills thousands by an effect that is not (yet) fully visible. You could alert the public, but you would automatically lose your job. There is a risk that the company's evil scientists would disprove you, causing additional humiliation. You are aware of what Monsanto shills did to the French scientist Gilles-Éric Séralini, who, until he won his defamation suit, lived in total scientific disgrace, the reputational equivalent of leprosy. Or the news will come and go and you may end up being ignored. You are familiar with the history of whistleblowers, which shows that even if you end up vindicated, it may take time for the truth to emerge over the noise created by corporate shills. Meanwhile you will pay the price. A smear campaign against you will destroy any hope of getting another job.

You have nine children, a sick parent, and as a result of taking a stand, your children's future may be compromised. Their college hopes will evaporate—you may even have trouble feeding them properly. You are severely conflicted between your obligation to the collective and to your progeny. You feel you are part of the crime, and unless you do something, you are an agent: thousands are dying from the hidden poisoning by the corporation. Being ethical comes at a huge cost *to others*.

In the James Bond movie *Spectre,* agent Bond found himself fighting—on his own, whistleblower style—a conspiracy of dark forces that took over the British service, including his supervisors. Q, who built the new fancy car and other gadgets for him, when asked to help against the conspiracy, said, "I have a mortgage and two cats"—in jest of course, because he ended up risking the lives of his two cats to fight the bad guys.

Society likes saints and moral heroes to be celibate so they do not have family pressures that may force them into the dilemma of needing to compromise their sense of ethics to feed their children. The entire human race, something rather abstract, becomes their family. Some martyrs, such as Socrates, had young children (although he was in his seventies), and overcame the dilemma at their expense.* Many can't.

The vulnerability of heads of households has been remarkably exploited in history. The samurai had to leave their families in Edo as hostages, thus guaranteeing to the authorities that they would not take positions against the rulers. The Romans and Huns partook of the practice of exchanging permanent "visitors," the children of rulers on both sides, who grew up at the courts of the foreign nation in a form of gilded captivity.

The Ottomans relied on janissaries, who were extracted as babies from Christian families and never married. Having no family (or no contact with their family), they were entirely devoted to the sultan.

It is no secret that large corporations prefer people with families; those with downside risk are easier to own, particularly when they are choking under a large mortgage.

And of course most fictional heroes such as Sherlock Holmes or James Bond don't have the encumbrance of a family that can become a target of, say, evil professor Moriarty.

---

* In Plato's *Apology,* Socrates behaved like a mensch: "I, Sir, have a family, you know, and was not born 'from oak or from rock' "—this is again an expression of Homer—"but from human beings, so that I have a family too, and indeed sons, men of Athens, three of them, one already a teenager and two who are children. But nonetheless I will not beg you to acquit me by bringing any of them here."

Let us go one step further.

To make ethical choices you cannot have dilemmas between the particular (friends, family) and the general.

Celibacy has been a way to force men to implement such heroism: for instance, the rebellious ancient sect the Essenes were celibate. So by definition they did not reproduce—unless one considers that their sect mutated to merge with what is known today as Christianity. A celibacy requirement might help with rebellious causes, but it isn't the greatest way to multiply your sect through the ages.

Financial independence is another way to solve ethical dilemmas, but such independence is hard to ascertain: many seemingly independent people aren't particularly so. While, in Aristotle's days, a person of independent means was free to follow his conscience, this is no longer as common in modern days.

Intellectual and ethical freedom requires the absence of the skin of others in one's game, which is why the free are so rare. I cannot possibly imagine the activist Ralph Nader, when he was the target of large motor companies, raising a family with 2.2 kids and a dog.

But neither celibacy nor financial independence makes one unconditionally immune, as we see next.

FINDING HIDDEN VULNERABILITIES

So far we have seen that the requirement of celibacy is enough evidence that society has, traditionally, been implicitly penalizing some layer of a collective for the actions of a person. This is never done explicitly: nobody says, "I will punish your family because you are criticizing the big agrichemical firms," when in effect this is what happens in practice when there is the threat of the reduction in the volume of the objects under the Christmas tree, or the degradation of the quality of food in the refrigerator.

I have *f*** you money*, so I appear to be fully independent (though I am certain that my independence is unrelated to my finances). But there are people I care about who can be affected by my actions, and those who want to harm me may want to go after them. In the campaign against me waged by Big Ag, the public relation firms (hired to discredit those who were skeptical of the risk of transgenics) couldn't threaten my livelihood. Nor could they tag me with the "antiscience" label (the central part of their arsenal) since I have a history of standing for probabilistic rigor in science expressed in technical language, and several million readers who understand my reasoning. It is a bit too late for that now. In fact, by creating analogies between some cherry-picked passages from my writings taken out of context and those of the new age guru Deepak Chopra, they have caused some people to suspect that Chopra was a logician, an application of Wittgenstein's ruler*: *by measuring the table with a ruler am I measuring the ruler or measuring the table?* Far-fetched comparisons are more likely to discredit the commentator than the commentated.

So these P.R. firms resorted to harassing New York University's staff by using web-mobs to flood them with emails—which includes overwhelming a defenseless assistant and people who had no idea I worked for the university since I am there only quarter-time. This method—of hitting you where they *think* it hurts—implies hitting people around you who are more vulnerable than you. General Motors, in the campaign against Ralph Nader (who uncovered flaws in their products), desperate to stop him, resorted to harassing Rose Nader, his mother, calling her at three in the morning—in the days when it was hard to trace a telephone call. Clearly it was meant to make Ralph Nader feel he was guilty of harming his own mother. It turned out that Rose Nader was herself an activist and felt flattered by the calls (at least she was not left out of the battle).

I am privileged to have other enemies than Big Ag. A couple of years ago, a university in Lebanon offered me an honorary doctorate. I accepted out of respect, counter to my habit of refusing honors, (largely) because I get very bored during ceremonies. Plus, in my experience, people who collect honorary doctorates are typically hierarchy-conscious, and I abide by Cato's injunction: he preferred to be asked why he didn't have a statue rather than why he had one. The staff of the university became automatically the target of my detractors, of Salafi-sympathizers among the student body, and of people who were ticked off by my enthusiasm for and defense of Shiite Islam, and my desire to return Lebanon to the Eastern Mediterranean, the Greco-Roman world to which it tangi-

---

* In *Fooled by Randomness.*

bly belongs, away from the disastrous and fictional construction called Arabism. Visibly, deans and presidents of universities are far more vulnerable than independent persons, and animals know where weakness lies. By the minority rule, all it takes is a very small number of detractors using misplaced buzzwords of the type that makes people cringe (such as "racist") to scare an entire institution. Institutions are employees—vulnerable, reputation-conscious employees. Being Salafi is not a race but a political movement–cum–criminal organization, yet people fear being labeled racists so much that they lose their logical faculties. But in the end the efforts of the detractors were to no avail: on one hand I cannot be harmed; on the other the university would have more to lose from the withdrawal of an honor than from harassment by Pan-Arabists and Salafis.

These methods of going after vulnerable people associated with you are eventually ineffective. For one thing, odious people (and Salafi sympathizers) tend to be dumb, along with people who act only in mobs. In addition, those who engage in smear campaigning as a profession are necessarily incompetent at everything else—hence at that business too—so the industry accumulates rejects who are prone to ethical stretches. Did any of your business-smart, streetwise, or academically gifted peers in high school declare that their dream was to become the world's expert in smearing whistleblowers? Or even work as a lobbyist or public relations expert? These jobs are indicative of necessary failure in other things.

Further:

To be free of conflict you need to have no friends.

Which is why Cleon was said to have renounced all of his friendships during his office.

So far we have seen that the link between the individual and the collective is too fuzzy to interpret naively. So let us consider the classical situation of the terrorist who thinks he is immune to harm.

HOW TO PUT SKIN IN THE GAME OF SUICIDE BOMBERS

Can someone punish a family for the crimes of an individual? The scriptures are self-contradictory—you can get both answers from the

Old Testament. *Exodus* and *Numbers* show God as "visiting the iniquity of the fathers on the children to the third or fourth generation." *Deuteronomy* makes a separation: "Fathers shall not be put to death because of their children, nor shall children be put to death because of their fathers. Each one shall be put to death for his own sin." Even today the question isn't fully settled, nor is the answer clear-cut. You are not responsible for the debts of your parents, but German taxpayers are still responsible for war reparations for crimes committed by their grandparents and great-grandparents. And even in ancient times, when debt was a burden that crossed generations, the answer wasn't clear-cut: there was a balancing mechanism of periodic (literal) cleaning of the slate, with jubilee debt forgiveness.

However, the answer is clear in the case of terrorism. The rule should be: *You kill my family with supposed impunity; I will make yours pay* some *indirect price for it.* Indirect responsibility isn't part of the standard crime-and-punishment methodology of a civilized society, but confronting terrorists (who threaten innocents) isn't standard either. For we have rarely in history faced a situation in which the perpetrator of a crime has a completely asymmetric payoff and upside from death itself.*

Hammurabi's code actually makes such a provision, transferring liability across generations. For, on that same basalt stele surrounded by Korean selfie sticks, is written the following: "If the architect built a house and the house subsequently collapses, killing the firstborn son of the master, the firstborn son of the architect shall be put to death." The individual as we understand it today did not exist as a standalone unit; the family did.

Gypsies have rules that remained for a long time opaque to outsiders; it was probably not until the movie *Vengo* (2000) that the general public discovered a dark custom among Gitano tribes. In a case where a member of one family kills a member of another, a direct relative of the killer will be delivered to the family of the victim.

The unusual nuisance with jihadi terrorism is that we are totally defenseless in front of a deluded person willing to kill scores of innocents without any true downside, that is, no skin in the game. In Northern

---

* The current narrative is that terrorists think they are going to heaven and will meet virgins that look like their next-door neighbors. Not quite true: many just seek a perceived heroic death, or to impress their friends. The desire to be a hero can be quite blinding.

Phoenicia, Alawis are terrorized by Salafis wearing bomb-filled jackets that they can activate in a public place. There is almost no way they can be "caught" without activation. Killing them on sight leads to false positives, but we can't afford false negatives. As a result, we have instances of private citizens cornering and "hugging" perceived self-bombers in places where detonation would be least harmful. This is a form of counter-suicide bombing.

Explicit communal punishment can be used where other methods of justice have failed, provided they are not based on an emotional reaction, but on a well-outlined method of justice defined prior to the event, so that it becomes a deterrent. One who is sacrificing himself for a perceived upside for a given collective needs a deterrent, so it is a form of injection of skin in the game where there are no other methods. And the skin is visible: that very collective.

The only way we have left to control suicide-terrorists would be precisely to convince them that blowing themselves up is not the worst-case scenario for them, nor the end scenario at all. Making their families and loved ones bear a financial burden—just as Germans still pay for war crimes—would immediately add consequences to their actions. The penalty needs to be properly calibrated to be a true disincentive, without imparting any sense of heroism or martyrdom to the families in question.

But I feel queasy about transferring a crime from one unit, an individual, to another, a collective. What I do not feel bad about is preventing the family of the perpetrators of terrorist acts from benefiting from those acts—many terrorist groups reward the families of suicide bombers, and this can be safely terminated without any ethical dilemma.

NEXT

In the last two chapters we examined the good and the bad of dependence and the constraints on our freedoms coming from skin in the game. Next, let us look at the thrills (of the right type) of risk taking.

BOOK 5

BEING ALIVE MEANS TAKING CERTAIN RISKS

CHAPTER 5

Life in the Simulation Machine

*How to dress while reading Borges and Proust—There are many ways
to convince with an ice pick—Councils of bickering bishops—Theosis—
Why Trump will win (he actually did win)*

––––––

I once sat in a dinner party at a large round table across from a courteous fellow called David. The host was a physicist, Edgar C., in his New York club, a literary sort of club, where, except for David, almost everyone was dressed like people who either read Borges and Proust, wanted to be known as readers of Borges and Proust, or just liked to spend time with people who read Borges and Proust (corduroy, ascot, suede shoes, or just business suit). As for David, he was dressed like someone who didn't know that people who read Borges and Proust needed to dress in a certain way when they congregated. At some point during the dinner, David unexpectedly pulled out an ice pick and made it go through his hand. I had no clue what the fellow did for a living—nor was I aware that Edgar was into magic as a side hobby. It turned out that the David in question was a magician (his name is David Blaine), and that he was very famous.

I knew very little about magicians, assumed it was all about optical illusions—the central inverse problem we mentioned in Prologue 2 that makes it easier to engineer than reverse-engineer. But something struck me at the end of the party. David was standing by the coat check using a handkerchief to sop up drops of blood coming out of his hand.

So the fellow was really making an icepick go through his hand—with all the risks that entailed. He suddenly became another person in my eyes. He was now real. He took risks. He had skin in the game.

I met him again a few months later and, as I tried to shake hands with him, noticed a scar where the icepick had come out of his hand.

JESUS WAS A RISK TAKER

This allowed me to finally figure out this business of the Trinity. The Christian religion, throughout Chalcedon, Nicea, and other ecumenical councils and various synods of argumentative bishops, kept insisting on the dual nature of Jesus Christ. It would be theologically simpler if God were god and Jesus were man, just like another prophet, the way Islam views him, or the way Judaism views Abraham. But no, he had to be both man and god; the duality is so central it kept coming back though all manner of refinement: whether the duality allowed sharing the same substance (Orthodoxy), the same will (Monothelites), the same nature (Monophysites). The trinity is what caused other monotheists to see traces of polytheism in Christianity, and caused many Christians who fell into the hands of the Islamic State to be beheaded.

So it appears that the church founders really wanted Christ to have skin in the game; he did actually suffer on the cross, sacrifice himself, and experience death. He was a risk taker. More crucially to our story, he sacrificed himself *for the sake of others*. A god stripped of humanity cannot have skin in the game in such a manner, cannot really suffer (or, if he does, such a redefinition of a god injected with a human nature would back up our argument). A god who didn't really suffer on the cross would be like a magician who performed an illusion, not someone who actually bled after sliding an icepick between his carpal bones.

The Orthodox Church goes further, making the human side flow upward rather than downward. The fourth-century bishop Athanasius of Alexandria wrote: "Jesus Christ was incarnate so *we* could be made God" (emphasis mine). It is the very human character of Jesus that can allow us mortals to access God and merge with him, become part of him, in order to partake of the divine. That fusion is called *theosis*. The human nature of Christ makes the divine possible for all of us.*

---

* "The Son of God shares our nature so we can share His; as He has us in Him, so we have Him in us."—Chrysostom

PASCAL'S WAGER

This argument (that real life is risk taking) reveals the theological weakness of Pascal's wager, which stipulates that believing in the creator has a positive payoff in case he truly exists, and no downside in case he doesn't. Hence the wager would be to believe in God as a free option. But there are no free options. If you follow the idea to its logical end, you can see that it proposes religion without skin in the game, making it a purely academic and sterile activity. But what applies to Jesus should also apply to other believers. We will see that, traditionally, there is no religion without some skin in the game.

THE MATRIX

Philosophers, unlike the equally argumentative but vastly more sophisticated (and more colorfully dressed) bishops, don't get the point with their *experience machine* thought experiment. The procedure is as follows. Simply, you sit in an apparatus and a technician plugs a few cables into your brain, after which you undergo an "experience." You feel exactly as if an event took place, except that it all happened in virtual reality; it was all mental. Alas, such an experience will never be in the same category as the real—only an academic philosopher who never took risk can believe such nonsense. Why?

Because, to repeat, life is sacrifice and risk taking, and nothing that doesn't entail some moderate amount of the former, under the constraint of satisfying the latter, is close to what we can call life. If you do not undertake a risk of real harm, reparable or even potentially irreparable, from an adventure, it is not an adventure.

Our argument—that the real requires peril—can lead to niceties about the mind-body problem, but don't tell your local philosopher.

Now, one may argue: once inside the machine, you may *believe* that you have skin in the game, and experience the pains and consequences as if you were living the actual harm. But this is once *inside,* not outside, and there is no risk of irreversible harm, things that linger and make time flow in one direction not the other. The reason a dream is not reality is that when you suddenly wake up from falling from a Chinese skyscraper, life continues, and there is no *absorbing barrier,* the mathematical name for that irreversible state that we will discuss at length in Chapter 19, along with *ergodicity,* the most powerful concept I know.

Next, let us consider the signaling benefits of overt flaws.

THE DONALD

I have a tendency to watch television with the sound off. When I saw Donald Trump in the Republican primary standing next to other candidates, I became certain he was going to win that stage of the process, no matter what he said or did. Actually, it was *because* he had visible deficiencies. Why? Because he was real, and the public—composed of people who usually take risks, not the lifeless non-risk-taking analysts we will present in the next chapter—would vote anytime for someone who actually bled after putting an icepick in his hand rather than someone who did not. Arguments that Trump was a failed entrepreneur, even if true, actually prop up this argument: you'd even rather have a failed real person than a successful one, as blemishes, scars, and character flaws increase the distance between a human and a ghost.*

> *Scars signal skin in the game.*

And

> *People can detect the difference between front- and back-office operators.*

NEXT

Before we end, take some Fat Tony wisdom: always do more than you talk. And precede talk with action. For it will always remain that *action without talk supersedes talk without action.*

Otherwise you will resemble the person we expose in the next chapter (which hopefully will offend many "intellectuals"), the insidious disease of modern times: back-office people (that is, support staff) acting as front-office ones (business generators).

---

* I note that even the fact that Trump expressed himself in an unconventional manner was a signal that he never had a boss before, no supervisor to convince, impress, or seek approval from: people who have been employed are more careful in their choice of words.

CHAPTER 6

The Intellectual Yet Idiot

People who don't have skin in the game—Lipid phobias—Teach a professor how to deadlift

———

Whathat we saw worldwide from 2014 to 2018, from India to the U.K. to the U.S., was a rebellion against the inner circle of no-skin-in-the-game policymaking "clerks" and journalists-insiders, that class of paternalistic semi-intellectual experts with some Ivy League, Oxford-Cambridge or similar label-driven education who are telling the rest of us 1) what to do, 2) what to eat, 3) how to speak, 4) how to think, and . . . 5) whom to vote for.

WHERE TO FIND A COCONUT

But the problem is the one-eyed following the blind: these self-described members of the "intelligentsia" can't find a coconut on Coconut Island, meaning they aren't intelligent enough to define intelligence, hence fall into circularities—their main skill is a capacity to pass exams written by people like them, or to write papers read by people like them. Some of us—not Fat Tony—have been blind to their serial incompetence. With psychology studies replicating less than 40 percent of the time, dietary advice reversing after thirty years of dietary fat phobia, macroeconomics and financial economics (while trapped in an intricate Gargantuan patch of words) scientifically worse than astrology (this is what the reader of the *Incerto* has known since *Fooled by Randomness*), the reappointment of Bernanke (in 2010) who was less than clueless about financial risk as the Federal Reserve boss, and pharmaceutical trials replicating at best only a third of the time, people are perfectly entitled to rely on their own ancestral instincts and to listen to their grandmothers (or to Montaigne and such filtered classical knowledge), who have a better track record than these policymaking goons.

SCIENCE AND SCIENTISM

Indeed, one can see that these academico-bureaucrats who feel entitled to run our lives aren't even rigorous, whether in medical statistics or policymaking. They can't tell science from *scientism*—in fact in their eyes scientism looks more scientific than real science. For instance, it is trivial to show the following: much of what the Cass Sunstein and Richard Thaler types—those who want to "nudge" us into some behavior—much of what they would classify as "rational" or "irrational" (or some such categories indicating deviation from a desired or prescribed protocol) comes from their misunderstanding of probability theory and cosmetic use of first-order models. They are also prone to mistake the ensemble for the linear aggregation of its components—that is, they think that our understanding of single individuals allows us to understand crowds and markets, or that our understanding of ants allows us to understand ant colonies.

The *Intellectual Yet Idiot* (IYI) is a product of modernity, hence has been proliferating since at least the mid-twentieth century, to reach a local supremum today, to the point that we have experienced a takeover by people without skin in the game. In most countries, the government's role is between five and ten times what it was a century ago (expressed in percentage of gross domestic product). The IYI seems ubiquitous in our lives but is still a small minority and is rarely seen outside specialized outlets, think tanks, the media, and university social science departments—most people have proper jobs and there are not many openings for the IYI, which explains how they can be so influential in spite of their low numbers.

The IYI pathologizes others for doing things he doesn't understand without ever realizing it is *his* understanding that may be limited. He thinks people should act according to their best interests *and* he knows their interests, particularly if they are "rednecks" or from the English non-crisp-vowel class who voted for Brexit. When plebeians do something that makes sense to themselves, but not to him, the IYI uses the term "uneducated." What we generally call participation in the political process, he calls by two distinct designations: "democracy" when it fits the IYI, and "populism" when plebeians dare to vote in a way that contradicts IYI preferences. While rich people believe in *one tax dollar one vote*, more humanistic ones in *one man one vote*, Monsanto in *one lobbyist one vote*, the IYI believes in *one Ivy League degree one vote*, with some equivalence for foreign elite schools and PhDs, as these are needed in the club.

They are what Nietzsche called *Bildungsphilisters*—educated philistines. Beware the slightly erudite who thinks he is an erudite, as well as the barber who decides to perform brain surgery.

The IYI also fails to naturally detect sophistry.

INTELLECTUAL YET PHILISTINE

The IYI subscribes to *The New Yorker,* a journal designed so philistines can learn to fake a conversation about evolution, neurosomething, cognitive biases, and quantum mechanics. He never curses on social media. He speaks of "equality of races" and "economic equality," but never goes out drinking with a minority cab driver (again, no real skin in the game, as, I will repeat until I am hoarse, the concept is fundamentally foreign to the IYI). The modern IYI has attended more than one TED talk in person or watched more than two TED talks on YouTube. Not only did he vote for Hillary Monsanto-Malmaison because she seemed electable or some such circular reasoning, but he holds that anyone who didn't do so is mentally ill.

The IYI mistakes the Near East (ancient Eastern Mediterranean) for the Middle East.

The IYI has a copy of the first hardback edition of *The Black Swan* on his shelf, but mistakes absence of evidence for evidence of absence. He believes that GMOs are "science," that their "technology" is in the same risk class as conventional breeding.

Typically, the IYI get first-order logic right, but not second-order (or higher) effects, making him totally incompetent in complex domains.

The IYI has been wrong, historically, about Stalinism, Maoism,

GMOs, Iraq, Libya, Syria, lobotomies, urban planning, low carbohydrate diets, gym machines, behaviorism, trans-fats, Freudianism, portfolio theory, linear regression, HFCS (High-Fructose Corn Syrup), Gaussianism, Salafism, dynamic stochastic equilibrium modeling, housing projects, marathon running, selfish genes, election-forecasting models, Bernie Madoff (pre-blowup), and p-values. But he is still convinced that his current position is right.*

NEVER GOTTEN DRUNK WITH RUSSIANS

The IYI joins a club to get travel privileges; if he is a social scientist, he uses statistics without knowing how they are derived (like Steven Pinker and psycholophasters in general); when in the United Kingdom, he goes to literary festivals and eats cucumber sandwiches, taking small bites at a time; he drinks red wine with steak (never white); he used to believe that dietary fat was harmful and has now completely reversed himself (information in both cases is derived from the same source); he takes statins because his doctor told him to do so; he fails to understand ergodicity, and, when explained to him, he forgets about it soon after; he doesn't use Yiddish words even when talking business; he studies grammar before speaking a language; he has a cousin who worked with someone who knows the Queen; he has never read Frédéric Dard, Libanius Antiochus, Michael Oakeshott, John Gray, Ammianus Marcellinus, Ibn Battuta, Saadia Gaon, or Joseph de Maistre; he has never gotten drunk with Russians; he never drinks to the point where he starts breaking glasses (or, preferably, chairs); he doesn't even know the difference between Hecate and Hecuba (which in Brooklynese is "can't tell sh**t from shinola"); he doesn't know that there is no difference between "pseudointellectual" and "intellectual" in the absence of skin in the game; he has mentioned quantum mechanics at least twice in the past five years in conversations that had nothing to do with physics.

The IYI likes to use buzzwords from philosophy of science when discussing unrelated phenomena; he goes two or three levels too theoretical for a given problem.

---

* Pareto's comments are harsher than mine on this topic.

TO CONCLUDE

The Intellectual Yet Idiot knows at any given point in time what his words or actions are doing to his reputation.

But a much easier marker: he doesn't even deadlift.*

POSTSCRIPT

From the reactions to this chapter (which was posted before the presidential elections of 2016), I discovered that the typical IYI has difficulty, when reading, in differentiating between the satirical and the literal.

Next, we stop the satirical and return to the main book with the sooooo misunderstood topic of economic inequality. By IYIs.

---

* Also the IYI thinks this criticism of IYIs means "everybody is an idiot," not realizing that their group represents, as we said, a tiny minority—but they don't like their sense of entitlement to be challenged, and although they treat the rest of humans as inferiors, they don't like it when the water hose is turned to the opposite direction (what the French call *arroseur arrosé*). For instance, the economist and psycholophaster Richard Thaler, partner of the dangerous GMO advocate übernudger Cass Sunstein, interpreted this piece as saying that "there are not many non-idiots not called Taleb," not realizing that people like him are less than 1 percent or even less than one-tenth of 1 percent of the population.

CHAPTER 7

Inequality and Skin in the Game

The static and the dynamic—How to go bankrupt and be loved by the many—Piketty's equals

———

INEQUALITY VS. INEQUALITY

There is inequality and inequality.

The first is the inequality people tolerate, such as one's understanding compared to that of people deemed heroes, say, Einstein, Michelangelo, or the recluse mathematician Grisha Perelman, in comparison to whom one has no difficulty acknowledging a large surplus. This applies to entrepreneurs, artists, soldiers, heroes, the singer Bob Dylan, Socrates, the current local celebrity chef, some Roman Emperor of good repute, say, Marcus Aurelius; in short, those for whom one can naturally be a "fan." You may like to imitate them, you may aspire to be like them, but you don't resent them.

The second is the inequality people find intolerable because the subject appears to be just a person like you, except that he has been playing the system, and getting himself into rent-seeking, acquiring privileges that are not warranted—and although he has something you would not mind having (which may include his Russian girlfriend), you cannot possibly become a fan. The latter category includes bankers, bureaucrats who get rich, former senators shilling for the evil firm Monsanto, clean-shaven chief executives who wear ties, and talking heads on television making outsized bonuses. You don't just envy them; you take umbrage at their fame, and the sight of their expensive or even semi-expensive car triggers some feeling of bitterness. They make you feel smaller.*

There may be something dissonant in the spectacle of a rich slave.

The author Joan C. Williams, in an insightful article, explains that the American working class is impressed by the rich, as role models—something people in the media, who communicate with one another but rarely with subjects in the real world, don't realize, as they impart normative ideas to people ("this is how they should think"). Michèle Lamont, the author of *The Dignity of Working Men*, cited by Williams, did a systematic interview of blue-collar Americans and found a resentment of high-paid professionals but, unexpectedly, not of the rich.

It is safe to say that the American public—actually all publics—despises people who make a lot of money on a salary, or, rather, salarymen who make a lot of money. This is indeed generalized to other countries: a few years ago the Swiss, of all people, ran a referendum for a law capping salaries of managers to a set multiple of the lowest wage. The law didn't pass, but the fact that they thought in these terms is rather significant. For the same Swiss hold rich entrepreneurs, and people who have derived their celebrity by other means, in some respect.

Further, in countries where wealth comes from rent-seeking, political patronage, or regulatory capture (which, I remind the reader, is how the powerful and the insiders use regulation to scam the public, or red tape to slow down competition), wealth is seen as zero-sum.† What Peter gets is extracted from Paul. Someone getting rich is doing so at other people's expense. In countries such as the U.S., where wealth can come from destruction, people can easily see that someone getting rich is not taking dollars from your pocket; odds are he is even putting some in yours. On the other hand, inequality, by definition, is zero sum.

In this chapter, I will propose that what people resent—or should resent—is the person at the top who has *no skin in the game,* that is, because he doesn't bear his allotted risk, he is immune to the possibility of falling from his pedestal, exiting his income or wealth bracket, and

---

* It came to my notice that in countries with high rent-seeking, wealth is seen as something zero-sum: you take from Peter to give to Paul. On the other hand, in places with low rent-seeking (say the United States before the Obama administration), wealth is seen as a positive-sum game, benefiting everybody.

† Complex regulations allow former government employees to find jobs helping firms navigate the regulations they themselves created.

waiting in line outside the soup kitchen. Again, on that account, the detractors of Donald Trump, when he was still a candidate, not only misunderstood the value of scars as risk signaling, but they also failed to realize that, by advertising his episode of bankruptcy and his personal losses of close to a billion dollars, he removed the resentment (the second type of inequality) people may have had toward him. There is something respectable in losing a billion dollars, provided it is your own money.

In addition, someone without skin in the game—say, a corporate executive with upside and no financial downside (the type to speak clearly in meetings)—is paid according to some metrics that do not necessarily reflect the health of his company; these he can manipulate, hide risks, get the bonus, then retire (or go do the same thing at another company) and blame his successor for subsequent results.

We will also, in the process, redefine inequality and put the notion on more rigorous grounds. But we first need to introduce the difference between two types of approaches, the static and the dynamic, as *skin in the game* can transform one type of inequality into another.

Take also the two following remarks:

True equality is equality in probability.

and

Skin in the game prevents systems from rotting.

THE STATIC AND THE DYNAMIC

Visibly, a problem with economists (particularly those who never took risk) is that they have mental difficulties with *things that move* and are unable to consider that things that move have different attributes from things that don't. That's the reason complexity theory and fat tails (which we will explain a few pages down) are foreign to most of them; they also have (severe) difficulties with the mathematical and conceptual intuitions required for deeper probability theory. Blindness to ergodicity, which we will begin to define a few paragraphs down, is indeed in my opinion the best marker separating a genuine scholar who understands something about the world from an academic hack who partakes of ritualistic paper writing.

A few definitions:

Static inequality is a snapshot view of inequality; it does not reflect what will happen to you in the course of your life.

Consider that about 10 percent of Americans will spend at least a year in the top 1 percent, and more than half of all Americans will spend a year in the top 10 percent.* This is visibly not the same for the more static—but nominally more equal—Europe. For instance, only 10 percent of the wealthiest five hundred American people or dynasties were so thirty years ago; more than 60 percent on the French list are heirs and a third of the richest Europeans were the richest centuries ago. In Florence, it was just revealed that things are even worse: the same handful of families have kept the wealth for five centuries.

Dynamic (ergodic) inequality takes into account the entire future and past life.

You do not create dynamic equality just by raising the level of those at the bottom, but rather by making the rich rotate—or by forcing people to incur the possibility of creating an opening.

The way to make society more equal is by forcing (through skin in the game) the rich to be subjected to the risk of exiting from the 1 percent.†

Our condition here is stronger than mere income mobility. Mobility means that someone can become rich. The *no-absorbing-barrier* condition means that someone who is rich should never be certain to stay rich.

Now, even more mathematically,

---

* Thirty-nine percent of Americans will spend a year in the top 5 percent of the income distribution, 56 percent will find themselves in the top 10 percent, and 73 percent will spend a year in the top 20 percent.

† Or, more mathematically: Dynamic equality assumes Markov chain with no absorbing states.

Dynamic equality is what restores ergodicity, making time and ensemble probabilities substitutable.

Let me explain *ergodicity*—something that we said is foreign to the intelligentsia. Chapter 19 at the back of the book goes into the details; it cancels most crucial psychological experiments related to probability and rationality. The intuition for now is as follows. Take a cross-sectional picture of the U.S. population. You have, say, a minority of millionaires in the one percent, some overweight, some tall, some humorous. You also have a high majority of people in the lower middle class, yoga instructors, baking experts, gardening consultants, spreadsheet theoreticians, dancing advisors, and piano repairpersons—plus of course the Spanish grammar specialist. Take the percentages of each income or wealth bracket (note that the inequality of income is typically flatter than that of wealth). Perfect ergodicity means that each one of us, should he live forever, would spend a proportion of time in the economic conditions of the entire cross-section: out of, say, a century, an average of sixty years in the lower middle class, ten years in the upper middle class, twenty years in the blue-collar class, and perhaps one single year in the one percent.*†

The exact opposite of perfect ergodicity is an absorbing state. The term *absorption* is derived from particles that, when they hit an obstacle, get absorbed or stick to it. An absorbing barrier is like a trap, once in, you can't get out, good or bad. A person gets rich by some process, then, having arrived, he stays rich. And if someone enters the lower middle class (from above), he will never have the chance to exit from it and become rich *should he want to,* of course—hence will be justified to resent the rich. You will notice that where the state is large, people at the top tend to have little downward mobility—in such places as France, the state is chummy with large corporations and protects their executives

---

* A technical comment (for nitpickers): what we can call here imperfect ergodicity means that each one of us has long-term, ergodic probabilities that have some variation among individuals: your probability of ending in the one percent may be higher than mine; nevertheless no state will have a probability of 0 for me, and no state will have a transition probability of 1 for you.

† Another comment for nitpickers. Rawls's veil, discussed in *Fooled by Randomness,* assumes that a fair society is the one which you would select if there were some type of a lottery. Here we go further and discuss a dynamic structure, in other words, how such a society would move, as it obviously will not be static.

and shareholders from experiencing such descent; it even encourages their ascent.

And no downside for some means no upside for the rest.

PIKETTISM AND THE REVOLT OF THE MANDARIN CLASS[*]

There is a class often called the *Mandarins,* after the fictionalized memoirs of the French author Simone de Beauvoir, named after the scholars of the Ming dynasty (the high Chinese language is also called Mandarin). I have always been aware of their existence, but a salient—and pernicious—attribute came to me while observing the reactions of its members to the works of the French economist Thomas Piketty.

Piketty followed Karl Marx by writing an ambitious book on capital. A friend gave me the book as a gift when it was still in French (and unknown outside France) because I find it commendable that people publish their original, nonmathematical work in social science in book format. The book, *Capital in the Twenty-first Century,* makes aggressive claims about the alarming rise of inequality, adding to it a theory of why capital tends to command too much return in relation to labor and how the absence of redistribution and dispossession might make the world collapse. Piketty's theory about the increase in the return of capital in relation to labor is patently wrong, as anyone who has witnessed the rise of what is called the "knowledge economy" (or anyone who has had investments in general) knows.

Clearly, when you say that inequality changes from year one to year two, you need to show that those who are at the top are the *same people*—something Piketty doesn't do (remember that he is an economist and has trouble with things that move). But the problem doesn't stop there. Soon, I discovered that—aside from deriving conclusions from static measures of inequality—the methods he used were flawed: Piketty's tools did not match what he purported to show about the rise in inequality. There was no mathematical rigor. I soon wrote two articles (one in collaboration with Raphael Douady, another with Andrea Fontanari and Pasquale Cirillo, published in *Physica A: Statistical Me-*

---

[*] This section is technical and can be skipped by those who aren't particularly impressed with economists.

chanics and Applications), about the measure of inequality that consists in taking the ownership of, say, the top 1 percent and monitoring its variations. The flaw is that if you take the inequality thus measured in Europe as a whole, you will find it is higher than the average inequality across component countries; the bias increases in severity with processes that deliver a high degree of inequality. All in all, the papers had enough theorems and proofs to make them about as ironclad a piece of work as one can have in science; although it was not necessary, I insisted on putting the results in theorem form because someone cannot contest a formally proved theorem without putting in question his own understanding of mathematics.

The reason these errors were not known was because economists who work with inequality were not familiar with . . . inequality. Inequality is the disproportion of the role of the tail—rich people were in the tails of the distribution.* The more inequality in the system, the more the winner-take-all effect, the more we depart from the methods of thin-tailed Mediocristan (see Glossary) in which economists were trained. The wealth process is dominated by winner-take-all effects. Any form of control of the wealth process—typically instigated by bureaucrats—tends to lock people with privileges in their state of entitlement. So the solution is to allow the system to destroy the strong, something that works best in the United States.

But there was something far, far more severe than a scholar being wrong.

The problem is never the problem; it is how people handle it. What was worse than Piketty's flaws was the discovery of how that Mandarin class operates. They got so prematurely excited by the "evidence" of the rise in inequality that their reactions were like fake news. Actually, they were fake news. Economists got so carried away; they praised Piketty for his "erudition" because he discussed Balzac and Jane Austen, the equivalent to hailing as a weight lifter someone spotted carrying a briefcase across Terminal B. And they completely ignored my results—and when they didn't, it was to declare that I was "arrogant"(recall the strategy of using formal mathematics as a way to make it impossible to say you are

---

* The type of distributions—called fat tails—associated with it made the analyses more delicate, far more delicate, and it had become my mathematical specialty. In Mediocristan, changes over time are the result of the collective contributions of the center, the middle. In Extremistan these changes come from the tails. Sorry if you don't like it, but that is purely mathematical.

wrong)—which is a form of scientific compliment. Even Paul Krugman (a currently famous economist and public intellectual) wrote, "If you think you've found an obvious hole, empirical or logical, in Piketty, you're very probably wrong. He's done his homework!" When I met him in person and pointed out the flaw to him, he evaded it—not necessarily out of malice, but most likely because probability and combinatorics eluded him, by his own admission.

Now consider that the likes of Krugman and Piketty have no downside in their existence—lowering inequality brings them up in the ladder of life. Unless the university system or the French state goes bust, they will continue receiving their paychecks. The fellow you just saw in the steak restaurant dripping with gold chains is exposed to the risk of the soup kitchen, not them. Just as those who live by the sword die by the sword, those who earn their living taking risks will lose their livelihood taking risks.*

We've made a big deal out of Piketty here because the widespread enthusiasm for his book was representative of the behavior of that class of people who love to theorize and engage in false solidarity with the oppressed, while consolidating their privileges.

COBBLER ENVIES COBBLER

The reason regular people are not as acrimonious as the "intellectuals" and bureaucrats is because envy does not travel long distance or cross many social classes. Envy does not originate with the impoverished, concerned with the betterment of their condition, but with the clerical class. Simply, it looks like it was the university professors (who have "arrived") and people who have permanent stability of income, in the form of tenure, governmental or academic, who bought heavily into Piketty's argument. From conversations, I became convinced that people who counterfactual upwards (i.e., compare themselves to those richer) want to actively dispossess the rich. As with all communist movements, it is

---

* If the process is fat-tailed (Extremistan), then wealth is generated at the top, which means increases in wealth lead to increases of measured inequality. Within populations, wealth creation is a series of small probability bets. So it is natural that the pool of wealth (measured in years of spending, as Piketty does) increases with wealth. Consider one hundred people in a 80/20 world: the additional wealth should come from one person, with the remaining bottom fifty contributing nothing. It is not a zero-sum gain: eliminate that person, and there will be almost no wealth increases. In fact the rest are already benefiting from the contribution of the minority.

often the bourgeois or clerical classes who are the early adopters of revolutionary theories. So class envy doesn't originate from a truck driver in South Alabama, but from a New York or Washington, D.C., Ivy League–educated IYI (say Paul Krugman or Joseph Stiglitz) with a sense of entitlement, upset some "less smart" persons are much richer.

Aristotle, in his *Rhetoric,* postulated that envy is something you are more likely to encounter in your own kin: lower classes are more likely to experience envy toward their cousins or the middle class than toward the very rich. And the expression *Nobody is a prophet in his own land,* making envy a geographical thing (mistakenly thought to originate with Jesus), originates from that passage in the *Rhetoric.* Aristotle himself was building on Hesiod: *cobbler envies cobbler, carpenter envies carpenter.* Later, Jean de La Bruyère wrote that jealousy is to be found within the same art, talent, and condition.*

So I doubt Piketty bothered to ask blue-collar Frenchmen what they want, as Michelle Lamont did (as we saw earlier in the chapter). I am certain that they would ask for better beer, a new dishwasher, or faster trains for their commute, not to bring down some rich businessman invisible to them. But, again, people can frame questions and portray enrichment as theft, as was done before the French Revolution, in which case the blue-collar class would ask, once again, for heads to roll.†

INEQUALITY, WEALTH, AND VERTICAL SOCIALIZATION

If intellectuals are overly worried about inequality, it is because they tend to view themselves in hierarchical terms, and thus think that others do too. Furthermore, as if by pathology, discussions in "competitive" universities are all about hierarchy. Most people in the real world don't obsess over it.‡

In the more rural past, envy was rather controlled; wealthy people were not as exposed to other persons of their class. They didn't have the pressure to keep up with other wealthy persons and compete with them.

---

* La Bruyère: *L'émulation et la jalousie ne se rencontrent guère que dans les personnes du même art, de même talent et de même condition.*

† What happened with the U.K. Parliament expenses scandal: MPs were giving themselves TVs and dishwashers, which the public could easily imagine, and revolted against. One MP said, "It's not like I took one million in bonds." The public understands TVs, not bonds.

‡ There is a technical argument that, if one looks at the issue dynamically, not statically, a wealth tax favors the salaryperson over the entrepreneur.

The wealthy stayed within their region, surrounded by people who depended on them, say a lord on his property. Except for the occasional season in the cities, their social life was quite vertical. Their children played with the children of the servants.

It was in mercantile urban environments that socializing within social classes took place. And, over time, with industrialization, the rich started moving to cities or suburbs surrounded by other people of similar—but not completely similar—condition. Hence they needed to keep up with each other, racing on a treadmill.

For a rich person isolated from vertical socializing with the poor, the poor become something entirely theoretical, a textbook reference. As I mentioned in the past chapter, I have yet to see a *bien pensant* Cambridge don hanging out with Pakistani cab drivers or lifting weights with cockney speakers. The intelligentsia therefore feels entitled to deal with the poor as a construct; one they created. Thus they become convinced that they know what is best for them.

EMPATHY AND HOMOPHILY

Recall the scaling problem, the idea that people's ethical rules are not universal; they vary according to whether someone is "Swiss," that is, an outsider or not.

The same applies to empathy (the reverse of envy). You can see that people feel more for those of their class. Traditionally, the upper class engaged in rescuing those from ruined families by making them "stewards" or *dames de compagnie*. Such in-group protection has a self-insurance attribute—something that can only work for a limited number of people and can't be universalized: *you take care of my progeny if they are ruined; I will take care of yours.*

DATA, SHMATA

Another lesson from Piketty's ambitious volume: it was loaded with charts and tables. There is a lesson here: what we learn from professionals in the real world is that data is not necessarily rigor. One reason I—as a probability professional—left data out of *The Black Swan* (except for illustrative purposes) is that it seems to me that people flood their stories with numbers and graphs in the absence of solid or logical arguments. Further, people mistake empiricism for a flood of data. Just a little bit of significant data is needed when one is right, particularly when it is disconfirmatory empiricism, or counterexamples: only one data point (a single extreme deviation) is sufficient to show that Black Swans exist.

Traders, when they make profits, have short communications; when they lose they drown you in details, theories, and charts.

Probability, statistics, and data science are principally logic fed by observations—and absence of observations. For many environments, the relevant data points are those in the extremes; these are rare by definition, and it suffices to focus on those *few but big* to get an idea of the story. If you want to show that a person has more than, say $10 million, all you need is to show the $50 million in his brokerage account, not, in addition, list every piece of furniture in his house, including the $500 painting in his study and the silver spoons in the pantry. So I've discovered, with experience, that when you buy a thick book with tons of graphs and tables used to prove a point, you should be suspicious. It means something didn't distill right! But for the general public and those untrained in statistics, such tables appear convincing—another way to substitute the true with the complicated.

For instance, the science journalist Steven Pinker played that trick with his book *The Better Angels of Our Nature,* which claims a decline of violence in modern human history, and attributes this to modern institutions. My collaborator Pasquale Cirillo and I, when we put his "data" under scrutiny, found out that either he didn't understand his own numbers (actually, he didn't), or he had a story in mind and kept adding charts, not realizing that statistics isn't about data but distillation, rigor, and avoiding being *fooled by randomness*—but no matter, the general public and his state-worshipping IYI colleagues found it impressive (for a while).

ETHICS OF CIVIL SERVICE

Let us finish this discussion with an unfairness that is worse than inequality: the sore sight of back office, non-risk-takers getting rich from public service.

When, on leaving office, Barack Obama accepted a sum of more than $40 million to write his memoirs, many people were outraged. His supporters, statists who were defending him, on the other hand, were critical of the rich entrepreneurs hired by the subsequent administration. Money is greed, for them—but *those who did not earn the money via commerce were illogically exempt*. I had a rough time explaining that having rich people in a public office is very different from having public people become rich—again, it is the dynamics, the sequence, that matters.

Rich people in public office have shown some evidence of lack of total incompetence—success may come from randomness, of course, but we at least have a hint of some skill in the real world, some evidence that the person has dealt with reality. This is of course conditional on the person having had skin in the game—and it is better if the person felt a blowup, has experienced at least once the loss of part of his or her fortune and the angst associated with it.

As usual, there is a mix of the ethical and the effective here.

It is downright unethical to use public office for enrichment.

A good rule for society is to oblige those who start in public office to pledge never subsequently to earn from the private sector more than a set amount; the rest should go to the taxpayer. This will ensure sincerity in, literally, "service"—where employees are supposedly underpaid because of their emotional reward from serving society. It would prove that they are not in the public sector as an investment strategy: you do not become a Jesuit priest because it may help you get hired by Goldman Sachs later, after your eventual defrocking—given the erudition and the masterly control of casuistry generally associated with the Society of Jesus.

Currently, most civil servants tend to stay in civil service—except for those in delicate areas that industry controls: the agro-alimentary segment, finance, aerospace, anything related to Saudi Arabia . . .

A civil servant can make rules that are friendly to an industry such as banking—and then go off to J.P. Morgan and recoup a multiple of the difference between his or her current salary and the market rate. (Regulators, you may recall, have an incentive to make rules as complex as possible so their expertise can later be hired at a higher price.)

So there is an implicit bribe in civil service: you act as a servant to an industry, say, Monsanto, and they take care of you later on. They do not do it out of a sense of honor: simply, it is necessary to keep the system going and encourage the next guy to play by these rules. The IYI-cum-cronyist former Treasury Secretary Tim Geithner—with whom I share the Calabrese barber of the Prologue—was overtly rewarded by the industry he helped bail out. He helped bankers get bailouts, let them pay themselves from the largest bonus pool in history *after* the crisis, in 2010 (that is, using taxpayer money), and then got a multimillion-dollar job at a financial institution as his reward for good behavior.

NEXT

There is a vicious domain-dependence of expertise: the electrician, dentist, scholar of Portuguese irregular verbs, assistant colonoscopist, London cabby, and algebraic geometer are experts (plus or minus some local variations), while the journalist, State Department bureaucrat, clinical psychologist, management theorist, publishing executive, and macro-economist are not. This allows us to answer the questions: Who is the real expert? Who decides who is and who is not an expert? Where is the meta-expert?

Time is the expert. Or, rather, the temperamental and ruthless Lindy, as we see in the next chapter.

An Expert Called Lindy

She is the one and only expert—Don't eat their cheesecake—Meta-experts judged by meta-meta-experts—Prostitutes, nonprostitutes, and amateurs

———

L indy is a deli in New York, now a tourist trap, that proudly claims to be famous for its cheesecake, but in fact has been known for fifty or so years by physicists and mathematicians thanks to the heuristic that developed there. Actors who hung out there gossiping about other actors discovered that Broadway shows that lasted for, say, one hundred days, had a future life expectancy of a hundred more. For those that lasted two hundred days, two hundred more. The heuristic became known as the Lindy effect.

Let me warn the reader: while the Lindy effect is one of the most useful, robust, and universal heuristics I know, Lindy's cheesecake is . . . much less distinguished. Odds are the deli will not survive, by the Lindy effect.

There had been a bevy of mathematical models that sort of fit the story, though not really, until a) yours truly figured out that the Lindy effect can be best understood using the theory of fragility and antifragility, and b) the mathematician Iddo Eliazar formalized its probabilistic structure. Actually the theory of fragility *directly* leads to the Lindy effect. Simply, my collaborators and I managed to define fragility as sensitivity to disorder: the porcelain owl sitting in front of me on the writing desk, as I am writing these lines, wants tranquility. It dislikes shocks, disorder, variations, earthquakes, mishandling by dust-phobic cleaning service operators, travel in a suitcase transiting through Terminal 5 in Heathrow, and shelling by Saudi Barbaria–sponsored Islamist militias. Clearly, it has no upside from random events and, more generally, disorder. (More technically, being fragile, it *necessarily* has a nonlinear reaction to stressors: up until its breaking point, shocks of larger intensity affect it disproportionally more than smaller ones).

Now, crucially, time is equivalent to disorder, and resistance to the ravages of time, that is, what we gloriously call survival, is the ability to handle disorder.

> That which is fragile has an asymmetric response to volatility and other stressors, that is, will experience more harm than benefit from it.

In probability, volatility and time are the same. The idea of fragility helped put some rigor around the notion that the only effective judge of things is time—by *things* we mean ideas, people, intellectual productions, car models, scientific theories, books, etc. You can't fool Lindy: books of the type written by the current hotshot Op-Ed writer at *The New York Times* may get some hype at publication time, manufactured or spontaneous, but their five-year survival rate is generally less than that of pancreatic cancer.

WHO IS THE "REAL" EXPERT?

Effectively Lindy answers the age-old meta-questions: Who will judge the expert? Who will guard the guard? (*Quis custodiet ipsos custodes?*) Who will judge the judges? Well, survival will.

For time operates through skin in the game. Things that have survived are hinting to us *ex post* that they have some robustness—conditional on their being exposed to harm. For without skin in the game, via exposure to reality, the mechanism of fragility is disrupted: things may survive for no reason for a while, at some scale, then ultimately collapse, causing a lot of collateral harm.

A few more details (for those interested in the intricacies, the Lindy effect has been covered at length in *Antifragile*). There are two ways things handle time. First, there is aging and perishability: things die because they have a biological clock, what we call senescence. Second, there is hazard, the rate of accidents. What we witness in physical life is the combination of the two: when you are old and fragile, you don't handle accidents very well. These accidents don't have to be external, like falling from a ladder or being attacked by a bear; they can also be internal, from random malfunctioning of your organs or circulation. On the other hand, animals that don't really age, say turtles and crocodiles, seem to have a remaining life expectancy that stays constant for a long time. If a twenty-year-old crocodile has forty more years to live (owing to the perils of the habitat), a forty-year-old one will also have about forty years to live.

Let us use as shorthand "Lindy proof," "is Lindy," or "Lindy compatible" (one can substitute for another) to show something that seems to belong to the class of things that have proven to have the following property:

> *That which is "Lindy" is what ages in reverse, i.e., its life expectancy lengthens with time, conditional on survival.*

Only the nonperishable can be Lindy. When it comes to ideas, books, technologies, procedures, institutions, and political systems under Lindy, there is no intrinsic aging and perishability. A physical copy of *War and Peace* can age (particularly when the publisher cuts corners to save twenty cents on paper for a fifty-dollar book); the book itself as an idea doesn't.

Note that thanks to Lindy, no expert is the final expert anymore and we do not need meta-experts judging the expertise of experts one rank below them. We solve the "turtles all the way down" problem.* Fragility is the expert, hence time and survival.

THE LINDY OF LINDY

The idea of the Lindy effect is itself Lindy-proof. The pre-Socratic thinker Periander of Corinth wrote, more than twenty-five hundred years ago: *Use laws that are old but food that is fresh.*

Likewise, Alfonso X of Spain, nicknamed El Sabio, "the wise," had

---

* The "turtles all the way down" expression expresses an infinite regress problem, as follows. The logician Bertrand Russell was once told that the world sits on turtles. "And what do these turtles stand on?" he asked. "It's turtles all the way down," was the answer.

as a maxim: *Burn old logs. Drink old wine. Read old books. Keep old friends.*

The insightful and luckily nonacademic historian Tom Holland once commented: "The thing I most admire about the Romans was the utter contempt they were capable of showing the cult of youth." He also wrote: "The Romans judged their political system by asking not whether it made sense but whether it worked," which is why, while dedicating this book, I called Ron Paul a Roman among Greeks.

DO WE NEED A JUDGE?

As I mentioned earlier in Prologue 3, I have held for most of my (sort of) academic career no more than a quarter position. A quarter is enough to have somewhere to go, particularly when it rains in New York, without being emotionally socialized and losing intellectual independence for fear of missing a party or having to eat alone. But one (now "resigned") department head one day came to me and emitted the warning: "Just as, when a businessman and author you are judged by other businessmen and authors, here as an academic you are judged by other academics. Life is about peer assessment."

It took me a while to overcome my disgust—I am still not fully familiar with the way non-risk-takers work; they actually don't realize that others are not like them, and can't get what makes real people tick. No, businessmen *as risk takers* are not subjected to the judgment of other businessmen, only to that of their personal accountant. They just need to avoid having a documented record of (some) ethical violations. Furthermore, not only did you not want peer approval, you wanted disapproval (except for ethical matters): an old fellow pit trader once shared his wisdom: "If people over here like you, you are doing something wrong."

Further,

> *You can define a free person precisely as someone whose fate is not centrally or directly dependent on peer assessment.*

And as an essayist, I am not judged by other writers, book editors, and book reviewers, but by readers. Readers? Maybe, but wait a minute . . . not today's readers. Only those of tomorrow, and the day after tomorrow. So, my only real judge being time, it is the stability and robustness of the readership (that is, *future* readers) that counts. The fashion-oriented steady reader of the most recently reviewed book in *The New York Times* is of no interest to me. And as a risk taker, only time counts—for I could fool my accountant with steady earnings with a lot of hidden risk, but time will eventually reveal them.

> *Being reviewed or assessed by others matters if and only if one is subjected to the judgment of future—not just present—others.*

And recall that, a free person does not need to win arguments—just win.*

TEA WITH THE QUEEN

Peers devolve honors, memberships in academies, Nobels, invitations to Davos and similar venues, tea (and cucumber sandwiches) with the Queen, requests by rich name-droppers to attend cocktail parties where you see only people who are famous. Believe me, there are rich people whose lives revolve around these things. They usually claim to be trying to save the world, the bears, the children, the mountains, the deserts—all the ingredients of the broadcasting of virtue.

But clearly they can't influence Lindy—in fact, it is the reverse. If you spend your time trying to impress others in the New York club 21, there may be something wrong with you.

> *Contemporary peers are valuable collaborators, not final judges.†*

---

* An observation about modernity. Change for the sake of change, as we see in architecture, food, and lifestyle, is frequently the opposite of progress. As I have explained in *Antifragile,* too high a rate of mutation prevents locking in the benefits of previous changes: evolution (and progress) requires some, but not too frequent, variation.

† Prizes as a Curse: In fact, there is a long-held belief among traders that praise by journalists is a reverse indicator. I learned about it the hard way. In 1983, right before I became a trader, the computer giant IBM made the front cover of *BusinessWeek*, a U.S. magazine then influential, as the ultimate company. I naively rushed to buy the stock. I got shellacked. Then it hit me that, if anything, I should be shorting the company, to benefit from its decline. So I reversed the trade, and learned that collective praise by journos is at the least suspicious and, at best, a curse. IBM went into a decline that lasted a decade and a half; it almost went bust. Further, I learned to avoid honors and prizes partly because, given that they are awarded by the wrong judges, they are likely to hit you at the peak (you'd rather be ignored, or, better, disliked by the general media). A former trader who invests in the restaurant business, Brian Hinchcliffe, conveyed to me the following heuristic: Shops that get awards as "The Best" *something* (best atmosphere, best waiter service, best fer-

INSTITUTIONS

In fact, there is something worse than peer-assessment: the bureaucratization of the activity creates a class of new judges: university administrators, who have no clue what someone is doing except via external signals, yet become the actual arbiters.

These arbiters fail to realize that "prestigious" publication, determined by peer-reviewers in a circular manner, are not Lindy-compatible—they only mean that a certain set of (currently) powerful people are happy with your work.

Hard science might be robust to the pathologies—even then. So let us take a look at social science. Given that the sole judges of a contributor are his "peers," there is a citation ring in place that can lead to all manner of rotting. Macroeconomics, for instance, can be nonsense since it is easier to macrobull***t than microbull***t—nobody can tell if a theory really works.

If you say something crazy you will be deemed crazy. But if you create a collection of, say, twenty people who set up an academy and say crazy things accepted by the collective, you now have "peer-reviewing" and can start a department in a university.

Academia has a tendency, when unchecked (from lack of skin in the game), to evolve into a ritualistic self-referential publishing game.

Now, while academia has turned into an athletic contest, Wittgenstein held the exact opposite viewpoint: if anything, knowledge is the reverse of an athletic contest. In philosophy, the winner is the one who finishes last, he said.

Further,

Anything that smacks of competition destroys knowledge.

In some areas, such as gender studies or psychology, the ritualistic publishing game gradually maps less and less to real research, by the

---

mented yoghurt and other nonalcoholic beverages for visiting Sheikhs, etc.) close down before the awards ceremony. Empirically, if you want an author to cross a few generations, make sure he or she never gets that something called the Nobel Prize in Literature.

very nature of the agency problem, to reach a Mafia-like divergence of interest: researchers have their own agenda, at variance with what their clients, that is, society and the students, are paying them for. The opacity of the subject to outsiders helps them control the gates. Knowing "economics" doesn't mean knowing anything about economics in the sense of the real activity, but rather the theories, most of which are bull***t, produced by economists. And courses in universities, for which hard-working parents need to save over decades, easily degenerate into fashion. You work hard and save for your children to be taught a post-colonial study-oriented critique of quantum mechanics.

But there is a ray of hope. Actually, recent events indicate how the system will fold: alumni (who happen to have worked in the real world) are starting to cut funds to spurious and farcical disciplines (though not to the farcical approaches within traditional disciplines). After all, it so happens that someone needs to pay the salaries of macroeconomists and post-colonial gender "experts." And university education needs to compete with professional training workshops: once upon a time, studying post-colonial theories could help one get a job other than serving French fries. No longer.

AGAINST ONE'S INTEREST

The most convincing statements are those in which one stands to lose, ones in which one has maximal skin in the game; the most unconvincing ones are those in which one patently (but unknowingly) tries to enhance one's status without making a tangible contribution (like, as we saw, in the great majority of academic papers that say nothing and take no risks). But it doesn't have to be that way. Showing off is reasonable; it is human. As long as the substance exceeds the showoff, you are fine. Stay human, take as much as you can, under the condition that you give more than you take.

> One should give more weight to research that, while being rigorous, contradicts other peers, particularly if it entails costs and reputational harm for its author.

Further,

> *Someone with a high public presence who is controversial and takes risks for his opinion is less likely to be a bull***t vendor.**

SOUL IN THE GAME, AGAIN

The deprostitutionalization of research will eventually be done as follows. Force people who want to do "research" to do it on their own time, that is, to derive their income from other sources. Sacrifice is necessary. It may seem absurd to brainwashed contemporaries, but *Antifragile* documents the outsized historical contributions of the nonprofessional, or, rather, the non-meretricious. For their research to be genuine, they should first have a real-world day job, or at least spend ten years as: lens maker, patent clerk, Mafia operator, professional gambler, postman, prison guard, medical doctor, limo driver, militia member, social security agent, trial lawyer, farmer, restaurant chef, high-volume waiter, firefighter (my favorite), lighthouse keeper, etc., while they are building their original ideas.

It is a filtering, nonsense-expurgating mechanism. I have no sympathy for moaning professional researchers. I for my part spent twenty-three years in a full-time, highly demanding, extremely stressful profession while studying, researching, and writing my first three books at night; it lowered (in fact, eliminated) my tolerance for career-building research.

(There is this illusion that just as businessmen are motivated and rewarded by profits, scientists should be motivated and rewarded by honors and recognition. That's not how it works. Remember, science is a minority rule: a few will run it, others are just back-office clerks.)

SCIENCE IS LINDY-PRONE

We said earlier that without skin in game, survival mechanisms are severely disrupted. This also applies to ideas.

Karl Popper's idea of science is an enterprise that produces claims

---

* I am usually allergic to some public personalities, but not others. It took me a while to figure out how to draw the line explicitly. The difference is risk-taking and whether the person worries about his or her reputation.

that can be contradicted by eventual observations, not a series of verifiable ones: science is fundamentally disconfirmatory, not confirmatory. This mechanism of falsification is entirely Lindy-compatible; it actually requires the operation of the Lindy effect (in combination with the minority rule). Although Popper saw the statics, he didn't study the dynamics, nor did he look at the risk dimension of things. The reason science works isn't because there is a proper "scientific method" derived by some nerds in isolation, or some "standard" that passes a test similar to the eye exam of the Department of Motor Vehicles; rather it is because scientific ideas are Lindy-prone, that is, subjected to their own natural fragility. Ideas need to have skin in the game. You know an idea will fail if it is not useful, and can be therefore vulnerable to the *falsification* of time (and not that of naive falsificationism, that is, according to some government-printed black-and-white guideline). The longer an idea has been around without being falsified, the longer its future life expectancy. For if you read Paul Feyerabend's account of the history of scientific discoveries, you can clearly see that anything goes in the process—but not with the test of time. That appears to be nonnegotiable.

Note that I am here modifying Popper's idea; we can replace "true" (rather, *not false*) with "useful," even "not harmful," even "protective to its users." So I will diverge from Popper in the following. For things to survive, they necessarily need to fare well in the risk dimension, that is, be good at *not dying*. By the Lindy effect, if an idea has skin in the game, it is not in the truth game, but in the harm game. An idea survives if it is a good risk manager, that is, not only doesn't harm its holders, but favors their survival—this also applies to superstitions that have crossed centuries because they led to some protective actions. More technically, an idea needs to be convex (antifragile), or at least bring about a beneficial reduction of fragility somewhere.

EMPIRICAL OR THEORETIC?

Academics divide research into theoretical and empirical areas. Empiricism consists in looking at data on a computer in search for what they call "statistically significant," or doing experiments in the laboratory under some purposefully narrow conditions. Doing things in the real world, in some professions (such as medicine), bears the name *clinical,* which is not deemed to be scientific. Many disciplines lack this third dimension, the clinical one.

For in fact, by the Lindy effect, robustness to time, that is, doing things under risk-taking conditions, is checked by survival. Things work 1) if those who have been doing the doing took some type of risk, and 2) their work manages to cross generations.

Which brings me to the grandmother.

THE GRANDMOTHER VS. THE RESEARCHERS

If you hear advice from a grandmother or elders, odds are that it works 90 percent of the time. On the other hand, in part because of scientism and academic prostitution, in part because the world is hard, if you read anything by psychologists and behavioral scientists, odds are that it works at less than 10 percent, unless it is has also been covered by the grandmother and the classics, in which case why would you need a psychologist?* Consider that a recent effort to replicate the hundred psychology papers in "prestigious" journals of 2008 found that, out of a hundred, only thirty-nine replicated. Of these thirty-nine, I believe that fewer than ten are actually robust and transfer outside the narrowness of the experiment. Similar defects have been found in medicine and neuroscience; more on those later. (I will discuss the point further in Chapters 18 and (mostly) 19, as well as why the warnings of your grandmother or interdicts aren't "irrational"; most of what is called "irrational" comes from misunderstanding of probability.)

It is critical that it is not just that the books of the ancients are still around and have been filtered by Lindy, but that those populations who read them have survived as well.

While our knowledge of physics was not available to the ancients, human nature was. So everything that holds in social science and psychology has to be Lindy-proof, that is, have an antecedent in the classics; otherwise it will not replicate or not generalize beyond the experiment. By classics we can define the Latin (and late Hellenistic) moral literature (moral sciences meant something else than they do today): Cicero, Seneca, Marcus Aurelius, Epictetus, Lucian, or the poets:

---

* In a technical note called "Meta-distribution of p-values" around the stochasticity of "p-values" and their hacking by researchers, I show that the statistical significance of these papers is at least one order of magnitude smaller than claimed.

Juvenal, Horace, or the later French so-called "moralists" (La Roche-foucauld, Vauvenargues, La Bruyère, Chamfort). Bossuet is a class on his own. One can use Montaigne and Erasmus as a portal to the ancients: Montaigne was the popularizer of his day; Erasmus was the thorough compiler.

A BRIEF TOUR OF YOUR GRANDPARENTS' WISDOM

Let us now close by sampling a few ideas that exist in both ancient lore and are sort of reconfirmed by modern psychology. These are sampled organically, meaning they are not the result of research but of what spontaneously comes to mind (remember this book is called *Skin in the Game*), then verified in the texts.

Cognitive dissonance (a psychological theory by Leon Festinger about *sour grapes*, by which people, in order to avoid inconsistent beliefs, rationalize that, say, the grapes they can't reach got to be sour). It is seen first in Aesop, of course, repackaged by La Fontaine. But its roots look even more ancient, with the Assyrian Ahiqar of Nineveh.

Loss aversion (a psychological theory by which a loss is more painful than a gain is pleasant): in Livy's Annals (XXX, 21) *Men feel the good less intensely than the bad.** Nearly all the letters of Seneca have some element of loss aversion.

Negative advice (*via negativa*): We know the wrong better than what's right; recall the superiority of the Silver over the Golden Rule. *The good is not as good as the absence of bad,*† Ennius, repeated by Cicero.

Skin in the game (literally): We start with the Yiddish proverb: *You can't chew with somebody else's teeth.* "Your fingernail can best scratch your itch,"‡ picked up by Scaliger circa 1614 in *Proverborum Arabicorum*.

Antifragility: There are tens of ancient sayings. Let us just mention Cicero. *When our souls are mollified, a bee can sting.* See also Machiavelli and Rousseau for its application to political systems.

Time discounting: "A bird in the hand is better than ten on the tree."§ (Levantine proverb)

---

* *Segnius homines bona quam mala sentiunt.*

† *Nimium boni est, cui nihil est mali.*

‡ *Non scabat caput praeter unges tuo, Ma biḣikkak illa ḋifrak.*

§ *xasfour bil 'id aḣsan min xaṡra xalṡajra.*

Madness of crowds: Nietzsche: *Madness is rare in individuals, but in groups, parties, nations, it is the rule.* (This counts as ancient wisdom since Nietzsche was a classicist; I've seen many such references in Plato.)

Less is more: *Truth is lost with too much altercation,** in Publilius Syrus. But of course the expression "less is more" is in an 1855 poem by Robert Browning.

Overconfidence: "I lost money because of my excessive confidence,"† Erasmus inspired by Theognis of Megara (*Confident, I lost everything; defiant, I saved everything*) and Epicharmus of Kos (*Remain sober and remember to watch out*).

The Paradox of progress, and the **paradox of choice:** There is a familiar story of a New York banker vacationing in Greece, who, from talking to a fisherman and scrutinizing the fisherman's business, comes up with a scheme to help the fisherman make it a big business. The fisherman asked him what the benefits were; the banker answered that he could make a pile of money in New York and come back to vacation in Greece; something that seemed ludicrous to the fisherman, who was already there doing the kind of things bankers do when they go on vacation in Greece.

The story was well known in antiquity, under a more elegant form, as retold by Montaigne (my translation): When King Pyrrhus tried to cross into Italy, Cynéas, his wise adviser, tried to make him feel the vanity of such action. "To what end are you going into such enterprise?" he asked. Pyrrhus answered, "To make myself the master of Italy." Cynéas: "And so?" Pyrrhus: "To get to Gaul, then Spain." Cynéas: "Then?" Pyrrhus: "To conquer Africa, then . . . come rest at ease." Cynéas: "But you are already there; why take more risks?" Montaigne then cites the well-known passage in Lucretius' *De Rerum Natura* (V, 1431) on how human nature knows no upper bound, as if to punish itself.

---

* *Nimium allercando veritas amittitur.*

† *Fiducia pecunias amici.*

———

BOOK 6

DEEPER INTO AGENCY

CHAPTER 9

Surgeons Should Not
Look Like Surgeons

Literature doesn't look like literature—Donaldo hiring practitioners—
The glory of bureaucracy—Teach a professor how to deadlift—Looking
the part

———

LOOKING THE PART

Say you had the choice between two surgeons of similar rank in the same department in some hospital. The first is highly refined in appearance; he wears silver-rimmed glasses, has a thin build, delicate hands, measured speech, and elegant gestures. His hair is silver and well combed. He is the person you would put in a movie if you needed to impersonate a surgeon. His office prominently boasts Ivy League diplomas, both for his undergraduate and medical schools.

The second one looks like a butcher; he is overweight, with large hands, uncouth speech, and an unkempt appearance. His shirt is dangling from the back. No known tailor on the East Coast of the U.S. is capable of making his shirt button at the neck. He speaks unapologetically with a strong New Yawk accent, as if he wasn't aware of it. He even has a gold tooth showing when he opens his mouth. The absence of diplomas on the wall hints at the lack of pride in his education: he perhaps went to some local college. In a movie, you would expect him to impersonate a retired bodyguard for a junior congressman, or a third-generation cook in a New Jersey cafeteria.

Now if I had to pick, I would overcome my sucker-proneness and take the butcher any minute. Even more: I would seek the butcher as a third option if my choice was between two doctors who looked like doctors. Why? Simply the one who *doesn't* look the part, conditional on having made a (sort of) successful career in his profession, had to have much to overcome in terms of perception. And if we are lucky enough to have people who do not look the part, it is thanks to the presence of some skin in the game, the contact with reality that filters out incompetence, as reality is blind to looks.

When results come from dealing directly with reality rather than through the agency of commentators, image matters less, even if it correlates to skills. But image matters quite a bit when there is hierarchy and standardized "job evaluation." Consider the chief executive officers of corporations: they don't just look the part, they even look the same. And, worse, when you listen to them talk, they sound the same, down to the same vocabulary and metaphors. But that's their job: as I will keep reminding the reader, counter to the common belief, executives are different from entrepreneurs and are supposed to look like actors.

Now there may be some correlation between looks and skills (someone who looks athletic is likely to be athletic), but, conditional on having had some success *in spite of not looking the part,* it is potent, even crucial, information.

So it becomes no wonder that the job of chief executive of the country was once filled by a former actor, Ronald Reagan. Actually, the best actor is the one nobody realizes is an actor: a closer look at Barack Obama shows that he was even more of an actor: a fancy Ivy League education combined with a liberal reputation is compelling as an image builder.

Much has been written about the *millionaire next door:* the person who is actually rich, on balance, but doesn't look like the person you would expect to be rich, and vice versa. About every private banker is taught to not be fooled by the looks of the client and avoid chasing Ferrari owners at country clubs. As I am writing these lines, a neighbor in my ancestral village (and like almost everyone there, a remote relative), who led a modest but comfortable life, ate food he grew by himself, drank his own pastis (arak), that sort of thing, left an estate of a hundred million dollars, a hundred times what one would have expected him to leave.

So the next time you randomly pick a novel, avoid the one with the author photo representing a pensive man with an ascot standing in front of wall-to-wall bookshelves.

By the same reasoning, and flipping the arguments, skilled thieves at large should not look like thieves. Those who do are more likely to be in jail.

Next, we will get deeper into the following:

> *In any type of activity or business divorced from the direct filter of skin in the game, the great majority of people know the jargon, play the part, and are intimate with the cosmetic details, but are clueless about the subject.*

THE GREEN LUMBER FALLACY

The idea of this chapter is Lindy-compatible. Don't think that beautiful apples taste better, goes the Latin saying.* This is a subtler version of the common phrase "all that glitters is not gold"—something it has taken consumers half a century to figure out; even then, as they have been continuously fooled by the aesthetics of produce.

An expert rule in my business is to never hire a well-dressed trader. But it goes beyond:

> *Hire the successful trader, conditional on a solid track record, whose details you can understand the least.*

Not the most: the least. Why so?

I've introduced this point in *Antifragile*, where I called it *the green lumber fallacy*. A fellow made a fortune in green lumber without knowing what appears to be essential details about the product he traded—he wasn't aware that green lumber stood for freshly cut wood, not lumber that was painted green. Meanwhile, by contrast, the person who related the story went bankrupt while knowing every intimate detail about the green lumber. The fallacy is that what one may need to know in the real world does not necessarily match what one can perceive through intellect: it doesn't mean that details are not relevant, only that those we

---

* *Non teneas aurum totum quod splendet ut aurum/nec pulchrum pomum quodlibet esse bonum.*

tend (IYI-style) to believe are important can distract us from more central attributes of the price mechanism.

In any activity, hidden details are only revealed via Lindy.

Another aspect:

What can be phrased and expressed in a clear narrative that convinces suckers will be a sucker trap.

My friend Terry B., who taught an investment class, invited two speakers. One looked the part of the investment manager, down to a tee: tailored clothes, expensive watch, shiny shoes, and clarity of exposition. He also talked big, projecting the type of confidence you would desire in an executive. The second looked closer to our butcher-surgeon and was totally incomprehensible; he even gave the impression that he was confused. Now, when Terry asked the students which of the two they believed was more successful, they didn't even get close. The first, not unexpectedly, was in the equivalent of the soup kitchen of that business; the second was at least a centimillionaire.

The late Jimmy Powers, a die-hard New York Irishman with whom I worked in an investment bank early in my trading career, was successful in spite of being a college dropout, with the background of a minor Brooklyn street gangster. He would discuss our trading activities in meetings with such sentences as: "We did this and then did that, badaboom, badabing, and then it was all groovy," to an audience of extremely befuddled executives who didn't mind not understanding what he was talking about, so long as our department was profitable. Remarkably, after a while, I learned to effortlessly understand what Jimmy meant. I also learned, in my early twenties, that the people you understand most easily were necessarily the bull***tters.

BEST-DRESSED BUSINESS PLAN

Literature *should* not look like literature. The author Georges Simenon worked as a teenager in journalism as an assistant to the famous French writer Colette; she taught him to resist the idea of putting imperfect subjunctives and references to zephyrs, rhododendrons, and firmaments in his text—the kind of stuff one does when waxing literary. Simenon took this advice to the extreme: his style is similar to that of, say, Graham Greene; it is stripped to the core, and as a result, words do not stand in the way of conveying atmosphere—you feel wetness penetrating your shoes just reading his accounts of commissar Maigret spending endless hours in the Parisian rain; it is as if his central character is the background.

Likewise, the illusion prevails that businesses work via business plans and science via funding. This is strictly not true: a business plan is a useful narrative for those who want to convince a sucker. It works because, as I said in Prologue 2, firms in the entrepreneurship business make most of their money packaging companies and selling them; it is not easy to sell without some strong narrative. But for a real business (as opposed to a fund-raising scheme), something that should survive on its own, business plans and funding work backward. At the time of writing, most big recent successes (Microsoft, Apple, Facebook, Google) were started by people with skin and soul in the game and grew organically—if they had recourse to funding, it was to expand or allow the managers to cash out; funding was not the prime source of creation. You don't create a firm by creating a firm; nor do you do science by doing science.

A BISHOP FOR HALLOWEEN

Which brings me back to social science. I have in many instances quickly jotted down ideas on a piece of paper, along with mathematical proofs, and posted them somewhere, planning to get them published. No fluff or the ideas-free verbose circularity of social science papers. In some fake fields like economics, ritualistic and dominated by citation rings, I discovered that *everything* is in the presentation. So the criticism I've received has never been about the content, but rather the looks. There is a certain language one needs to learn through a long investment, and papers are just iterations around that language.

> *Never hire an academic unless his function is to partake of the*
> *rituals of writing papers or taking exams.*

Which brings us to the attributes of scientism. For it is not just some presentation that matters to these idiots. It is unnecessary complication.

But there is a logic behind these academic complications and rituals. Did you ever wonder why a bishop is dressed for Halloween?

Mediterranean societies are traditionally ones in which the highest-ranking person is the one with the most skin in the game. And if anything characterizes today's America, it is economic risk taking, thanks to a happy transfer of martial values to business and commerce in Anglo-Saxon society—remarkably, traditional Arabic culture also puts the same emphasis on the honor of economic risk-taking. But history shows that there were—and still are—societies in which the intellectual was at the top. The Hindus held the Brahman to be first in the hierarchy, the Celts had the druids (so do their Druze possible-cousins), the Egyptians had their scribes, and the Chinese had for a relatively brief time the scholar. Let me add postwar France. You can notice a remarkable similarity to the way these intellectuals held power and separated themselves from the rest: through complex, extremely elaborate rituals, mysteries that stay within the caste, and an overriding focus on the cosmetic.

Even within the "normal" warrior-run or doer-run societies, the class of intellectuals is all about rituals: without pomp and ceremony, the intellectual is just a talker, that is, pretty much nothing. Consider the bishop in my parts, the Greek-Orthodox church: it's a show of dignity. A bishop on rollerblades would no longer be a bishop. There is nothing wrong with the decorative if it remains what it is, decorative, as remains true today. However, science and business must not be decorative.

Next, we examine the following points:

> *Just as the slick fellow in a Ferrari looks richer than the rumpled centimillionaire, scientism looks more scientific than real science.*

> *True intellect should not appear to be intellectual.*

THE GORDIAN KNOT

Never pay for complexity of presentation when all you need is results.

Alexander the Magnus was once called to solve the following challenge in the Phrygian city of Gordium (as usual with Greek stories, in modern-day Turkey). When he entered Gordium, he found an old wagon, its yoke tied with a multitude of knots, all so tightly entangled that it was impossible to figure out how they were fastened. An oracle had declared that he who would untie the knot would rule all of what was then called "Asia," that is, Asia Minor, the Levant, and the Middle East.

After wrestling with the knot, the Magnus drew back from the lump of gnarled ropes, then made a proclamation that it didn't matter for the prophecy how the tangle was to be unraveled. He then drew his sword and, with a single stroke, cut the knot in half.

No "successful" academic could ever afford to follow such a policy. And no Intellectual Yet Idiot. It took medicine a long time to realize that when a patient shows up with a headache, it is much better to give him aspirin or recommend a good night's sleep than do brain surgery, although the latter appears to be more "scientific." But most "consultants" and others paid by the hour are not there yet.

OVERINTELLECTUALIZATION OF LIFE

The researchers Gerd Gigerenzer and Henry Brighton contrast the approaches of the "rationalistic" school (in quotation marks, as there is little that is rational in these rationalists) and that of the heuristic one, in the following example on how a baseball player catches the ball by Richard Dawkins:

> Richard Dawkins (. . .) argues that "He behaves as if he had solved a set of differential equations in predicting the trajectory of the ball. At some subconscious level, something functionally equivalent to the mathematical calculations is going on."
> (. . .) Instead, experiments have shown that players rely on several heuristics. The gaze heuristic is the simplest one and works if the ball is already high up in the air: Fix your gaze on the ball, start running, and adjust your running speed so that the angle of gaze remains constant.

This error by the science writer Richard Dawkins generalizes to, simply, overintellectualizing humans in their responses to all manner of natural phenomena, rather than accepting the role of a collection of mental heuristics used *for specific purposes*. The baseball player has no clue about the exact heuristic, but he goes with it—otherwise he would lose the game to another, nonintellectualizing, competitor. Likewise, as we will see in Chapter 18, religious "beliefs" are simply mental heuristics that solve a collection of problems—without the agent really knowing how. Solving equations in order to make a decision isn't a skill we humans can aspire to have—it is computationally impossible. What we can rationally do is neutralize some harmful aspects of these heuristics, defang them so to speak.

ANOTHER BUSINESS OF INTERVENTION

People who have always operated without skin in the game (or without their skin in the right game) seek the complicated and centralized, and avoid the simple like the plague. Practitioners, on the other hand, have opposite instincts, looking for the simplest heuristics. Some rules:

> *People who are bred, selected, and compensated to find complicated solutions do not have an incentive to implement simplified ones.*

And it gets more complicated as the remedy has itself a skin-in-the-game problem.

> *This is particularly acute in the meta-problem, when the solution is about solving this very problem.*

In other words, many problems in society come from the interventions of people who sell complicated solutions because that's what their position and training invite them to do. There is absolutely no gain for someone in such a position to propose something simple: you are rewarded for perception, not results. Meanwhile, they pay no price for the side effects that grow nonlinearly with such complications.

This also holds true when it comes to solutions that are profitable to technologists.

GOLD AND RICE

Now, indeed, we know by instinct that brain surgery is not more "scientific" than aspirin, any more than flying the forty or so miles between

JFK and Newark airports represent "efficiency," although there is more technology involved. But we don't easily translate this to other domains and remain victims of *scientism,* which is to science what a Ponzi scheme is to investment, or what advertisement or propaganda are to genuine scientific communication. You magnify the cosmetic attributes.

Recall the genetic modifications of Book 3 (and the smear campaign of Chapter 4). Let us consider the story of the genetically modified Golden Rice. There has been a problem of malnutrition and nutrient deficiency in many developing countries, which my collaborators Yaneer Bar-Yam and Joe Norman attribute to a simple and very straightforward transportation issue. Simply, we waste more than a third of our food supply, and the gains from simple improvement in distribution would far outweigh those from modification of supply. Simply consider that close to 80 or 85 percent of the cost of a tomato can be attributed to transportation, storage, and waste (unsold inventories), rather than the cost at the farmer level. So visibly our efforts should be on low-tech distribution.

Now the "techies" saw an angle of intervention. First, you show pictures of starving children to elicit sympathy and prevent further discussion—anyone who argues in the presence of dying children is a heartless a**hole. Second, you make it look like any critic of your method is arguing *against* saving the children. Third, you propose some scientific-looking technique that is lucrative to you and, should it cause a catastrophe or blight, insulates you from the long-term effects. Fourth, you enlist journalists and useful idiots, people who hate things that appear "unscientific" in their unscientific eyes. Fifth, you create a smear campaign to harm the reputations of researchers who, not having *f*** you money,* are very vulnerable to the slightest blemish to their reputations.

The technique in question consists in genetically modifying rice to have the grains include vitamins. My colleagues and I made an effort to show the following, which is a criticism of the method in general. First, transgenics, that is the type of genetic modifications thus obtained, was not analytically in the same category as the crossbreeding of plants and animals that have characterized human activities since husbandry—say, potatoes or mandarin oranges. We skipped complexity classes, and the effects on the environment are not foreseeable—nobody studied the interactions. Recall that fragility is in the dosage: falling from the 20th floor is not in the same risk category as falling from your chair. We even showed that there was a patent increase in systemic risk. Second, there was no proper risk study, and the statistical methods in the papers in support of the argument were flawed. Third, we invoked the principle of simplicity, which was called *antiscience*. Why don't we give these people rice and vitamins separately? After all, we don't have genetically modified coffee that has milk with it. Fourth, we were able to show that GMOs brought a bevy of hidden risk to the environment, because of the higher use of pesticide, which kills the microbiome (that is, the bacteria and other life in the soil).

I realized soon after that, owing to the minority rule, there was no point continuing. As I said in Book 3, GMOs lost simply because a minority of intelligent and intransigent people stood against them.

THE COMPENSATION

Simply, the minute one is judged by others rather than by reality, things become warped as follows. Firms that haven't gone bankrupt yet have something called personnel departments. So there are metrics used and "evaluation forms" to fill.

The minute one has evaluation forms, distortions occur. Recall that in *The Black Swan* I had to fill my evaluation form asking for the percentage of profitable days, encouraging traders to make steady money at the expense of hidden risks of Black Swans, consequential losses. Russian Roulette allows you to make money five times out of six. This has bankrupted banks, as banks lose less than one in one hundred quarters, but then they lose more than they ever made. My declared approach was to try to make money infrequently. I tore the evaluation form in front of the big boss and they left me alone.

Now the mere fact that an evaluation causes you to be judged not by the end results, but by some intermediary metric that invites you to look sophisticated, brings some distortions.

EDUCATION AS LUXURY GOOD

Ivy League universities are becoming in the eyes of the new Asian upper class the ultimate status luxury good. Harvard is like a Vuitton bag and a Cartier watch. It is a huge drag on the middle class, who have been plowing an increased share of their savings into educational institutions, transferring their money to bureaucrats, real estate developers,

SURGEONS SHOULD NOT LOOK LIKE SURGEONS   **165**

tenured professors of some discipline that would not otherwise exist (gender studies, comparative literature, or international economics), and other parasites. In the United States, we have a buildup of student loans that automatically transfer to these rent extractors. In a way it is no different from racketeering: one needs a decent university "name" to get ahead in life. But we have evidence that collectively society doesn't advance with organized education, rather the reverse: the level of (formal) education in a country is the result of wealth.[*]

A BS DETECTION HEURISTIC

The heuristic here would be to use education in reverse: hire, conditional on an equal set of skills, the person with the least label-oriented education. It means that the person had to succeed in spite of the credentialization of his competitors and overcome more serious hurdles. In addition, people who didn't go to Harvard are easier to deal with in real life.

You can tell if a discipline is BS if the degree depends severely on the prestige of the school granting it. I remember when I applied to MBA programs being told that anything outside the top ten or twenty would be a waste of time. On the other hand a degree in mathematics is much less dependent on the school (conditional on being above a certain level, so the heuristic would apply to the difference between top ten and top two thousand schools).

The same applies to research papers. In math and physics, a result posted on the repository site arXiv (with a minimum hurdle) is fine. In low-quality fields like academic finance (where papers are usually some form of complicated storytelling), the "prestige" of the journal is the sole criterion.

REAL GYMS DON'T LOOK LIKE GYMS

This education labeling provides a lot of cosmetic things but misses something essential about antifragility and true learning, reminiscent of gyms. People are impressed with expensive equipment—fancy, compli-

---

[*] The same argument applies to biographies of scientists and mathematicians written by science journalists—or professional biographers. They will find some narrative and, worse, put scientists on pedestals.

cated, multicolored—meant to look as if it belonged on a spaceship. Things appear maximally sophisticated and scientific—but remember that what looks scientific is usually scientism, not science. As with label universities, you pay quite a bit of money to join, largely for the benefit of the real estate developer. Yet people into strength training (those who are actually strong across many facets of real life) know that users of these machines gain no strength beyond an initial phase. By having recourse to complicated equipment that typically targets very few muscles, regular users will eventually be pear-shaping and growing weaker over time, with skills that do not transfer outside of the very machine that they trained on. The equipment may have some use in a hospital or a rehabilitation program, but that's about it. On the other hand, the simpler barbell (a metal bar with two weights on both ends) is the only standard piece of equipment that gets you to recruit your entire body for exercises—and it is the simplest and cheapest to get. All you need to learn are the safety skills to move off the floor at your maximum while avoiding injury. Lindy again: weight lifters have known the phenomenology for at least two and a half millennia.

All you need are shoes to run outside when you can (and perhaps some pants that don't make you look ridiculous), and a barbell with weights. As I am writing these lines I am checking the brochure of a fancy hotel where I will be spending the next two days. The brochure was put together by some MBA: it is glossy, shows all the machines and the jars of the color-rich juices to "improve" your health. They even have a swimming pool; but no barbell.

And if gyms should not look like gyms, exercise should not look like exercise. Most gains in physical strength come from working the tails of the distribution, close to your limit.

NEXT

This chapter managed to mix weight lifting and fundamental research under the single argument that, while the presence of skin in the game does away with the cosmetic, its absence causes multiplicative nonsense. Next, let us consider the divergence of interest between you and yourself when you become rich.

CHAPTER 10

Only the Rich Are Poisoned:
The Preferences of Others

The salesman is the boss—How to drink poison—Advertising and manipulation—The unbearable silence of large mansions on Sunday evening

————

When people get rich, they shed their skin-in-the-game-driven experiential mechanism. They lose control of their preferences, substituting constructed preferences for their own, complicating their lives unnecessarily, triggering their own misery. And these constructed preferences are of course the preferences of those who want to sell them something. This is a skin-in-the-game problem, as the choices of the rich are dictated by others who have something to gain, and no side effects, from the sale. And given that they are rich, and their exploiters not often so, nobody would shout *victim*.

I once had dinner in a Michelin-starred restaurant with a fellow who insisted on eating there instead of my selection of a casual Greek taverna with a friendly owner-operator whose second cousin was the manager and third cousin once removed was the friendly receptionist. The other customers seemed, as we say in Mediterranean languages, to have a cork plugged in their behind obstructing proper ventilation, causing the vapors to build on the inside of the gastrointestinal walls, leading to the irritable type of decorum you only notice in the educated semi-upper classes. I noted that, in addition to the plugged corks, all the men wore ties.

Dinner consisted of a succession of complicated small things, with microscopic ingredients and contrasting tastes that forced you to concentrate as if you were taking some entrance exam. You were not eating, rather visiting some type of museum with an affected English major lecturing you on some artistic dimension you would have never considered on your own. There was so little that was familiar and so little that fit my taste buds: once something on the occasion tasted like something real, there was no chance to have more as we moved on to the next dish. Trudging through the dishes and listening to some bull***t by the sommelier about the paired wine, I was afraid of losing concentration. It costs a lot of energy to fake that you're not bored. In fact, I discovered an optimization in the wrong place: the only thing I cared about, the bread, was not warm. It appears that this is not a Michelin requirement for three stars.

VENENUM IN AURO BIBITUR

I left the place starving. Now, if I had a choice, I would have had some time-tested recipe (say a pizza with very fresh ingredients, or a juicy hamburger) in a lively place—for a twentieth of the price. But because the dinner partner could afford the expensive restaurant, we ended up the victims of some complicated experiments by a chef judged by some Michelin bureaucrat. It would fail the Lindy effect: food does better through minute variations from Sicilian grandmother to Sicilian grandmother. It hit me that the rich were natural targets; as the eponymous Thyestes shouts in Seneca's tragedy, thieves do not enter impecunious homes, and one is more likely to be drinking poison in a golden cup than an ordinary one. Poison is drunk in golden cups (*Venenum in auro bibitur*).

It is easy to scam people by getting them into complications—the poor are spared that type of scamming. This is the same complication we saw in Chapter 9 that makes academics sell the most possibly complicated solution when a simple one can do. Further, the rich start using "experts" and "consultants." An entire industry meant to swindle you will swindle you: financial consultants, diet advisors, exercise experts, lifestyle engineers, sleeping councilors, breathing specialists, etc.

Hamburgers, to many of us, are vastly tastier than filet mignon because of the higher fat content, but people have been convinced that the latter is better because it is more expensive to produce.

My idea of the good life is to *not* attend a gala dinner, one of those situations where you find yourself stuck seated for two hours between the wife of a Kansas City real estate developer (who just visited Nepal) and a Washington lobbyist (who just returned from a vacation in Bali).

LARGE FUNERAL HOMES

Same with real estate: most people, I am convinced, are happier in close quarters, in a real barrio-style neighborhood, where they can feel human warmth and company. But when they have big bucks they end up pressured to move into outsized, impersonal, and silent mansions, far away from neighbors. On late afternoons, the silence of these large galleries has a funereal feel to it, but without the soothing music. This is something historically rare: in the past, large mansions were teeming with servants, head-servants, butlers, cooks, assistants, maids, private tutors, impoverished cousins, horse grooms, even personal musicians. And nobody today will come to console you for having a mansion—few will realize that it is quite sad to be there on Sunday evening.

As Vauvenargues, the French moralist, figured out, small is preferable owing to what we would call in today's terms scale properties. Some things can be, simply, too large for your heart. Rome, he wrote, was easy to love by its denizens when it was a small village, harder when it became a large empire.

Prosperous people of the type who don't look rich are certainly aware of the point—they live in comfortable quarters and instinctively know that a move will be a mental burden. Many still live in their original houses.

Very few people understand their own choices, and end up being manipulated by those who want to sell them something. In that sense, impoverishment might even be desirable. Looking at Saudi Arabia, which should progressively revert to the pre-oil level of poverty, I wonder if taking away some things from them—including the swarm of fawning foreigners coming to skin them—will make them better off.

To put it another way: if wealth is giving you fewer options instead of more (and more varied) options, you're doing it wrong.

CONVERSATION

If anything, being rich you need to hide your money if you want to have what I call friends. This may be known; what is less obvious is that you may also need to hide your erudition and learning. People can *only* be social friends if they don't try to upstage or outsmart one another. Indeed, the classical art of conversation is to avoid any imbalance, as in Baldassare Castiglione's *Book of the Courtier:* people need to be equal, at least for the purpose of the conversation, otherwise it fails. It has to be hierarchy-free and equal in contribution. You'd rather have dinner with your friends than with your professor, unless of course your professor understands "the art" of conversation.

Indeed, one can generalize and define a community as a space within which many rules of competition and hierarchy are lifted, where the collective prevails over one's interest. Of course there will be tension with the outside, but that's another discussion. This idea of competition being lifted within a group or a tribe was, once again, present in the notion of a group as studied by Elinor Ostrom.

NONLINEARITY OF PROGRESS

Now let us generalize to progress in general. Do you want society to get wealthy, or is there something else you prefer—avoidance of poverty? Are your choices yours or those of salespeople?

Let's return to the restaurant experience and discuss constructed preferences as compared to natural ones. If I had a choice between paying $200 for a pizza or $6.95 for the French complicated experience, I would readily pay $200 for the pizza, plus $9.95 for a bottle of Malbec wine. Actually I would pay to *not* have the Michelin experience.

This reasoning shows that sophistication can, at some level, cause degradation, what economists call "negative utility." This tells us something about wealth and the growth of gross domestic product in society; it shows the presence of an inverted U curve with a level beyond which you get incremental harm. It is detectable only if you get rid of constructed preferences.

Now, many societies have been getting wealthier and wealthier, many beyond the positive part of the inverted U curve, not counting the effect of the increased comfort on their spoiled children. And I am certain that if pizza were priced at $200, the people with corks plugged in their behinds would be lining up for it. But it is too easy to produce, so they opt for the costly, and pizza with fresh natural ingredients will be always cheaper than the complicated crap.

So long as society is getting richer, someone will try to sell you something until the point of degradation of your well-being, and a bit beyond that.

NEXT

The next chapter will present the rule of *no verbal threat* through the history of the experts of the craft, the sect of the Assassins.

CHAPTER 11

Facta non Verba
(Deeds Before Words)

Dead horse in your bed—Friendship via poisoned cake—Roman emperors and U.S. presidents—A living enemy is worth ten dead ones

———

The best enemy is the one you own by putting skin in his game and letting him know the exact rules that come with it. You keep him alive, with the knowledge that he owes his life to your benevolence. The notion that an enemy you own is better than a dead one was perfected by the order of the Assassins, so we will do some digging into the work of that secret society.

AN OFFER VERY HARD TO REFUSE

There is this formidable scene in the Godfather when a Hollywood executive wakes up with the bloody severed head of his cherished race horse in his bed.

He had refused to hire a Sicilian-American actor for reasons that appeared iniquitous, as while he knew the latter was the best for the role, he was resentful of the "olive oil voice" that had charmed one of his past mistresses and fearful of its powers to seduce future ones. It turned out that the actor, who in real life was (possibly) Frank Sinatra, had friends and friends of friends, that type of thing; he was even the godson of a capo. A visit from the consigliere of the "family" neither succeeded to sway the executive, nor softened his Hollywood abrasiveness—the fellow failed to realize that by flying across the country to make the request, the high-ranking mobster was not just providing the type of recommendation letter you mail to the personnel department of a state university. He had made him *an offer that he could not refuse* (the expression was popularized by that scene in the movie).

It was a threat, and not an empty threat.

As I am writing these lines, people discuss terrorism and terrorist groups while making severe category mistakes; there are in fact two totally distinct varieties. The first group are terrorists for about everyone, that is, for every person equipped with the ability to discern and who isn't a resident of Saudi Arabia and doesn't work for a think tank funded by sheikhs; the second are militia groups largely called terrorists by their enemies, and "resistance" or "freedom fighters" by those who don't dislike them.

The first includes nonsoldiers who indiscriminately kill civilians for effect and don't bother with military targets, as their aim isn't to make military gains, just to make a statement, harm some living humans, produce some noise, and, for some, find a low-error way to go to paradise. Most Sunni jihadis, of the type who take incommensurable pleasure in blowing up civilians, such as Al Qaeda, ISIS, and the "moderate rebels" in Syria sponsored by former U.S. president Obama, are in that category. The second group is about strategic political assassination—the Irish Republican Army, most Shiite organizations, Algerian independence fighters against France, French resistance fighters during the German occupation, etc.

For Shiites and similar varieties in the Near and Middle East, the ancestry, methods, and rules originate in the order of the Assassins, itself following the modus of the Judean Sicarii during Roman times. The Sicarii are named after the daggers they used to kill Roman soldiers and, mostly, their Judean collaborators, due to what they perceived as the profanation of their temple and the land.

I have the misfortune to know a bit about the subject. My high school, the Franco-Lebanese Lycée of Beirut, has a list of "notable" former students. I am the only one who is "notable" for reasons other than being the victim of a successful or attempted assassination (although I have enough Salafi enemies and there is still time to satisfy such requirement—skin in the game).

THE ASSASSINS

The most interesting thing about the Assassins is that actual assassination was low on their agenda. They understood non-cheap messaging. They preferred to own their enemies. And the only enemy you cannot manipulate is a dead one.

In 1118, Ahmad Sanjar became the sultan of the Seljuk Turkish Empire of Asia minor (that is, modern-day Turkey), Iran, and parts of Afghanistan. Soon after his accession, he woke up one day with a dagger next to his bed, firmly planted in the ground. In one version of the legend, a letter informed him that the dagger thrust in hard ground was preferable to the alternative, being plunged in his soft breast. It was a characteristic message of the Hashishins, aka Assassins, making him aware of the need to leave them alone, send them birthday gifts, or hire their actors for his next movie. Sultan Sanjar had previously snubbed their peace negotiators, so they moved to phase two of a demonstrably well planned-out process. They convinced him that his life was in *their* hands and that, crucially, he didn't have to worry if he did the right thing. Indeed Sanjar and the Assassins had a happy life together ever after.

You will note that no explicit verbal threat was issued. Verbal threats reveal nothing beyond weakness and unreliability. Remember, once again, *no* verbal threats.

The Assassins were an eleventh- through fourteenth-century sect related to Shiite Islam, and were (and still are through their reincarnations) violently anti-Sunni. They were often associated with the Knights Templar as they fought frequently on the side of the crusaders—and if they seem to share some of the values of the Templars, in sparing the innocent and the weak, it is likely because the former group transmitted some of their values to the latter. The chivalric code of honor has, for its second clause: *I shall respect and defend the weak, the sick, and the needy*.

The Assassins supposedly sent the same message to Saladin (the Kurdish ruler of Syria who conquered Jerusalem from the Crusaders), informing him that the cake he was about to eat was poisoned . . . by themselves.

The ethical system of the Assassins held that political assassination helped prevent war; threats of the dagger-by-your-bed variety are even better for bloodless control.* They supposedly aimed at sparing civilians and people who were not directly targeted. Their precision was meant to reduce what is now called "collateral damage."

ASSASSINATION AS MARKETING

Those readers who may have tried to get rid of *pebbles in their shoes* (that is, someone who bothers you and doesn't get the hint) might know that "contracts" on ordinary citizens (that is, to trigger their funeral) are relatively easy to perform and inexpensive to buy. There is a relatively active underground market for these contracts. In general, you need to pay a bit more to "make it look like an accident." However, skilled historians and observers of martial history would recommend the exact opposite: in politics, you should have to pay more to make it look intentional.

In fact, what Captain Mark Weisenborn, Pasquale Cirillo, and I discovered, when we tried doing a systematic study of violence (debunking the confabulatory thesis by Steven Pinker that we mentioned earlier, holding that violence has dropped), was that war numbers have been historically inflated . . . by both sides. Both the Mongols (during their sweep across Eurasia in the Middle Ages) and their panicky victims had an incentive to exaggerate, which acted as a deterrent. Mongols weren't interested in killing everybody; they just wanted submission, which came cheaply through terror. Further, having spent some time perusing the genetic imprints of invaded populations, it is clear that if the warriors coming from the Eastern steppes left a cultural imprint, they certainly left their genes at home. Gene transfer between areas happens by group migrations, inclement climate, and unaccommodating soil rather than war.

More recently, the Hama "massacre" in 1982 of Syrian jihadis by Assad senior caused documented casualties (by my estimation) at least an order of magnitude lower than what is reported; the rest came from inflation—numbers swelling over time from two thousand to close to forty thousand without significant new information. Both the Syrian regime and its enemies had an interest in numbers being inflated. Interestingly the number has continued to climb in recent years. We will return to historians in Chapter 14, where we show how empirical rigor is quite foreign to their discipline.

---

* It appears that what we read about the Assassins can be smear by their enemies, including the apocryphal accounts according to which their name comes from consumption of hashish (cannabis in Arabic), as they would get into a trance before their assassination.

ASSASSINATION AS DEMOCRACY

Now, political life; if the democratic system doesn't fully deliver governance—it patently doesn't, owing to cronyisms and the Hillary Monsanto-Malmaison style of covert legal corruption—we have known forever what does: an increased turnover at the top. Count Ernst zu Münster's epigrammatic description of the Russian Constitution explains it: "Absolutism tempered by assassination."

While today's politicians have no skin in the game and do not have to worry so long as they play the game, they stay longer and longer on the job, thanks to the increased life expectancy of modern times. France's caviar socialist François Mitterrand reigned for fourteen years, longer than many French kings; and thanks to technology he had more power over the population than most French kings. Even a United States president, the modern kind of emperor (unlike Napoleon and the czars, Roman emperors before Diocletian were not absolutists), tends to last at least four years on the throne, while Rome had five emperors in a single year and four in another. The mechanism worked: consider that all the bad emperors—Caligula, Caracalla, Elagabalus, and Nero—ended their careers either murdered by the Praetorian Guard or, in the case of Nero, dead by suicide in anticipation. Recall that in the first four hundred years of empire, less than a third of emperors died a natural death, assuming these deaths were truly natural.*

THE CAMERA FOR SKIN IN THE GAME

Thanks to the camera, you no longer need to put horses' heads in boutique hotels or villas in the Hamptons to own people. You may no longer even need to assassinate anyone.

We used to live in small communities; our reputations were directly determined by what we did—we were watched. Today, anonymity brings out the a**hole in people. So I accidentally discovered a way to change the behavior of unethical and abusive persons *without verbal threat*. Take their pictures. Just the act of taking their pictures is similar to holding their lives in your hands and controlling their future behavior

---

* This is an argument for term limits for politicians that match former life expectancy on the job.

thanks to your silence. They don't know what you can do with it, and will live in a state of uncertainty.

I discovered the magic of the camera in reestablishing civil/ethical behavior as follows. One day, in the New York subway underground corridor, I hesitated for a few seconds trying to get my bearings in front of the list of exits. A well-dressed man with a wiry build and neurotic personality started heaping insults at me "for stopping." Instead of hitting him as a conversation starter, as I would have done in 1921, I pulled my cell out and took his picture while calmly calling him a "mean idiot, abusive to lost persons." He freaked out and ran away from me, hiding his face in his hands to prevent further photographs.

Another time, a man in upstate New York got into my parking spot as I was backing into it. I told him it was against etiquette, he acted as an a**hole. Same thing, I silently photographed him and his license plate. He rapidly drove away and liberated the parking spot. Finally, near my house, there is a forest preserve banned to bicycles as they harm the environment. Two mountain cyclists rode on it every weekend during my 4 P.M. walk. I admonished them to no avail. One day I calmly took a dozen pictures, making sure they noticed. The bigger guy complained, but they then left rapidly. They have never returned.

Of course, I destroyed their pictures. But I never thought handhelds could be such a weapon. And it would be unfair to use their pictures for web-mobbing. In the past, bad deeds were only transmitted to acquaintances who knew how to put things in perspective. Today, strangers, incapable of judging a person's general character, have become self-appointed behavior police. Web-shaming is much more powerful than past reputational blots, and more of a tail risk.

In Book 2 of Plato's *Republic*, there is a discussion between Socrates and Plato's brother, Glaucon, about the ring of the Gyges, which gives its holder the power to be invisible at will and watch others. Clearly Plato anticipated the later Christian contrivance "you are watched." The discussion was whether people behave in a right manner because they are watched—or, according to Socrates, because of their character. Of course we side with Socrates, but we will even go beyond, by defining virtue as something that goes beyond pleasing the watchers, and can actually irritate them. Remember that Socrates was put to death because he would not compromise his standards. More on that, in a few chapters, when we discuss real virtue.

CHAPTER 12

The Facts Are True,
the News Is Fake

I never said that I said—No news is mostly news—Information flows in both directions

---

HOW TO DISAGREE WITH YOURSELF

In the summer of 2009, I partook of an hour-long public discussion with David Cameron, who was in the running for, and later became, the U.K. prime minister. The discussion was about how to make society robust, even immune to Black Swans, what structure was needed for both decentralization and accountability, and how the system should be built, *ce genre de trucs*. It was an interesting fifty-nine minutes around the topics of the *Incerto,* and I felt great communicating all the points in bulk for the first time. The room in the elegant Royal Society for the Arts was full of journalists. I subsequently went to a Chinese restaurant in (London's) Soho to celebrate with a few people when I received a phone call from a horrified friend. All London newspapers were calling me a "climate denier," portraying me as part of a dark anti-environment conspiracy.

The entire fifty-nine minutes were summarized by the press and reported from a tangential comment that lasted twenty seconds taken in reverse of the intended meaning. Someone who didn't attend the conference would have been under the impression that that was the whole conversation.

It turned out that I presented my version of the precautionary principle during the conversation, worth restating here. It asserts that one does not need complex models as a justification to avoid a certain action. If we don't understand something and it has a systemic effect, just avoid it. Models are error-prone, something I knew well with finance; most risks only appear in analyses after harm is done. As far as I know, we only have one planet. So the burden is on those who pollute—or who introduce new substances in larger than usual quantities—to show a lack of tail risk. In fact, the more uncertainty about the models, the more conservative one should be. The same newspapers had lauded *The Black Swan* in which this very point was fleshed out clearly—so visibly the attack had nothing to do with the point I was making, rather they wanted to weaken Cameron by demonizing me. I realized that they would have found another reason to tarnish me no matter what I said.

I managed to defend myself by making a lot of noise, and, with explicit legal threats, forced every newspaper to publish my correction. Even then someone at *The Guardian* tried (unsuccessfully) to tone down my letter by showing that it was some type of *disagreement* with what *I* said, not a correction of their misrepresentation. In other words, they wanted me to say that I was disagreeing with myself.

The London newspapers were actively misrepresenting something to *their* own public. Someone who read the paper was mistaking the journalist for an intermediary between him- or herself and the product, the piece of news. But if I eventually set the record straight, thanks to my bully pulpit, many can't do the same.

So clearly there is an agency problem. There is no difference between a journalist at *The Guardian* and the restaurant owner in Milan, who, when you ask for a taxi, calls his cousin who does a tour of the city to inflate the meter before showing up. Or the doctor who willfully misdiagnoses you to sell you a drug in which he has a vested interest.

INFORMATION DOESN'T LIKE TO BE OWNED

Journalism isn't Lindy compatible. Information transmits organically by word of mouth, which circulates in a two-way manner. In Ancient Rome, people got information without a centralized filter. In the ancient Mediterranean marketplaces, people talked; they were the receivers and the purveyors of news. Barbers offered comprehensive services; they doubled as surgeons, dispute-resolution experts, and news reporters. If people were left to filter their own rumors, they were also part of the transmission. Same with pubs and London coffee houses. In the Eastern Mediterranean (currently Greece and the Levant), condolences were the source of gathering and transmission—and represented the bulk of social life. Dissemination of the news took place at these gatherings. My social grandmother would have her "rounds" of visits of condolences some days in Beirut's then-significant Greek Orthodox community, and knew practically everything down to the most insignificant details. If the child of someone prominent flunked an exam, she knew it. Practically every affair in town was detected.

Unreliable people carried less weight than reliable ones. You can't fool people more than twice.*

The period of time that corresponds to reliance on one-sided accounts such as television and newspapers, which can be controlled by the mandarins, lasted from the middle of the twentieth century until the U.S. election of 2016. At that point, social networks, allowing a two-way flow of information, returned the mechanism of tidings to its natural format—Lindy had to strike. As with participants in markets and souks, there is a long-term advantage to being dependable.

Further, such an agency problem as that of the current press is systemic, as its interests will keep diverging from that of its public until the eventual systemic blowup as we saw with the Bob Rubin trade. As an illustration: I was less frustrated by the misinterpretation of my ideas than by the fact that no reader would have realized that 99 percent of my discussion with Cameron was about things other than climate change. If the former could have been a misunderstanding, the latter is a structural defect. And you never cure structural defects; the system corrects itself by collapsing.†

The divergence is evident in that journos worry considerably more

---

* There were some occasional episodes of collective frenzy, with the spread of false rumors, but, owing to the low level of connectivity between communities, these did not travel as fast as they do today.

† One way journalism will self-destruct from its growing divergence from the public is illustrated by the Gawker story. Gawker was a voyeurism outfit that specialized in publicizing people's private lives in industrial proportions. Eventually Gawker, which bullied its financially weaker victims (often twenty-one-year-olds in revenge porn scenes), got bullied by someone richer and went bankrupt. It was revealing that journalists overwhelmingly sided with Gawker on grounds of "freedom of information," the most misplaced exploitation of that concept, rather than with the public, who sided, naturally, with the victim. This is to remind the reader that journalism has the mother of all agency problems.

about the opinion of other journalists than the judgment of their readers. Compare this to a healthy system, say, that of restaurants. As we saw in Chapter 8, restaurant owners worry about the opinion of their customers, not those of other restaurant owners, which keeps them in check and prevents the business from straying collectively away from its interests. Further, skin in the game creates diversity, not monoculture. Economic insecurity worsens the condition. Journalists are currently in the most insecure profession you can find: the majority live hand to mouth, and ostracism by their friends would be terminal. Thus they become easily prone to manipulation by lobbyists, as we saw with GMOs, the Syrian wars, etc. You say something unpopular in that profession about Brexit, GMOs, or Putin, and you become history. This is the opposite of business where me-tooism is penalized.

THE ETHICS OF DISAGREEMENT

Now let us get deeper into the application of the Silver Rule in intellectual debates. You can criticize either what a person *said* or what a person *meant*. The former is more sensational, hence lends itself more readily to dissemination. The mark of a charlatan—say the writer and pseudo-rationalist Sam Harris—is to defend his position or attack a critic by focusing on some specific statement ("look at what he said") rather than blasting his exact position ("look at what he means" or, more broadly, "look at what he stands for")—for the latter requires an extensive grasp of the proposed idea. Note that the same applies to the interpretation of religious texts, often extracted from their broader circumstances.

It is impossible for anyone to write a perfectly rationally argued document without a segment that, out of context, can be transformed by some dishonest copywriter to appear totally absurd and lend itself to sensationalization, so politicians, charlatans, and, more disturbingly, journalists hunt for these segments. "Give me a few lines written by any man and I will find enough to get him hung" goes the saying attributed to Richelieu, Voltaire, Talleyrand, a vicious censor during the French revolution phase of terror, and a few others. As Donald Trump said, "The facts are true, the news is fake"—ironically at a press conference in which he subsequently suffered the same selective reporting as my RSA event.

The great Karl Popper often started a discussion with an unerring representation of his opponent's positions, often exhaustive, as if he were marketing them as his own ideas, before proceeding to systematically dismantle them. Also, take Hayek's diatribes *Contra Keynes and Cambridge:* it was a "contra," but not a single line misrepresents Keynes or makes an overt attempt at sensationalizing. (It helped that people were too intimidated by Keynes's intellect and aggressive personality to risk triggering his ire.)

Read Aquinas's *Summa Theologica,* written eight centuries ago; you will notice sections titled "Questio," then "Praeteria," "Objectiones," "Sed Contra," etc., describing with a legalistic precision the positions being challenged and looking for a flaw in them before submitting a compromise. If you notice a similarity with the *Talmud,* it is no accident: it appears that both methods originate with Roman legal reasoning.

Note the associated *straw man* arguments by which one not only extracts a comment but *also* provides an interpretation or promotes misinterpretation. As an author, I consider *straw man* no different from theft.

Some types of lies in an open market cause others to treat the perpetrator as if he were invisible. It is not about the lie; it is about the system that requires some modicum of trust. For purveyors of calumnies did not survive in ancient environments.

The principle of charity stipulates that you try to understand a message as if you were yourself its author. It, and revulsion at its violations, are Lindy compatible. For instance, Isaiah 29:21 states: *That make a man an offender for a word, and lay a snare for him that reproveth in the gate, and turn aside the just for a thing of nought.* The wicked ensnare you. Calumny was already a very severe crime in Babylon, where the person who made a false accusation was punished as if he committed the exact crime.

However, in philosophy, the principle of charity—as principle—is only sixty years old. As with other things, if the principle of charity had to become a principle, it must be because some old ethical practices were abandoned.

NEXT

The next chapter will take us to virtue as skin in the game.

CHAPTER 13

The Merchandising of Virtue

Sontag is about Sontag—Virtue is what you do when nobody is looking—Have the guts to be unpopular—Meetings breed meetings— Call someone lonely on Saturdays after tennis

———

Lycurgus, the Spartan lawmaker, responded to a suggestion to allow democracy there, saying "begin with your own family."

I will always remember my encounter with the writer and cultural icon Susan Sontag, largely because I met the great Benoit Mandelbrot on the same day. It took place in 2001, two months after the terrorist event of September, in a radio station in New York. Sontag, who was being interviewed, was piqued by the idea of a fellow who "studies randomness" and came to engage me. When she discovered that I was a trader, she blurted out that she was "against the market system" and turned her back to me as I was in mid-sentence, just to humiliate me (note here that courtesy is an application of the Silver Rule), while her assistant gave me a look as if I had been convicted of child killing. I sort of justified her behavior in order to forget the incident, imagining that she lived in some rural commune, grew her own vegetables, wrote with pencil and paper, engaged in barter transactions, that type of stuff.

No, she did not grow her own vegetables, it turned out. Two years later, I accidentally found her obituary (I waited a decade and a half before writing about the incident to avoid speaking ill of the departed). People in publishing were complaining about her rapacity; she had squeezed her publisher, Farrar, Straus and Giroux, for what would be several million dollars today for a novel. She shared, with a girlfriend, a mansion in New York City, later sold for $28 million. Sontag probably felt that insulting people with money inducted her into some unimpeachable sainthood, exempting her from having skin in the game.

> *It is immoral to be in opposition to the market system and not live (somewhere in Vermont or Northwestern Afghanistan) in a hut or cave isolated from it.*

But there is worse:

> *It is much more immoral to claim virtue without fully living with its direct consequences.*

This will be the main topic of this chapter: exploiting virtue for image, personal gain, careers, social status, these kinds of things—and by personal gain I mean anything that does not share the downside of a negative action.

By contrast with Sontag, I have met a few people who live their public ideas. Ralph Nader, for instance, leads the life of a monk, identical to a member of a monastery in the sixteenth century. And the secular saint Simone Weil, while coming from the French Jewish upper class, spent a year in a car factory so the working class could be something other than an abstract construct for her.

THE PUBLIC AND THE PRIVATE

As we saw with the interventionistas, a certain class of theoretical people can despise the details of reality. If you manage to convince yourself that you are right in theory, you don't really care how your ideas affect others. Your ideas give you a virtuous status that makes you impervious to how they affect others.

Likewise, if you believe that you are "helping the poor" by spending money on PowerPoint presentations and international meetings, the type of meetings that lead to more meetings (and PowerPoint presentations) you can completely ignore individuals—the poor become an abstract reified construct that you do not encounter in your real life. Your efforts at conferences give you license to humiliate them in person. Hillary Monsanto-Malmaison, sometimes known as Hillary Clinton, found it permissible to heap abuse on secret service agents. I was recently told that a famous Canadian socialist environmentalist, with whom I was part of a lecture series, abused waiters in restaurants, between lectures on equity, diversity, and fairness.

Kids with rich parents talk about "class privilege" at privileged colleges such as Amherst—but in one instance, one of them could not answer Dinesh D'Souza's simple and logical suggestion: Why don't you go to the registrar's office and give your privileged spot to the minority student next in line?

Clearly the defense given by people under such a situation is that they want others to do so as well—they require a systemic solution to every local perceived problem of injustice. I find that immoral. I know of no ethical system that allows you to let someone drown without helping him because other people are not helping, no system that says, "I will save people from drowning only if others too save other people from drowning."

Which brings us to the principle:

> If your private life conflicts with your intellectual opinion, it cancels your intellectual ideas, not your private life.

And a solution to the vapid universalism we discussed in the Prologue:

> If your private actions do not generalize, then you cannot have general ideas.

This is not strictly about ethics, but information. If a car salesman tries to sell you a Detroit car while driving a Honda, he is signaling that the wares he is touting may have a problem.

THE VIRTUE MERCHANTS

In about every hotel chain, from Argentina to Kazakhstan, the bathroom will have a sign meant to get your attention: PROTECT THE ENVIRONMENT. They want you to hold off from sending the towels to the laundry and reuse them for a while, because avoiding excess laundry saves them tens of thousands of dollars a year. This is similar to the salesperson telling you what is good for you when it is mostly (and centrally) good for him. Hotels, of course, love the environment, but you can bet that they wouldn't advertise it so loudly if it weren't good for their bottom line.

So these global causes—poverty (particularly children's), the environment, justice for some minority trampled upon by colonial powers, or some as-yet-unknown gender that will be persecuted—are now the last refuge of the scoundrel advertising virtue.

Virtue is not something you advertise. It is not an investment strategy. It is not a cost-cutting scheme. It is not a bookselling (or, worse, concert-ticket-selling) strategy.

Now I have wondered why, by the Lindy effect, there is so little mention of what is called virtue signaling in the ancient texts. How could it be new?

Well, it is not new, but was not seen as prevalent enough in the past to warrant much complaining and get named a vice. But mention there is; let's check Matthew 6:1–4, where the highest mitzvah is the one done secretly:

> *Be careful not to practice your righteousness in front of others to be seen by them. If you do, you will have no reward from your Father in heaven.*
>
> *So when you give to the needy, do not announce it with trumpets, as the hypocrites do in the synagogues and on the streets, to be honored by others. Truly I tell you, they have received their reward in full. But when you give to the needy, do not let your left hand know what your right hand is doing, so that your giving may be in secret. Then your Father, who sees what is done in secret, will reward you.*

TO BE OR TO SEEM?

The investor Charlie Munger once said: "Look it. Would you rather be the world's greatest lover, but have everyone think you're the world's worst lover? Or would you rather be the world's worst lover but have everyone think you're the world's greatest lover?" As usual, if it makes sense, it has to be in the classics, where it is found under the name *esse quam videri,* which I translate as *to be or to be seen as such.* It can be found in Cicero, Sallust, even Machiavelli, who, characteristically, inverted it to *videri quam esse,* "show rather than be."

SIMONY

At some point in history, if you had money, you could part with some of it to exonerate your sins. The opulent could clear their conscience thanks to the purchase of ecclesiastical favors and indulgences, and while the practice peaked in the ninth and tenth centuries, it continued in a milder and more subtle form later, and most certainly contributed to the exasperation with church practices that led to the Reformation.

Simony was a convenient way for the church to raise funds, by selling offices, and everybody was happy with the arrangement. Same with indulgences: the buyer had an inexpensive option on paradise, the seller was selling something that cost nothing. It was, as we call it in trading, "free money." Yet technically it was a violation of canon law, as it commuted something temporal for the spiritual and intemporal. It was most certainly Lindy compatible: technically, indulgences were not markedly different from the pagan practice of giving offerings to propitiate the gods, a part of which went to line the pockets of the high priest.

Now consider publicly giving a million dollars to some "charity." Part of that money will be spent to advertise that you are giving money, a charity being defined as some organization that aims to make no profit, and to "spend" a chunk of the money on its specialization: meetings, future fundraising, and multiplicative intercompany emails (all meant to help a country after an earthquake, for instance). Do you see any difference between this and simony and indulgences? Indeed, simony and indulgences reincarnated themselves in lay society in the form of charity dinners (for some reason, black tie), of people feeling useful engaging in the otherwise selfish activity of running marathons—no longer selfish as it aims at saving other people's kidneys (as if kidneys could not be saved by people writing checks to save kidneys), and of executives giving their names to buildings so they could be remembered as virtuous. So you can scam the world for a billion; all you need to do is spend part of it, say, a million or two, to enter the section of paradise reserved for the "givers."

Now, I am not saying that all those who put their names on a building are necessarily non-virtuous and buying a spot in paradise. Many are forced by peer and social pressures to do so, so it could be a way to get some people off their backs.

We have argued that virtue is not an ornament, not something one can buy. Let us go a step beyond and see where virtue requires skin in the game in terms of risk taking, particularly when it is one's reputation that is at risk.

VIRTUE IS ABOUT OTHERS AND THE COLLECTIVE

From the scaling property, we can safely establish that virtue is doing something for the collective, particularly when such an action conflicts with your narrowly defined interests. Virtue isn't in just being nice to people others are prone to care about.

So true virtue lies mostly in also being nice to those who are neglected by others, the less obvious cases, those people the grand charity business tends to miss. Or people who have no friends and would like someone once in while to just call them for a chat or a cup of fresh roasted Italian-style coffee.

UNPOPULAR VIRTUE

Further, the highest form of virtue is unpopular. This does not mean that virtue is inherently unpopular, or correlates with unpopularity, only that unpopular acts signal some risk taking and genuine behavior.

Courage is the only virtue you cannot fake.

If I were to describe the perfect virtuous act, it would be to take an uncomfortable position, one penalized by the common discourse.

Let us take an example. For some reason, during the Syrian war, thanks to Qatari-funded public relations firms, the monoculture succeeded in penalizing everyone who stood against jihadi headcutters (the Syrian so-called rebels who in fact were fighting for the establishment of a Salafi-Wahhabi state in Syria). The labels "Assadist" and "baby killer" were designed to scare journalists from questioning any support for these jihadists. And it is always the children. Recall that Monsanto shills often accuse those opposing them of "starving the children."

Sticking up for truth when it is unpopular is far more of a virtue, because it costs you something—your reputation. If you are a journalist and act in a way that risks ostracism, you are virtuous. Some people only express their opinions as part of mob shaming, when it is safe to do so, and, in the bargain, think that they are displaying virtue. This is not virtue but vice, a mixture of bullying and cowardice.

TAKE RISK

Finally, when young people who "want to help mankind" come to me asking, "What should I do? I want to reduce poverty, save the world," and similar noble aspirations at the macro-level, my suggestion is:

1) Never engage in virtue signaling;
2) Never engage in rent-seeking;
3) You *must* start a business. Put yourself on the line, start a business.

Yes, take risk, and if you get rich (which is optional), spend your money generously on others. We need people to take (bounded) risks. The entire idea is to move the descendants of *Homo sapiens* away from the macro, away from abstract universal aims, away from the kind of social engineering that brings tail risks to society. Doing business will always help (because it brings about economic activity without large-scale risky changes in the economy); institutions (like the aid industry) may help, but they are equally likely to harm (I am being optimistic; I am certain that except for a few most do end up harming).

Courage (risk taking) is the highest virtue. We need entrepreneurs.

CHAPTER 14

Peace, Neither Ink nor Blood

*Arabs fighting to the last Palestinian—Where are the lions?—Italians
don't die easily—Make historians build rockets—Commerce makes
people equal (or unequal, but that's another subject)*

———

One of the problems of the interventionista—wanting to get involved in other people's affairs "in order to help"—results in disrupting some of the peace-making mechanisms that are inherent in human affairs, a combination of collaboration and strategic hostility. As we saw in the Prologue 1, the error continues because someone else is paying the price.

I speculate that had IYIs and their friends not gotten involved, problems such as the Israeli-Palestinian one would have been solved, sort of—and both parties, especially the Palestinians, would have been better off. As I am writing these lines the problem has lasted seventy years, with way too many cooks in the same tiny kitchen, most of whom never have to taste the food. I conjecture that when you leave people alone, they tend to settle for practical reasons.

People on the ground, those with skin in the game, are not too interested in geopolitics or grand abstract principles, but rather in having bread on the table, beer (or, for some, nonalcoholic fermented beverages such as yoghurt drinks) in the refrigerator, and good weather at outdoor family picnics. Also they don't want to be humiliated in their human contact with others.

For imagine the absurdity of Arab states prodding the Palestinians to fight for their principles while their potentates are sitting in carpeted alcohol-free palaces (with well-stocked refrigerators full of nonalcoholic fermented beverages such as yoghurt) while the recipients of their advice live in refugee camps. Had the Palestinians settled in 1947, they would have been better off. But the idea was to throw the Jews and neo-crusaders in the Mediterranean; Arab rhetoric came from Arab parties who were hundreds, thousands of miles away arguing for "principles" when Palestinians were displaced, living in tents. Then came the war of 1948. Had Palestinians settled then, things would have worked out. But, no, there were "principles." But then came the war of 1967. Now they feel they would be lucky if they recovered the territory lost in 1967. Then in 1992 came the Oslo peace treaty, from the top. No peace proceeds from bureaucratic ink. If you want peace, make people trade, as they have done for millennia. They will be eventually forced to work something out.

We are largely collaborative—except when institutions get in the way. I surmise that if we put those "people wanting to help" in the State Department on paid vacation to do ceramics, pottery, or whatever low-testosterone people do when they take a sabbatical, it would be great for peace.

Further, these people tend to see everything as geopolitics, as if the world was polarized into two big players, not a collection of people with diverse interests. To spite Russia, the State Department is urged to perpetuate the war in Syria, which in fact just punishes Syrians.

Peace from the top differs from real peace: consider that today's Morocco, Egypt, and to some extent Saudi Arabia, with more or less overtly pro-Israeli governments (with well-stocked refrigerators full of nonalcoholic fermented drinks such as yoghurt), have local populations conspicuously hostile to Jews. Compare this to Iran, with a local population that is squarely pro-Western and tolerant of Jews. Yet some people with no skin in the game who have read too much about the Treaty of Westphalia (and not enough on complex systems) still insist on conflating relations between countries with relations between governments.

MARS VS. SATURN

If you understand nothing about the problem (like D.C. pundits) and have no skin in the game, then everything is seen through the prism of geopolitics. For these ignorant pundits, it is all Iran vs. Saudi Arabia, the U.S. vs. Russia, Mars vs. Saturn.

I recall, during the Lebanese war, noticing how the local conflict was metamorphosed into an "Israel vs. Iran" problem. I described in *The Black Swan* how war journalists who came to Lebanon got all their information from other war journalists who came to Lebanon, hence they could live in a parallel world without ever seeing the true problems—absence of skin in the game does wonders in distorting information. But to those of us on the ground, the objective was to make things work and have a life, not sacrifice our existence for the sake of geopolitics. Real people are interested in commonalities and peace, not conflicts and wars.

Let us now examine history as it runs by itself, as opposed to what's seen by "intellectuals" and institutions.

WHERE ARE THE LIONS?

As I was writing *Antifragile,* I spent some time in South Africa in a wild reserve, doing Safari-style tours during part of the day and tinkering with the book in the afternoons. I went to the reserve to "see the lions." In an entire week I only saw one lion and it was such a big event that it caused a traffic jam of tourists coming from all the neighboring camp-style resorts. People kept shouting "kuru" in Zulu as if they had found gold. Meanwhile, on the twice-daily failed tours to find the lions, I saw giraffes, elephants, zebras, wild boars, impalas, more impalas, even more impalas. Everyone else was like me, looking for *kurus* and getting peaceful animals: a South African fellow we encountered in another car in the middle of the savannah, after the usual sighting of boring (and bored) animals, cracked the joke while pointing his finger at a hill: "Look, we saw two giraffes and three impalas over there."

It turned out that I had squarely made the error that I warn against, of mistaking the lurid for the empirical: there are very, very few predators compared to what one can call collaborative animals. The camp in the wild reserve was next to a watering hole, and in the afternoon it got crowded with hundreds of animals of different species who apparently got along rather well with one another. But of the thousands of animals that I spotted cumulatively, the image of the lion in a state of majestic calm dominates my memory. It may make sense from a risk-management point of view to overestimate the role of the lion—but not in our interpretation of world affairs.

If the "law of the jungle" means anything, it means collaboration for the most part, with a few perceptional distortions caused by our otherwise well-functioning risk-management intuitions. Even predators end up in some type of arrangement with their prey.

HISTORY SEEN FROM THE EMERGENCY ROOM

History is largely peace punctuated by wars, rather than wars punctuated by peace. The problem is that we humans are prone to the availability heuristic, by which the salient is mistaken for the statistical, and the conspicuous and emotional effect of an event makes us think it is occurring more regularly than in reality. This helps us to be prudent and careful in daily life, forcing us to add an extra layer of protection, but it does not help with scholarship.

For when you read histories of international affairs, you might fall under the illusion that history is mostly wars, that states like to fight as a default condition, whenever they have the chance, and that the only coordination between entities takes place when two countries have a "strategic" alliance against a common danger. Or some unification under a top-down bureaucratic structure. Recent peace among European states is attributed to the rule of verbose bureaucrats devoid of "toxic masculinity" (the most recent pathologification in universities), rather than American and Soviet occupation.

We are fed a steady diet of histories of wars, fewer histories of peace. As a trader, I was trained to look for the first question people forget to ask: *who* wrote these books? Well, *historians, international affairs scholars, and policy experts* did. Can these people be fooled? Let's be polite and say that they are in the majority no rocket scientists, and operate under a structural bias. It looks like, in spite of quite a bit of lip service and introspection, an empirically rigorous approach in history and international relations is rare.

First, there are problems of "overfitting," overnarrating, extracting too much *via positiva* and not enough *via negativa* from past data. Even in the empirical sciences, positive results ("this works") tends to get more press than negative ones ("this doesn't work") so it should be no surprise that historians and international relations scholars fall squarely into the same trap.

Second, these scholars, as non–rocket scientists, fail to get a central mathematical property, confusing intensity with frequency. In the five centuries preceding the unification of Italy, there was supposed to be "a lot of warfare" ravaging the place. Therefore, many of these scholars insist, unification "brought peace." But more than six hundred thousand Italians died in the Great War, during the "period of stability," almost one order of magnitude higher than all the cumulative fatalities in the five hundred years preceding it. Many of the "conflicts" that took place between states or statelings were between professional soldiers, often mercenaries, and much of the population was unaware of them. Now, in my experience, after presenting these facts, I am almost always confronted with "Still, there were *more* wars and instability." This is the Robert Rubin trade argument, that trades that lose money *infrequently* are more stable, even if they end up eventually wiping you out.*

Third, there is a problem of representativeness, or to what extent the narrated maps to the empirical. Historians and international affairistas who reach us are more motivated by stories of conflict than by organic collaboration on the ground between a broader set of noninstitutional players, merchants, barbers, doctors, money changers, plumbers, prostitutes, and others. Peace and commerce might be of some interest, but it's not quite what interests people—and while the French *Annales* school brought some awareness that history is the whole life of an organism, not episodes of lurid wars, they failed to change much in the minds of the neighboring disciplines such as international affairs. Even I, while aware of the point and writing a chapter on it, tend to find accounts of real life boring.

Fourth, as we said before with the research done by Captain Mark Weisenborn, Pasquale Cirillo, and myself, accounts of past wars are fraught with overestimation biases. The lurid rises to the surface and keeps rising from account to account.

Journalism is about "events," not absence of events, and many historians and policy scholars are glorified journalists with high factchecking standards who allow themselves to be a little boring in order to be taken seriously. But being boring doesn't make them scientists, nor

---

* This is the elementary but very common error I pointed out in *Fooled by Randomness*, of confusing frequency with expectation (or average). It is very hard for nontraders to understand that if the bank J.P. Morgan made money trading on 251 out of 252 days, that it is not necessarily a good thing and very often it should be interpreted as a red flag.

does "fact checking" make them empirical, as these scholars miss the notion of absence of data points and silent facts. Learning from the Russian school of probability makes one conscious of the need to think in terms of one-sided inequalities: what is absent from the data should be taken into account—absence of Black Swans in the record doesn't mean these were not there. The record is insufficient, and such asymmetry needs to be permanently present in one's analysis. Silent evidence should be the driver. Reading a history book, without putting its events in perspective, offers a similar bias to reading an account of life in New York seen from an emergency room at Bellevue Hospital.

So always keep in mind that historians and policy scholaristas are selected from a cohort of people who derive their knowledge from books, not real life and business. The same is true for State Department employees, since these are not hired among adventurers and doers, but students of these scholars. Let's say it bluntly: spending part of your life reading archives in the stacks of the Yale Library doesn't fit the nonacademic temperament of someone who has to be aware and watch his back, say, a debt-collector for the Mafia or a pit speculator in fast commodities. (If you don't get this, you are an academic.)

Let us take for example the standard account of Arabs in Spain, Turks in parts of the Byzantine Empire, or Arabs and Byzantines. From a geopolitics standpoint, you would see all of these situations as a tug-of-war. Yes, there was a tug-of-war, but not in the sense that you suspect. Merchants were doing business very actively during these periods. My own existence as Greek-Orthodox of Byzantine rite living under Islam (though at a safe, very safe physical distance from Sunni Muslims) is witness to such collaboration. And never discount the theological rationalizations to justify collaboration with the economic powers—before the discovery of America, the business center of gravity was in the East. The expression "Better the turban of the Turk than the tiara of the Pope!" originated with the Grand Duke Lucas Notaras, who negotiated a friendship treaty with the Ottomans, and was repeated at various stages in history. It is also attributed to Saint Mark of Ephesus, and was often shouted by Balkan peasants to justify siding with the Turks against their Catholic lords.

As the reader will know by now, I have myself lived through the worst part of the civil war in Lebanon. Except for areas near the Green

Line, it didn't feel like war. But those reading about it in history books will not understand my experience.*

NEXT

We just saw in Book 6 various asymmetries in life coming from largely undetected agency problems, where absence of skin in the game contaminates fields and produces distortions.

But recall that religion is about skin in the game—not quite about "belief." We will spend the next few chapters with what people call "religion," which will take us deeper and deeper into the core of the book: rationality and risk bearing.

---

* What to read? It would not cure the *via negativa* problem, but, for a start, instead of studying Roman history in terms of Caesar and Pompey, or Peloponnesian balances of power or diplomatic intrigues in Vienna, consider studying instead the daily life and body of laws and customs. I accidentally discovered the book *A History of Private Life* (four volumes in English) by Paul Veyne, Philippe Ariès, and Georges Duby some thirty years ago. *Volume 1* (Ancient Rome) has been at a comfortable distance from my bed ever since. Another representative book for the approach is Emmanuel Le Roy Ladurie's *Montaillou Village Occitan*. And, for our beloved yet troubled Mediterranean, take Fernand Braudel's magnificent opus: *The Mediterranean and the Mediterranean World in the Age of Philip II.*

It is in a way more pleasant to read an account of Venice based on trade rather than abstract geopolitical bull***t. Some books make you smell the spices. Since the discovery of the works of Duby, Braudel, Bloch, Ariès, et al., I have been unable to read conventional history books, say, a book on the Ottoman Empire that focuses on the sultans, without irritation. It feels like historians across the board are engaging in the repulsive "narrative nonfiction" style of *The New Yorker.*

Other books: James Davidson's *Courtesans and Fishcakes,* where you see how the Greeks ate bread with the left hand. Or Graham Robb's *The Discovery of France,* which informs you that the French spoke little French in 1914. And many more.

BOOK 7

RELIGION, BELIEF, AND SKIN IN THE GAME

CHAPTER 15

They Don't Know What They Are Talking About When They Talk about Religion

The more they talk. the less you understand—Law or nomous?—
In religion, as in other things, you pay for the label

———

My lifetime motto is that *mathematicians think in (well, precisely defined and mapped) objects and relations, jurists and legal thinkers in constructs, logicians in maximally abstract operators, and . . . fools in words.*

Two people can be using the same word, meaning different things, yet continue the conversation, which is fine for coffee, but not when making decisions, particularly policy decisions affecting others. But it is easy to trip them, as Socrates did, simply by asking them *what they think they mean* by what they said—hence philosophy was born as rigor in discourse and disentanglement of mixed-up notions, in precise opposition to the sophist's promotion of rhetoric. Since Socrates we have had a long tradition of mathematical science and contract law driven by precision in mapping terms. But we have also had many pronouncements by fools using labels—outside of poetry, beware the verbalistic, that archenemy of knowledge.

Different people rarely mean the same thing when they say "religion," nor do they realize it. For early Jews and Muslims, religion was law. *Din* means law in Hebrew and religion in Arabic. For early Jews, religion was also tribal; for early Muslims, it was universal. For the Romans, religion was social events, rituals, and festivals—the word *religio* was a counter to *superstitio,* and while present in the Roman zeitgeist it had no equivalent concept in the Greek-Byzantine East. Throughout the ancient world, law was procedurally and mechanically its own thing. Early Christianity, thanks to Saint Augustine, stayed relatively away from the law, and, later, remembering its origins, had an uneasy relation with it. For instance, even during the Inquisition, a lay court formally handled final sentencing. Further, Theodosius's code (compiled in the fifth century to unify Roman law) was "Christianized" with a short introduction, a blessing of sorts—the rest remained identical to pagan Roman legal reasoning as expounded in Constantinople and (mostly) Berytus. The code remained dominated by the Phoenician legal scholars Ulpian and Papinian, who were pagan: contrary to theories by geopoliticalists, the Roman school of law of Berytus (Beirut) was not shut down by Christianity, but by an earthquake.

The difference is marked in that Christian Aramaic uses different words: *din* for religion and *nomous* (from the Greek) for law. Jesus, with his imperative "give to Caesar what belongs to Caesar," separated the holy and the profane: Christianity was for another domain, "the kingdom to come," only merging with this one in the *eschaton*.* Neither Islam nor Judaism have a marked separation between holy and profane. And of course Christianity moved away from the solely spiritual domain to embrace the ceremonial and ritualistic, integrating much of the pagan rites of the Levant and Asia Minor. As an illustration of the symbolic separation between church and state, the title Pontifex Maximus (head priest), taken by the Roman emperors after Augustus, reverted after Theodosius, in the late fourth century, to the bishop of Rome, and later, more or less informally, to the Catholic Pope.

For most Jews today, religion has become ethnocultural, without the law—and for many, a nation. Same for Armenians, Syriacs, Chaldeans, Copts, and Maronites. For Orthodox and Catholic Christians, religion is largely aesthetics, pomp, and rituals. For Protestants, religion is belief without aesthetics, pomp, or law. Further East, for Buddhists, Shintoists, and Hindus, religion is practical and spiritual philosophy, with a code of ethics (and for some, a cosmogony). So when Hindus talk about the Hindu "religion," it doesn't mean the same thing to a Pakistani, and would certainly mean something different to a Persian.

---

* The Egyptian Copts have been increasingly persecuted by Sunni Muslims, but the Coptic Church stands against the creation of a self-governing state somewhere in Egypt, using the argument that it was "not Christian" to want a political entity in this world.

When the nation-state dream came about, things got more, much more complicated. When an Arab used to say "Jew" he largely referred to a creed; to Arabs, a converted Jew was no longer a Jew. But for a Jew, a Jew was simply defined as someone whose mother was a Jew. But Judaism somewhat merged into nation-state and now, for many, indicates belonging to a nation.

In Serbia, Croatia, and Lebanon, religion means one thing at times of peace, and something quite different at times of war.

When someone discusses the "Christian minority" in the Levant, it doesn't amount to (as Arabs tend to think) promoting a Christian theocracy (full theocracies were rare in Christian history, just Byzantium and a short attempt by Calvin). He just means "secular," or wants a marked separation of church and state. Same for the gnostics (Druids, Druze, Mandeans, Alawis, Alevis) who have a religion largely unknown by its members, lest they leak and get persecuted by the dominant majority.

The problem with the European Union is that naive bureaucrats (those fellows who can't find a coconut on Coconut island) are fooled by the label. They treat Salafism, say, as just a religion—with its houses of "worship"—when in fact it is just an intolerant political system, which promotes (or allows) violence and rejects the institutions of the West—those very institutions that allow them to operate. We saw with the minority rule that the intolerant will run over the tolerant; cancer must be stopped before it becomes metastatic.

Salafism is very similar to atheistic Soviet Communism in its heyday: both have all-embracing control over all of human activity and thought, which makes discussions about whether religion or atheistic regimes are more murderous lacking in pertinence, precision, and realism.

BELIEF VS. BELIEF

We will see in the next chapter that "belief" can be epistemic, or simply procedural (or metaphorical)—leading to confusions about which sorts of beliefs are religious beliefs and which ones are not. For, on top of the "religion" problem, there is a problem with belief. Some beliefs are largely decorative, some are functional (they help in survival), others are literal. And to revert to our metastatic Salafi problem: when one of these fundamentalists talks to a Christian, he is convinced that the

Christian takes his own beliefs literally, while the Christian is convinced that the Salafi has the same oft-metaphorical concepts that he has, to be taken seriously but not literally—and, often, not very seriously. Religions such as Christianity, Judaism, and, to some extent Shiite Islam, evolved (or, rather, let their members evolve in developing a sophisticated society) precisely by moving away from the literal. The literal doesn't leave any room for adaptation.

As Gibbon wrote:

> The various modes of worship, which prevailed in the Roman world, were all considered by the people, as equally true; by the philosopher, as equally false; and by the magistrate, as equally useful. And thus toleration produced not only mutual indulgence, but even religious concord.

LIBERTARIANISM AND CHURCH-FREE RELIGIONS

As we mentioned, the Roman emperor Julian the Apostate tried to revert to ancient paganism after his father's cousin Constantine the Great started the process toward making Christianity a state religion almost half a century earlier. But he made a fatal reasoning error.

His problem was that, having been brought up as a Christian, he imagined that paganism required a structure similar to that of the church, *ce genre de trucs*. So he tried to create pagan bishops, synods, and these kinds of things. He did not realize that each pagan group had its own definition of religion, that each temple had its own practices, that *by definition* paganism was distributed in its execution, rituals, cosmogonies, practices, and "beliefs." Pagans did not have a category for paganism.

After Julian, a brilliant general and valiant warrior, died in battle (heroically), the dream of returning to ancient values ended with him.

Just as paganism cannot be pigeon-holed, the same applies to libertarianism. It does not fit the structure of a political "party"—only that of a decentralized political movement. The very concept doesn't allow for the straitjacket of a strong party line and unified policy with respect to, say, court locations or relations with Mongolia. Political parties are hierarchical, they are designed in a way to substitute someone's own decision making with a well-defined protocol. This doesn't work with libertarians. The *nomenklatura* that is necessary in the functioning of a party cannot exist in a libertarian environment fraught with fractious and vehemently independent people.

Nevertheless, we libertarians share a minimal set of beliefs, the central one being to substitute the rule of law for the rule of authority. Without necessarily realizing it, libertarians believe in complex systems. And, since libertarianism is a movement, it can still exist as splintered factions within other political parties.

NEXT

To conclude, beware labels when it comes to matters associated with beliefs. And avoid treating religions as if they are all the same animal. But there is a commonality. The next chapter will show us how religion does not like fair-weather friends; it wants commitment; it is based on skin in the game.

CHAPTER 16

No Worship Without Skin in the Game

Symmetry, symmetry everywhere—Belief requires an entry fee

———

I t is when you break a fast that you understand religion. I am writing this as I am ending the grueling Greek-Orthodox period of Lent, which, for the most part, allows no animal products. This diet is particularly hard to keep in the West where people use butter and dairy products. But once you fast, you feel entitled to celebrate Easter; it is like the exhilaration of fresh water when one is thirsty. You've paid a price.

Recall our brief discussion of the theological necessity of making Christ man—he had to sacrifice himself. Time to develop the argument here.

The main theological flaw in Pascal's wager is that belief cannot be a free option. It entails a symmetry between what you pay and what you receive. Things otherwise would be too easy. So the skin-in-the-game rules that hold between humans also hold in our rapport with the gods.

THE GODS DO NOT LIKE CHEAP SIGNALING

I will always remember the church altar in Saint Sergius (or, in the vernacular, *Mar Sarkis)* in the Aramaic-speaking town of Maaloula, even if I live 125 years. I visited the church a few decades ago, sparking an obsession with that ancient and neglected language. The town still spoke at the time the version of Western Aramaic that was used by Christ. At the time of Christ, the Levant spoke Greek in the coastal towns and Aramaic in the countryside. For those into Talmud, Western

Aramaic corresponds to "Yerushalmi" or "Palestinian Aramaic," as opposed to the Babylonian Aramaic closer to what is now Syriac. It was mesmerizing to see children speak, tease each other, and do what children usually do, but in an ancient language.

When a town holds the remnants of an ancient language, one needs to look for vestiges of an ancient practice. And indeed there was one. The detail that I will always remember is that the altar in Saint Sergius has a drain for blood. It had been recycled from an earlier pre-Christian practice. The appurtenances of the church came from a reconverted pagan temple used by early Christians. Actually, at the risk of upsetting a few people, it was not *that* reconverted: early Christians were sort of pagans. The standard theory is that before the council of Nicea (fourth century), it was common for Christians to recycle pagan altars. But there turns out to be evidence for what I always suspected: Christians and Jews *in practice* were not too differentiated from other Semitic cult followers, and shared places of worship with one another. The presence of saints in Christianity comes from that mechanism of recycling. There were no telephones, fax machines, or websites financed by Saudi princes to homogenize religions.

"Altar" in spoken Levantine and Aramaic is still *madbah* from DBH, "ritual slaying by cutting the guttural vein." It is an old tradition that left its mark on Islam: halal food requires such a method for slaughter. And *qorban*, the Semitic word QRB for "getting closer (to God)," originally done via sacrifice, is still used as a word for sacrament.

In fact, one of the main figures of Shiite Islam, the Imam Hussein son of Ali, addressed God before his death by offering himself as sacrifice: "let me be the *qorban* for you"—the supreme offering.*

And his followers, to this day, show literal skin in the game during the commemoration of his death, the day of Ashoura, engaging in self-flagellation that leads to open wounds. Self-flagellation is also present in Christianity, as commemoration of the suffering of the Christ—while prevalent in the Middle Ages, it is now gone except in some places in Asia and Latin America.

In the Eastern Mediterranean pagan world (Greco-Semitic), no worship was done without sacrifice. The gods did not accept cheap talk. It

---

* *Taraktu'l kalqa tarran fi hawaka, ayatamtul xiyala likay araka /Falaw qataxani fil hubbi irban, lama malil fu'ada(ou) ila siwaka/fakuth ma šu'ta ya mawlaya minni, ana lkurbanu wajjahani nidaka.* But, once again, this may be apocryphal.

was all about revealed preferences. Also, burnt offerings were precisely burnt so no human would consume them. Actually, not quite: the high priest got his share; priesthood was quite a lucrative position since in the pre-Christian, Greek-speaking Eastern Mediterranean, the offices of high priests were often auctioned off.

Physical sacrifice even applied to the Temple of Jerusalem. And even to later Jews, or early Christians, the followers of Pauline Christianity. Hebrews 9:22: *Et omnia paene in sanguine mundantur secundum legem et sine sanguinis fusione non fit remissio.* "And almost all things are by the law purged with blood; and without shedding of blood is no remission."

But Christianity ended up removing the idea of such sacrifice under the notion that Christ sacrificed himself for others. But if you visit a Catholic or Orthodox church on Sunday service, you will see a simulacrum. It has wine representing blood, which, at the close of the ceremony is flushed in the *piscina* (the drain). Exactly as in the Maaloula altar.

Christianity used the personality of the Christ for the simulacrum; he sacrificed himself for us.

> At the Last Supper, on the night when He was betrayed, our Savior instituted the Eucharistic sacrifice of His Body and Blood. He did this in order to perpetuate the sacrifice of the Cross throughout the centuries until He should come again.
> —Sacrosanctum Concilium, 47

Sacrifice was ended by making it metaphorical:

> I appeal to you therefore brothers, by the mercies of God, to present your bodies as a living sacrifice, holy and acceptable to God, which is your spiritual worship. —Romans 12:1

As for Judaism, the same progression took place: after the destruction of the Second Temple in the first century A.D., animal sacrifices ended. Before that, the parable of Isaac and Abraham marks the notion of progressive departure from human sacrifice by the Abrahamic sects—as well as an insistence of skin in the game. But actual animal sacrifice continued for a while—though under different terms. God tested Abraham's faith with an asymmetric gift: sacrifice your son for me—it was not as with other situations of just giving the gods part of your yield in return for future benefits and improved harvests, as with common gift-giving, with tacit reciprocal expectations. It was the mother of all unconditional gifts to God. It was not a transaction, the transaction to end all transactions. About a millennia later, Christians had their last transaction.

The philosopher Moshe Halbertal holds that, post the simulacrum of Isaac, dealings with the Lord became a reciprocal gift-giving affair. But why did animal sacrifice continue for a while?

Canaanite habits die hard. Maimonides explains why God did not proscribe immediately the then-common practice of animal sacrifice: the reason is that "to obey such a commandment would have been contrary to the nature of man, who generally cleaves to that to which he is used"; instead he "transferred to His service that which had served as a worship of created beings and of things imaginary and unreal." So animal sacrifice continued—largely voluntary—but, and this is the mark of Abrahamic religion, not the worship of animals, or the propitiation of deities through bribery. The latter practice even extended to the bribery of other tribes and others' gods, as continued to be practiced in Arabia until the sixth century. Then a United Nations of sorts, a communal marketplace for both goods, foreign relations, and various bilateral worship, took place in Mecca.

Love without sacrifice is theft (Procrustes). This applies to any form of love, particularly the love of God.

THE EVIDENCE

To summarize, in a Judeo-Christian place of worship, the focal point, where the priest stands, symbolizes skin in the game. The notion of belief without sacrifice, which is tangible proof, is new in history.

The strength of a creed did not rest on "evidence" of the powers of its gods, but evidence of the skin in the game on the part of its worshippers.

CHAPTER 17

Is the Pope Atheist?

It is dangerous to be a Pope, but you get good medical attention—Talk is just talk—Religion manages rituals

————

After Pope John Paul II was shot in 1981, he was rushed to the emergency room of the Agostino Gemelli University Polyclinic, where he met a collection of some of the most skilled doctors—modern doctors—Italy could produce, in contrast with the neighboring public hospital with lower-quality care. The Gemelli clinic later became the preferred destination for the pontiff at the first sign of a health problem.

At no point during the emergency period did the drivers of the ambulance consider taking John Paul the Second to a chapel for a prayer, or some equivalent form of intercession with the Lord, to give the sacred first right of refusal for the treatment. And not one of his successors seemed to have considered giving precedence to dealing with the Lord with the hope of some miraculous intervention in place of the trappings of modern medicine.

This is not to say that the bishops, cardinals, priests, and mere laypeople didn't pray and ask the Lord for help, nor that they *believed* that prayers weren't subsequently answered, given the remarkable recovery of the saintly man. But it remains that nobody in the Vatican seems to ever take chances by going first to the Lord, subsequently to the doctor, and, what is even more surprising, nobody seems to see a conflict with such inversion of the logical sequence. In fact the opposite course of action would have been considered madness. It would be in opposition to the tenets of the Catholic church, as it would be considered voluntary death, which is banned.

Note that the putative predecessors of the pope, the various Roman emperors, had a similar policy of seeking treatment first, and having recourse to theology after, although some of their treatments were packaged as delivered by the deities, such as the Greek god Asclepius or the weaker Roman equivalent Vediovis.

Now try to imagine a powerful head of an "atheist" sect, equivalent to the pope in rank, suffering a similar health exigency. He would have arrived at Gemelli (not some second-rate hospital in Latium) at the same time as John Paul. He would have had a similar-looking crowd of "atheist" well-*wishers* come to give him something called "hope" (or "wishes" for a good recovery) in their very atheistic language, with some self-consistent narrative about what they would like or "wish" to happen to their prominent man. The atheists would have been less colorfully dressed; their vocabulary would have been a bit less ornamental as well, but their actions would have been nearly identical.

Clearly, there are a lot of differences between the Most Holy Father and an atheist of equivalent rank, but these concern matters that are not life-threatening. These include sacrifices. His Holiness has given up on certain activities in the bedroom, other than reading and praying, though at least a dozen of his predecessors, the most famous one being Alexander VI, fathered a great deal of children, at least one when he was in his sixties, and by the conventional (not the immaculate) route. (There have been so many playboy popes that people are bored with their stories.) His Holiness spends considerable time praying, organizing every minute of his life according to certain Christian practices. And yet, while they devote less of their time to what they believe is not "religion," many atheists engage in yoga and similar collective activities, or sit in concert halls in awe and silence (you can't even smoke a cigar or shout buy orders on your cell phone), spending considerable time doing what to a Martian would look like similar ritualistic gestures.

There was a period, the Albigensian crusade, in the thirteenth century, during which Catholics engaged in the mass killing of heretics. Some slaughtered indiscriminately, heretics and nonheretics, as a time saver and complexity-reduction approach. To them, it did not matter who was who, since "The Lord would be able to tell them apart." Those times are long gone. Most Christians, when it comes to central medical, ethical, and decision-making situations (like myself, an Orthodox Christian) do not act any differently than atheists. Those who do (such as Christian scientists) are few. Most Christians have accepted the modern trappings of democracy, oligarchy, or military dictatorship, all these heathen political regimes, rather than seeking theocracies. Their decisions on central matters are indistinguishable from those of an atheist.

RELIGIOUS IN WORDS

So we define atheism or secularism in deeds, by the distance between one's actions and those of a nonatheistic person for an equivalent situation, not his beliefs and other decorative and symbolic matters— which, we will show in the next chapter, do not count.

Let us take stock here. There are people who are

> *atheists in actions, religious in words (most Orthodox and Catholic Christians)*

and others who are

> *religious in actions, religious in words (Salafi Islamists and suicide bombers)*

but I know of nobody who is atheist in both actions and words, completely devoid of rituals, respect for the dead, and superstitions (say a belief in economics, or in the miraculous powers of the mighty state and its institutions).

NEXT

This chapter will ease us to the next section: a) rationality resides in what you do, not in what you think or in what you "believe" (skin in the game), and b) rationality is about survival.

BOOK 8

RISK AND RATIONALITY

CHAPTER 18

How to Be Rational About Rationality

*Restaurants without kitchens—Science from the grave—Do not shoot
to the left of piano players—Merchants of rationality*

———

My friend Rory Sutherland claims that the real function of swimming pools is to allow the middle class to sit around in bathing
suits without looking ridiculous. Same with New York restaurants: you
think their mission is to feed people, but that's not what they are about.
They are in the business of overcharging you for liquor or Great Tuscan
wines by the glass, yet get you in the door by serving you your low-carb
(or low-something) dishes at break-even cost. (This business model, of
course, fails to work in Saudi Arabia.)

So when we look at religion, and, to some extent, ancestral superstitions, we should consider what purpose they serve, rather than focusing
on the notion of "belief," epistemic belief in its strict scientific definition. In science, belief is literal belief; it is right or wrong, never metaphorical. In real life, belief is an instrument to do things, not the end
product. This is similar to vision: the purpose of your eyes is to orient
you in the best possible way, and get you out of trouble when needed, or
help you find prey at a distance. Your eyes are not sensors designed to
capture the electromagnetic spectrum. Their job description is not to
produce the most accurate scientific representation of reality; rather the
most *useful* one for survival.

OCULAR DECEPTION

Our perceptional apparatus makes mistakes—distortions—in order to lead us to more precise actions: ocular deception, it turns out, is a necessary thing. Greek and Roman architects misrepresented the columns of their temples, by tilting them inward, in order to give us the impression that the columns are straight. As Vitruvius explains, the aim is to "counteract the visual reception by a change of proportions." A distortion is meant to bring about an enhancement for your aesthetic experience. The floor of the Parthenon is curved in reality so we can see it as straight. The columns are in truth unevenly spaced, so we can see them lined up like a marching Russian division in a parade.

Should one go lodge a complaint with the Greek Ministry of Tourism claiming that the columns are not vertical and that someone is taking advantage of our visual mechanisms?

ERGODICITY FIRST

The same applies to distortions of beliefs. Are visual deceits any different from leading someone to believe in Santa Claus, if it enhances his or her holiday aesthetic experience? No, unless it causes harm.

In that sense harboring superstitions is not irrational by any metric: nobody has managed to build a criterion for rationality based on actions that bear no cost. But actions that harm you are detectable, if not observable.

We will see in the next chapter that, unless one has an overblown and very unrealistic (Greek column–style) representation of some tail risks, one cannot survive—all it takes is a single event to cause an irreversible exit from the Social Security system. Is selective paranoia "irrational" if those individuals and populations who don't have it end up dying or extinct?

A statement that will orient us for the rest of the book:

Survival comes first, truth, understanding, and science later.

In other words, you do not need science to survive (we've survived for several hundred million years or more, depending on how you define the "we"), but you must survive to do science. As your grandmother would have said, *better safe than sorry*. Or as per the expression attributed to Hobbes: *Primum vivere, deinde philosophari* (First, live; then philosophize). This logical precedence is well understood by traders and people in the real world, as per the Warren Buffett truism "to make money you must first survive"—skin in the game again; those of us who take risks have their priorities firmer than vague textbook pseudo-rationalism. More technically, this brings us again to the ergodic property (which I keep promising to explain, but we are not ready yet): for the world to be "ergodic," there needs to be no absorbing barrier, no substantial irreversibilities.

And what do we mean by "survival"? Survival of whom? Of you? Your family? Your tribe? Humanity? Note for now that I have a finite shelf life; my survival is not as important as the survival of things that do not have a limited life expectancy, such as mankind or planet earth. Hence the more "systemic" things are, the more important survival becomes.

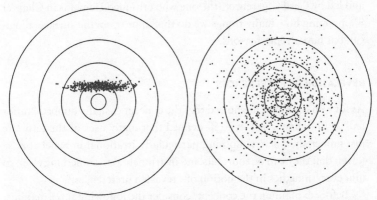

FIGURE 3. An illustration of the bias-variance tradeoff. Assume two people (sober) shooting at a target in, say, Texas. The left shooter has a bias, a systematic "error," but on balance gets closer to the target than the right shooter, who has no systematic bias but a high variance. Typically, you cannot reduce one without increasing the other. When fragile, the strategy at the left is the best: maintain a distance from ruin, that is, from hitting a point in the periphery should it be dangerous. This schema explains why if you want to minimize the probability of the plane crashing, you may make mistakes with impunity provided you lower your dispersion.

Rationality does not superficially look like rationality—just as science doesn't look like science as we've seen. Three rigorous thinkers (and their schools) orient my thinking on the matter: the cognitive scientist and polymath Herb Simon, who pioneered artificial intelligence;

the psychologist Gerd Gigerenzer; and the mathematician, logician, and decision theorist Ken Binmore, who spent his life formulating the logical foundations of rationality.

FROM SIMON TO GIGERENZER

Simon formulated the notion now known as *bounded rationality:* we cannot possibly measure and assess everything as if we were a computer; we therefore produce, under evolutionary pressures, some shortcuts and distortions. Our knowledge of the world is fundamentally incomplete, so we need to avoid getting into unanticipated trouble. And even if our knowledge of the world were complete, it would still be computationally near-impossible to produce a precise, unbiased understanding of reality. A fertile research program on *ecological rationality* came out of the effort to cure Simon's problem; it is mostly organized and led by Gerd Gigerenzer (the one who critiqued Dawkins in Chapter 9), mapping how many things we do that appear, on the surface, illogical, but have deeper reasons.

REVELATION OF PREFERENCES

As for Ken Binmore, he showed that the concept casually dubbed "rational" is ill-defined, in fact so ill-defined that many uses of the term are just gibberish. There is nothing particularly irrational in beliefs per se (given that they can be shortcuts and instrumental to something else): to him everything lies in the notion of "revealed preferences."

Before explaining the concept, consider the following three maxims:

Judging people by their beliefs is not scientific.

There is no such thing as the "rationality" of a belief, there is rationality of action.

The rationality of an action can be judged only in terms of evolutionary considerations.

The axiom of *revelation of preferences* (originating with Paul Samuelson, or possibly the Semitic gods), as you recall, states the following: you will not have an idea about what people *really* think, what predicts people's actions, merely by asking them—they themselves don't necessarily know. What matters, in the end, is what they pay for goods, not what they say they "think" about them, or the various possible reasons they give you or themselves for that. If you think about it, you will see that this is a reformulation of skin in the game. Even psychologists get it; in their experiments, their procedures require that actual dollars be spent for a test to be "scientific." The subjects are given a monetary amount, and they watch how the subject formulates choices by examining how they spend the money. However, a large share of psychologists fughedabout revealed preferences when they start bloviating about rationality. They revert to judging beliefs rather than action.

Beliefs are . . . cheap talk. There may be some type of a translation mechanism too hard for us to understand, with distortions at the level of the thought process that are actually necessary for things to work.

Actually, by a mechanism (more technically called the bias-variance tradeoff), you often get better results making "errors," as when you aim slightly away from the target when shooting. (See Figure 3.) I have shown in *Antifragile* that making some types of errors is the most rational thing to do, when the errors are of little cost, as they lead to discoveries. For instance, most medical "discoveries" are accidental to something else. An error-free world would have no penicillin, no chemotherapy . . . almost no drugs, and most probably no humans.

This is why I have been against the state dictating to us what we "should" be doing: only evolution knows if the "wrong" thing is really wrong, provided there is skin in the game to allow for selection.

WHAT IS RELIGION ABOUT?

It is therefore my opinion that religion exists to enforce tail risk management across generations, as its binary and unconditional rules are easy to teach and enforce. We have survived in spite of tail risks; our survival cannot be that random.

Recall that skin in the game means that you do not pay attention to what people say, only to what they do, and to how much of their necks they are putting on the line. Let survival work its wonders.

Superstitions can be vectors for risk management rules. We have as potent information that people who have them have survived; to repeat,

Incompleteness, decision making under opacity

Real World

🗇

Science

It is unscientific to use science outside its strictly bounded domains.

Science *itself* limits and qualifies claims on matters for which evidence is neither reliable nor sufficient, or in presence of a high degree of opacity.

FIGURE 4. The classical "large world vs small world" problem. Science is currently too incomplete to provide all answers—and says it itself. We have been so much under assault by vendors using "science" to sell products that many people, in their mind, confuse science and scientism. Science is mainly rigor in the process.

never discount anything that allows you to survive. For instance, Jared Diamond discusses the "constructive paranoia" of residents of Papua New Guinea, whose superstitions prevent them from sleeping under dead trees. Whether it is superstition or something else, some deep scientific understanding of probability that is stopping you, it doesn't matter, so long as you don't sleep under dead trees. And if you dream of making people use probability in order to make decisions, I have some news: more than ninety percent of psychologists dealing with decision making (which includes such regulators and researchers as Cass Sunstein and Richard Thaler) have no clue about probability, and try to disrupt our efficient organic paranoias.

Further, I find it incoherent to criticize someone's superstitions if these are meant to bring some benefits, while at the same time having no problemo with the optical illusions in Greek temples.

The notion of "rational" bandied about by all manner of promoters of *scientism* isn't defined well enough to be used for beliefs. To repeat, we do not have enough grounds to discuss "irrational beliefs." We do with irrational actions.

Extending such logic, we can show that much of what we call "belief" is some kind of background furniture for the human mind, more metaphorical than real. It may work as therapy.

Also recall from Chapter 3 that collective rationality might require some individual biases.

"TAWK" AND CHEAP "TAWK"

The first principle we draw:

> *There is a difference between beliefs that are decorative and different sorts of beliefs, those that map to action.*

There is no difference between them in words, except that the true difference reveals itself in risk taking, having something at stake, something one could lose in case one is wrong.

And the lesson, by rephrasing the principle:

> *How much you truly "believe" in something can be manifested only through what you are willing to risk for it.*

But this merits continuation. The fact that there is this decorative component to belief, life, these strange rules followed outside the Gemelli clinics of the world, merits a discussion. What are these for? Can we truly understand their function? Are we confused about their function? Do we mistake their rationality? Can we use them instead to *define* rationality?

WHAT DOES LINDY SAY?

Let us see what Lindy has to say about "rationality." While the notions of "reason" and "reasonable" were present in ancient thought, mostly embedded in the notion of precaution, or *sophrosyne*, this modern idea of "rationality" and "rational decision making" was born in the aftermath of Max Weber, with the works of psychologists, philosophasters, and psychosophasters. The classical *sophrosyne* means precaution, self-control, and temperance all in one. It was replaced with something a bit different. "Rationality" was forged during the post-enlightenment period, at a time when we thought that understanding the world was around the corner. It assumes absence of randomness, or a simplified random structure of our world. Also, of course, no interactions with the world.

The only definition of rationality that I've found that is practically, empirically, and mathematically rigorous is the following: what is rational is that which allows for *survival*. Unlike modern theories by psychosophasters, it maps to the classical way of thinking. Anything that hinders one's survival at an individual, collective, tribal, or general level is, to me, *irrational*.

Hence the precautionary principle and sound risk understanding.

THE NONDECORATIVE IN THE DECORATIVE

Now what I've called decorative is not necessarily superfluous, often to the contrary. The decorative may just have a function we do not know much about. We could consult for that the grandmaster statistician, time, through a very technical tool called the survival function, known by both old people and very complex statistics. We will resort here to the old-people version.

The fact to consider is not that beliefs have survived a long time—the Catholic church as an administration is close to twenty-four centuries old (it is largely the continuation of the Roman Republic). The point is that people who have religion—a certain religion—have survived.

Another principle:

When you consider beliefs in evolutionary terms, do not look at how they compete with each other, but consider the survival of the populations that have them.

Consider a competitor to the Pope's religion, Judaism. Jews have close to five hundred different dietary interdicts. These may seem irrational to an outsider who defines rationality in terms of what he can explain. Actually they will most certainly seem so. The Jewish kashrut prescribes keeping four sets of dishes, two sinks, the avoidance of mixing meat with dairy products or merely letting the two be in contact with each other, in addition to interdicts on some animals: shrimp, pork, etc. The good stuff.

These laws might have had an *ex ante* purpose. One can blame insalubrious behavior of pigs, exacerbated by the heat in the Levant (though heat in the Levant was not markedly different from that in pig-eating areas farther West). Or perhaps an ecological reason: pigs compete with humans in eating the same vegetables, while cows eat what we don't eat.

But it remains the case that whatever their purpose, kashrut laws survived several millennia not because of their "rationality" but because the populations that followed them survived. It most certainly brought cohesion: people who eat together hang together. (To be technical, it is a convex heuristic.) Such group cohesion might be also responsible for trust in commercial transactions with remote members of the community, thus creating a vibrant network. Or some other benefit—but it remains that Jews have survived in spite of a very hard history.

This allows us to summarize:

Rationality does not depend on explicit verbalistic explanatory factors; it is only what aids survival, what avoids ruin.

Why? Clearly as we saw in the Lindy discussion:

Not everything that happens happens for a reason, but everything that survives survives for a reason.

Rationality is risk management, period. The next chapter will make the final argument in support of this principle.

CHAPTER 19

The Logic of Risk Taking

The central chapter always comes last—Always bet twice—Do you know your uncle point?—Who is "you"?—The Greeks were almost always right

———

ENSEMBLE PROBABILITY

THE RUIN OF ONE DOES NOT AFFECT THE RUIN OF OTHERS

RUINED

SURVIVED

n OBSERVATIONS

APPROXIMATELY DONE IN $\frac{1}{n}$ FACE RUIN

TIME PROBABILITY

ONE SPECULATOR ACROSS TIME

RUINED, GAME STOPS

TIME

FIGURE 5. The difference between one hundred people going to a casino and one person going to a casino one hundred times, i.e. between path-dependent and conventionally understood probability. The mistake has persisted in economics and psychology since age immemorial.

Time to explain ergodicity, ruin, and (again) rationality. Recall that to do science (and other nice things) requires survival but not the other way around.

Consider the following thought experiment. First case, one hundred people go to a casino to gamble a certain set amount each over a set period of time, and have complimentary gin and tonic—as shown in the cartoon in Figure 5. Some may lose, some may win, and we can infer at the end of the day what the "edge" is, that is, calculate the returns simply by counting the money left in the wallets of the people who return. We can thus figure out if the casino is properly pricing the odds. Now assume that gambler number 28 goes bust. Will gambler number 29 be affected? No.

You can safely calculate, from your sample, that about 1 percent of the gamblers will go bust. And if you keep playing and playing, you will be expected to have about the same ratio, 1 percent of gamblers going bust, on average, over that same time window.

Now let's compare this to the second case in the thought experiment. One person, your cousin Theodorus Ibn Warqa, goes to the casino a hundred days in a row, starting with a set amount. On day 28 cousin Theodorus Ibn Warqa is bust. Will there be day 29? No. He has hit an uncle point; there is *no game no more*.

No matter how good or alert your cousin Theodorus Ibn Warqa is, you can safely calculate that he has a 100 percent probability of eventually going bust.

The probabilities of success from a collection of people do not apply to cousin Theodorus Ibn Warqa. Let us call the first set *ensemble* probability, and the second one *time* probability (since the first is concerned with a collection of people and the second with a single person through time). Now, when you read material by finance professors, finance gurus, or your local bank making investment recommendations *based on the long-term returns of the market*, beware. Even if their forecasts were true (they aren't), no individual can get the same returns as the market unless he has infinite pockets and no uncle points. This is conflating ensemble probability and time probability. If the investor has to eventually *reduce* his exposure because of losses, or because of retirement, or because he got divorced to marry his neighbor's wife, or because he suddenly developed a heroin addiction after his hospitalization for appendicitis, or because he changed his mind about life, his returns will be divorced from those of the market, period.

Anyone who has survived in the risk-taking business more than a few years has some version of our by now familiar principle that "in order to succeed, you must *first* survive." My own has been: "never cross a river if it is *on average* four feet deep." I effectively organized all my life around the point that *sequence matters* and the presence of ruin disqualifies cost-benefit analyses; but it never hit me that the flaw in decision theory was so deep. Until out of nowhere came a paper by the physicist Ole Peters, working with the great Murray Gell-Mann. They presented a version of the difference between ensemble and time probabilities with a thought experiment similar to mine above, and showed that just about everything in social science having to do with probability is flawed. Deeply flawed. Very deeply flawed. Largely, terminally flawed. For, in the quarter millennia since an initial formulation of decision making under uncertainty by the mathematician Jacob Bernoulli, one that has since become standard, almost all people involved in the field have made the severe mistake of missing the effect of the difference between ensemble and time.* Everyone? Not quite: every economist maybe, but not everyone: the applied mathematicians Claude Shannon and Ed Thorp, and the physicist J. L. Kelly of the Kelly Criterion got it right. They also got it in a very simple way. The father of insurance mathematics, the Swedish applied mathematician Harald Cramér, also got the point. And, more than two decades ago, practitioners such as Mark Spitznagel and myself built our entire business careers around it. (I mysteriously got it right in my writings and when I traded and made decisions, and detect deep inside when ergodicity is violated, but I never explicitly got Peters and Gell-Mann's mathematical structure—ergodicity is even discussed in *Fooled by Randomness,* two decades ago). Spitznagel and I even started an entire business to help investors eliminate uncle points so they could get the returns of the market. While I retired to do some flaneuring, Mark continued relentlessly (and successfully) at his Universa. Mark and I have been frustrated by economists who, not getting ergodicity, keep saying that worrying about the tails is "irrational."

The idea I just presented is very very simple. But how come nobody for 250 years quite got it? Lack of skin in the game, obviously.

---

* As with my "Fat Tails" project, economists may have been aware of the ensemble-time problem, but in a sterile way. Further, they keep saying "we've known about fat tails," but somehow they don't realize that taking the idea to the next step contradicts much of their work. It is the consequences that matter.

For it looks like you need a lot of intelligence to figure probabilistic things out when you don't have skin in the game. But for an overeducated nonpractitioner, these things are hard to figure out. Unless one is a genius, that is, has the clarity of mind to see through the mud, or has a sufficiently profound command of probability theory to cut through the nonsense. Now, certifiably, Murray Gell-Mann is a genius (and, likely, Peters). Gell-Mann discovered the subatomic particles he himself called *quarks* (which got him the Nobel). Peters said that when he presented the idea to Gell-Mann, "he got it instantly." Claude Shannon, Ed Thorp, J. L. Kelly, and Harald Cramér are, no doubt, geniuses— I can personally vouch for Thorp, who has an unmistakable clarity of mind combined with a depth of thinking that juts out in conversation. These people could get it without skin in the game. But economists, psychologists, and decision theorists have no geniuses among them (unless one counts the polymath Herb Simon, who did some psychology on the side), and odds are they never will. Adding people without fundamental insights does not sum up to insight; looking for clarity in these fields is like looking for aesthetic harmony in the cubicle of a self-employed computer hacker or the attic of a highly disorganized electrician.

ERGODICITY

To take stock: a situation is deemed non-ergodic when observed past probabilities do not apply to future processes. There is a "stop" somewhere, an absorbing barrier that prevents people *with skin in the game* from emerging from it—and to which the system will invariably tend. Let us call these situations "ruin," as there is no reversibility away from the condition. The central problem is that if there is a possibility of ruin, cost-benefit analyses are no longer possible.

Consider a more extreme example than the casino experiment. Assume a collection of people play Russian roulette a single time for a million dollars—this is the central story in *Fooled by Randomness*. About five out of six will make money. If someone used a standard cost-benefit analysis, he would have claimed that one has an 83.33 percent chance of gains, for an "expected" average return per shot of $833,333. But if you keep playing Russian roulette, you will end up in the cemetery. Your expected return is . . . not computable.

REPETITION OF EXPOSURES

Let us see why "statistical testing" and "scientific" statements are highly insufficient in the presence of both ruin problems and repetition of exposures. If one claimed that there is "statistical evidence that a plane is safe," with a 98 percent confidence level (statistics are meaningless without such confidence bands), and acted on it, practically no experienced pilot would be alive today. In my war with the Monsanto machine, the advocates of genetically modified organisms (transgenics) kept countering me with benefit analyses (which were often bogus and doctored up), not tail risk analyses for *repeated* exposures.

Psychologists determine our "paranoia" or "risk aversion" by subjecting a person to a single experiment—then declare that humans are rationally challenged, as there is an innate tendency to "overestimate" small probabilities. They manage to believe that their subjects will never ever again take any personal tail risk! Recall from the chapter on inequality that academics in social science are . . . dynamically challenged. Nobody could see the grandmother-obvious inconsistency of such behavior with our ingrained daily life logic, which is remarkably more rigorous. Smoking a single cigarette is extremely benign, so a cost-benefit analysis would deem it irrational to give up so much pleasure for so little risk! But it is the act of smoking that kills, at a certain number of packs per year, or tens of thousand of cigarettes—in other words, repeated serial exposure.

But things are even worse: in real life, every single bit of risk you take adds up to reduce your life expectancy. If you climb mountains *and* ride a motorcycle *and* hang around the mob *and* fly your own small plane *and* drink absinthe, *and* smoke cigarettes, *and* play parkour on Thursday night, your life expectancy is considerably reduced, although no single action will have a meaningful effect. This idea of repetition makes paranoia about some low-probability events, even that deemed "pathological," perfectly rational.

Further, there is a twist. If medicine is progressively improving your life expectancy, you need to be even more paranoid. Think dynamically.

If you incur a tiny probability of ruin as a "one-off" risk, survive it, then do it again (another "one-off" deal), you will eventually go bust with a probability of one hundred percent. Confusion arises because it may seem that if the "one-off" risk is reasonable, then *an additional one* is also reasonable. This can be quantified by recognizing that the probability of ruin approaches 1 as the number of exposures to individually small risks, say one in ten thousand, increases.

The flaw in psychology papers is to believe that the subject doesn't take any other tail risks anywhere outside the experiment and, crucially, will never again take any risk at all. The idea in social science of "loss aversion" has not been thought through properly—it is not measurable the way it has been measured (if it is at all measurable). Say you ask a subject how much he would pay to insure a 1 percent probability of losing $100. You are trying to figure out how much he is "overpaying" for "risk aversion" or something even more foolish, "loss aversion." But you cannot possibly ignore all the other financial risks he is taking: if he has a car parked outside that can be scratched, if he has a financial portfolio that can lose money, if he has a bakery that may risk a fine, if he has a child in college who may cost unexpectedly more, if he can be laid off, if he may be unexpectedly ill in the future. All these risks add up, and the attitude of the subject reflects them all. Ruin is indivisible and invariant to the source of randomness that may cause it.

Another common error in the psychology literature concerns what is called "mental accounting." The Thorp, Kelly, and Shannon school of information theory requires that, for an investment strategy to be ergodic and eventually capture the return of the market, agents increase their risks as they are winning, but contract after losses, a technique called "playing with the house money." In practice, it is done by threshold, for ease of execution, not complicated rules: you start betting aggressively whenever you have a profit, never when you have a deficit, as if a switch was turned on or off. This method is practiced by probably every single trader who has survived. Now it happens that this dynamic strategy is deemed out of line by behavioral finance econophasters such as the creepy interventionist Richard Thaler, who, very ignorant of probability, calls this "mental accounting"* a mistake (and, of course,

---

* Mental accounting refers to the tendency of people to mentally (or physically) put their funds in separate insulated accounts, focusing on the source of the money, and forgetting that as net owners the source should not matter. For instance, someone who would not buy a tie because it is expensive and appears superfluous gets excited when his wife buys for his birthday the same tie using funds from a joint checking account. In the case under discussion, Thaler finds it a mistake to vary one's strategy pending on whether the source of funds is gains from the casino or the original endowment. Clearly, Thaler, like other psycholophasters, is oblivious of the dynamics: social scientists are not good with things that move.

invites government to "nudge" us away from it, and prevent strategies from being ergodic).

I believe that risk aversion does not exist: what we observe is, simply, a residual of ergodicity. People are, simply, trying to avoid financial suicide and take a certain attitude to tail risks.

But we do not need to be overly paranoid about ourselves; we need to shift some of our worries to bigger things.

WHO IS "YOU"?

Let us return to the notion of "tribe." One of the defects modern education and thinking introduces is the illusion that each one of us is a single unit. In fact, I've sampled ninety people in seminars and asked them: "what's the worst thing that can happen to you?" Eighty-eight people answered "my death."

This can only be the worst-case situation for a psychopath. For after that, I asked those who deemed that their worst-case outcome was their own death: "Is your death *plus* that of your children, nephews, cousins, cat, dogs, parakeet, and hamster (if you have any of the above) worse than just *your* death?" Invariably, yes. "Is your death *plus* your children, nephews, cousins (. . .) *plus* all of humanity worse than just *your* death?" Yes, of course. Then how can your death be the worst possible outcome?*

> *Unless you are perfectly narcissistic and psychopathic—even then—your worst-case scenario is never limited to the loss of only your life.*

Thus, we see the point that individual ruin is not as big a deal as collective ruin. And of course ecocide, the irreversible destruction of our environment, is the big one to worry about.

To use the ergodic framework: my death at Russian roulette is not ergodic for me but it is ergodic for the system. The precautionary principle, as I formulated with a few colleagues, is precisely about the highest layer.

About every time I discuss the precautionary principle, some over-

---

* Actually, I usually joke that my death *plus* someone I don't like surviving, such as the journalistic professor Steven Pinker, is worse than just my death.

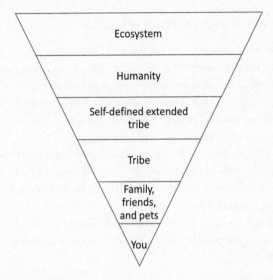

FIGURE 6. Taking personal risks to save the collective are "courage" and "prudence" since you are lowering risks for the collective.

educated pundit suggests that "we take risks by crossing the street," so why worry so much about the system? This sophistry usually causes a bit of anger on my part. Aside from the fact that the risk of being killed as a pedestrian is less than one in 47,000 years, the point is that my death is never the worst-case scenario *unless* it correlates to that of others.

I have a finite shelf life, humanity should have an infinite duration.

Or,

I am renewable, not humanity or the ecosystem.

Even worse, as I have shown in *Antifragile,* the fragility of the system's components (provided they are renewable and replaceable) is required to ensure the solidity of the system as a whole. If humans were immortals, they would go extinct from an accident, or from a gradual buildup of misfitness. But shorter shelf life for humans allows genetic changes across generations to be in sync with the variability of the environment.

COURAGE AND PRECAUTION AREN'T OPPOSITES

How can both courage and prudence be classical virtues? Virtue, as presented in Aristotle's *Nicomachean Ethics,* includes: *sophrosyne* (σωφροσύνη), prudence, and a form of sound judgment he called more broadly *phronesis*. Aren't these inconsistent with courage?

In our framework, they are not at all. They are actually, as Fat Tony would say, the same *ting*. How?

I can exercise courage to save a collection of kids from drowning, at the risk of my own life, and it would also correspond to a form of prudence. Were I to die, I would be sacrificing a lower layer in Figure 6 for the sake of a higher one.

Courage, according to the Greek ideal that Aristotle inherited from Homer (and conveyed by Solon, Pericles, and Thucydides) is never a selfish action:

> *Courage is when you sacrifice your own well-being for the sake of the survival of a layer higher than yours.*

Selfish courage is not courage. A foolish gambler is not committing an act of courage, especially if he is risking other people's funds or has a family to feed.*

RATIONALITY, AGAIN

The last chapter reframed rationality in terms of actual decisions, not what are called "beliefs," as these may be adapted to stimulate us in the most convincing way to avoid things that threaten systemic survival. If superstition is what it takes, not only is there absolutely no violation of the axioms of rationality there, but it would be technically irrational to stand in its way. If superstition is what's needed to satisfy ergodicity, let it be.

Let us return to Warren Buffett. He did not make his billions by cost-benefit analysis; rather, he did so simply by establishing a high filter, then

---

* To show the inanity of social science, they have to muster up the sensationalism of "mirror neurons" to explain the link between the individual and the collective. Relying on neuro-something is a form of scientism called "brain porn," discussed in *Antifragile*.

picking opportunities that pass such a threshold. "The difference between successful people and really successful people is that really successful people *say no* to almost everything," he said. Likewise our wiring might be adapted to "say no" to tail risk. For there are a zillion ways to make money without taking tail risk. There are a zillion ways to solve problems (say, feed the world) without complicated technologies that entail fragility and an unknown possibility of tail blowup. Whenever I hear someone saying "we need to take (tail) risks" I know it is not coming from a surviving practitioner but from a finance academic or a banker—the latter, we saw, almost always blows up, usually with other people's money.

Indeed, it doesn't cost us much to refuse some new shoddy technologies. It doesn't cost me much to go with my "refined paranoia," even if wrong. For all it takes is for my paranoia to be right once, and it saves my life.

LOVE *SOME* RISKS

Antifragile shows how people confuse risk of ruin with variations and fluctuations—a simplification that violates a deeper, more rigorous logic of things. I make the case for risk loving, for systematic "convex" tinkering, and for taking a lot of risks that don't have tail risks but offer tail profits. Volatile things are not necessarily risky, and the reverse is also true. Jumping from a bench would be good for you and your bones, while falling from the twenty-second floor will never be so. Small injuries will be beneficial, never larger ones, those that have irreversible effects. Fearmongering about some classes of events is fearmongering; about others it is not. Risk and ruin are different *tings*.

NAIVE EMPIRICISM

Not all risks are equal. We often hear that "Ebola is causing fewer deaths than people drowning in their bathtubs," or something of the sort, based on "evidence." This is another class of problems that your grandmother can get, but the semi-educated cannot.

> *Never compare a multiplicative, systemic, and fat-tailed risk to a non-multiplicative, idiosyncratic, and thin-tailed one.*

Recall that I worry about the correlation between the death of one person and that of another. So we need to be concerned with systemic effects: things that can affect more than one person should they happen.

A refresher here. There are two categories in which random events fall: Mediocristan and Extremistan. Mediocristan is thin-tailed and affects the individual without correlation to the collective. Extremistan, by definition, affects many people. Hence Extremistan has a systemic effect that Mediocristan doesn't. Multiplicative risks—such as epidemics—are *always* from Extremistan. They may not be lethal (say, the flu), but they remain from Extremistan.

More technically:

Mediocristan risks are subjected to the Chernoff bound.

The Chernoff bound can be explained as follows. The probability that the number of people who drown in their bathtubs in the United States doubles next year—assuming no changes in population or bathtubs—is one per several trillions lifetimes of the universe. This cannot be said about the doubling of the number of people killed by terrorism over the same period.

Journalists and social scientists are pathologically prone to such nonsense—particularly those who think that a regression and a graph are sophisticated ways to approach a problem. Simply, they have been trained with tools for Mediocristan. So we often see the headline that many more American citizens slept with Kim Kardashian than died of Ebola. Or that more people were killed by their own furniture than by terrorism. Your grandmother's logic would debunk these claims. Just consider that: it is impossible for a billion people to sleep with Kim Kardashian (even her), but that there is a non-zero probability that a multiplicative process (a pandemic) causes such a number of Ebola deaths. Or even if such events were not multiplicative, say, terrorism, there is a probability of actions such as polluting the water supply that can cause extreme deviations. The other argument is one of feedback: if terrorism casualties are low, it is because of vigilance (we tend to search passengers before boarding planes), and the argument that such vigilance is superfluous indicates a severe flaw in reasoning. Your bathtub is not trying to kill you.

I was wondering why the point appears to be unnatural to many "scientists" (which includes policymakers), but natural to some other people, such as the probabilist Paul Embrechts. Simply, Embrechts looks at things from the tail. Embrechts studies a branch of probability called extreme value theory and is part of a group we call "extremists"—a narrow group of researchers who specialize, as I do, in extreme events. Well, Embrechts and his peers look at the difference between processes for extremes, never the ordinary. Do not confuse this with Extremistan: they study what happens for extremes, which includes both Extremistan and Mediocristan—it just happens that Mediocristan is milder than Extremistan. They classify what can happen "in the tails" according to the generalized extreme value distribution. Things are a lot—a lot—clearer in the tails. And things are a lot—a lot—clearer in probability than they are in words.

SUMMARY

We close this chapter with a few summarizing lines.

One may be risk loving yet completely averse to ruin.

The central asymmetry of life is:

In a strategy that entails ruin, benefits never offset risks of ruin.

Further:

Ruin and other changes in condition are different animals.

Every single risk you take adds up to reduce your life expectancy.

Finally:

Rationality is avoidance of systemic ruin.

EPILOGUE

———

What Lindy Told Me

Now, reader, comes the end of the journey—and a fifth installment of the *Incerto*. So while trying to summarize the book, with the obligatory distillation, I saw the reflection of my face in a restaurant's mirror: dominated by a whitish beard, and a defiant East-Med (East Mediterranean) Greco-Phoenician pride in aging. It was more than two and a half decades ago that I put pen to paper for the *Incerto*, before my beard turned gray. Lindy was telling me that, for a certain class of things, I had less to prove, less to explain, and less to theorize. I had overheard someone in the restaurant saying emphatically, "It is what it is," and the phrase kept repeating itself in my head.

No summary this time, no summary anymore. Per Lindy:

When the beard (or hair) is black, heed the reasoning, but ignore
the conclusion. When the beard is gray, consider both reasoning
and conclusion. When the beard is white, skip the reasoning, but
mind the conclusion.

So let me finish this book with a (long) maxim, *via negativa* style:

No muscles without strength,
friendship without trust,
opinion without consequence,
change without aesthetics,

age without values,
life without effort,
water without thirst,
food without nourishment,
love without sacrifice,
power without fairness,
facts without rigor,
statistics without logic,
mathematics without proof,
teaching without experience,
politeness without warmth,
values without embodiment,
degrees without erudition,
militarism without fortitude,
progress without civilization,
friendship without investment,
virtue without risk,
probability without ergodicity,
wealth without exposure,
complication without depth,
fluency without content,
decision without symmetry,
science without skepticism,
religion without tolerance,

and, most of all:

nothing without skin in the game.

And thank you for reading my book.

ACKNOWLEDGMENTS

———

Ralph Nader; Ron Paul; Will Murphy (editor, advisor, proofreader, syntax expert and specialist); Ben Greenberg (editor); Casiana Ionita (editor); Molly Turpin; Mika Kasuga; Evan Camfield; Barbara Fillon; Will Goodlad; Peter Tanous; Xamer 'Bou Assaleh; Mark Baker (aka Guru Anaerobic); Armand d'Angour; Alexis Kirschbaum; Max Brockman; Russell Weinberger; Theodosius Mohsen Abdallah; David Boxenhorn; Marc Milanini; ETH participants in Zurich; Kevin Horgan; Paul Wehage; Baruch Gottesman, Gil Friend, Mark Champlain, Aaron Elliott, Rod Ripamonti, and Zlatan Hadzic (all on religion and sacrifice); David Graeber (Goldman Sachs); Neil Chriss; Amir-Reza Amini (automatic cars); Ektrit Kris Manushi (religion); Jazi Zilber (particularly Rav Safra); Farid Anvari (U.K. scandal); Robert Shaw (shipping and risk sharing); Daniel Hogendoorn (Cambyses); Eugene Callahan; Jon Elster, David Chambliss Johnson, Gur Huberman, Raphael Douady, Robert Shaw, Barkley Rosser, James Franklin, Marc Abrahams, Andreas Lind, and Elias Korosis (all on paper); John Durant; Zvika Afik; Robert Frey; Rami Zreik; Joe Audi; Guy Riviere; Matt Dubuque; Cesáreo González; Mark Spitznagel; Brandon Yarkin; Eric Briys; Joe Norman; Pascal Venier; Yaneer Bar-Yam; Thibault Lécuyer; Pierre Zalloua; Maximilian Hirner; Aaron Eliott; Jaffer Ali; Thomas Messina; Alexandru Panicci; Dan Coman; Nicholas Teague; Magued Iskander; Thibault Lécuyer; James Marsh; Arnie Schwarzvogel; Hayden Rei; John Mast-Finn; Rupert Read; Russell Roberts; Viktoria Martin; Ban Kanj Elsabeh; Vince Pomal; Graeme Michael Price; Karen Brennan; Jack Tohme; Marie-Christine Riachi; Jordan Thibodeau; Pietro Bonavita; Sharief Hendricks. I apologize for the near-certain omission.

GLOSSARY

—

Rent Seeking: trying to use protective regulations or "rights" to derive income without adding anything to economic activity, without increasing the wealth of others. As Fat Tony would define it, it is like being forced to pay protection money to the Mafia without getting the economic benefits of protection.

Revelation of Preferences: the theory, originating with Paul Samuelson (initially in the context of choice of public goods), that agents do not have full access to the reasoning behind their actions; actions are observables, while thought is not, which prevents the latter from being used for rigorous scientific investigation. In economics, experiments require an actual expenditure by the agent. Fat Tony's summary is "*tawk* is always cheap."

Regulatory Capture: situations where regulations end up being "gamed" by an agent, often in divergence from the original intent of the regulation. Some bureaucrats and businesspersons may owe part of their income to protective regulations and franchises, and lobby for them. Note that regulations are easier to put in than to correct and remove.

Scientism: the belief that science looks . . . like science, with too much emphasis on the cosmetic aspects, rather than its skeptical machinery. It prevails in domains with administrators judging contributions according to metrics. It also prevails in domains left to people who talk about science without "doing," such as journalists and schoolteachers.

Naive Rationalism: Belief that we have access to what makes the world work and that what we don't understand doesn't exist.

Intellectual Yet Idiot: an idiot.

Pseudo-rationalism: 1) focusing on the rationality of a belief rather than its consequences, 2) the use of bad probabilistic models to naively decry people's "irrationality" when they engage in a certain class of actions.

Agency Problem: misalignment of interest between the agent and the principal, say between the car salesman and you (the potential owner), or between the doctor and the patient.

Bob Rubin Trade: payoff in a skewed domain where the benefits are visible (and rewarded with some compensation) and the detriment is rare (and unpunished owing to absence of skin in the game). Can be generalized to politics, anything where the penalty is weak and the victims are abstract and distributed (say taxpayers or shareholders).

Interventionista: someone who causes fragility because he thinks he understands what's going on. He is not exposed to the filter and discipline of skin in the game. Also, usually lacks sense of humor.

Green Lumber Fallacy: mistaking the source of important or even necessary knowledge—the greenness of lumber—for another, less visible from the outside, less tractable one. How theoreticians impute wrong weights to what one should know in a certain business, or, more generally, how many things we call "relevant knowledge" aren't so much so.

Lecturing-Birds-How-to-Fly Effect: inverting the arrow of knowledge to read academia → practice, or education → wealth, to make it look as though technology owes more to institutional science than it actually does. See *Antifragile*.

Lindy Effect: when a technology, idea, corporation, or anything nonperishable has an increase in life expectancy with every additional day of survival—unlike perishable items (such as humans, cats, dogs, economic theories, and tomatoes). So a book that has been a hundred years in print is likely to stay in print another hundred years—provided its sales remain healthy.

Ergodicity: In our context here, ergodicity holds when a collection of players have the same statistical properties (particularly expectation) as a single player over time. Ensemble probabilities are similar to time probabilities. Absence of ergodicity makes the risk properties not directly transferable from observed probability to the payoff of a strategy subjected to ruin (or any absorbing barrier or "uncle point")—in other words, not probabilistically sustainable.

Mediocristan: a process dominated by the mediocre, with few extreme successes or failures (say, income for a dentist). No single observation can meaningfully affect the aggregate. Also called "thin-tailed," or member of the Gaussian family of distributions.

Extremistan: a process where the total can be conceivably impacted by a single observation (say, income for a writer). Also called "fat-tailed." Includes the fractal, or power-law, family of distributions. See *subexponentiality* in the Appendix.

Minority Rule: an asymmetry by which the behavior of the total is dictated by the preferences of a minority. Smokers can be in smoke-free areas but nonsmokers cannot be in smoking ones, so nonsmokers will prevail, not because they are initially a majority, but because they are asymmetric. It is held by the author that languages, ethics, and (some) religions spread by minority rule.

Via Negativa: in theology and philosophy, the focus on what something is not, an indirect definition, deemed less prone to fallacies than *via positiva*. In action, it is a recipe for what to avoid, what not to do—subtraction, not addition, works better in domains with multiplicative and unpredictable side effects. In medicine, stopping someone from smoking has fewer adverse effects than giving pills and treatments.

Scalability: The qualities of entities change, often abruptly, when they get smaller or larger: cities are different from large states, continents are very different from islands. Collective behavior switches when the size of the groups increases, an argument for localism and against unfettered globalism.

Intellectual Monoculture: Journalists, academics, and other slaves without skin in the game in a given subject converge to a "bien pensant" mode that can be manipulated and often resists empirical backing. The reason is that penalty from divergence is often penalized with labels such as "Putinist," "baby killer," or "racist" (children are always used by charlatans as a sensationalist argument). This is similar to the way ecological diversity decreases when an island gets larger (see *The Black Swan*).

Virtue Merchandising: the debasing of virtue by using it as a marketing strategy. Classically, virtue needs to be kept private, which clashes with modern "save the environment"–style messages. Virtue merchandisers are often hypocrites. Further, virtue devoid of courage, sacrifice, and skin in the game is never virtue. Virtue merchandising is similar to *simony*, which in the Middle Ages allowed someone of means to buy ecclesiastical positions or *indulgences*, to expunge his or her sins by payment.

Golden Rule (symmetry): Treat others the way you would like them to treat you.

Silver Rule (negative golden rule): Do not do to others what you would not like them to do to you. Note the difference from the Golden Rule, as the silver one prevents busybodies from attempting to run your life.

Principle of Charity: Exercise symmetry in intellectual debates; represent the argument of the opponent as accurately as you would like yours to be represented. The opposite of "strawman."

TECHNICAL APPENDIX

———

A. SKIN IN THE GAME AND TAIL PROBABILITIES

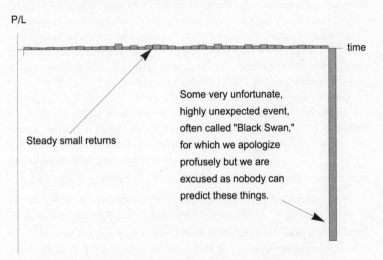

FIGURE 7. The Bob Rubin trade. Payoff in a skewed domain where the benefits are visible (and rewarded with some compensation) and the detriment is rare (and unpunished owing to absence of skin in the game). Can be generalized to politics, anything where the penalty is weak.

This section will analyze the probabilistic mismatch of tail risks and returns in the presence of a principal-agent problem.

Transfer of Harm: If an agent has the upside of the payoff of the random variable, with no downside, and is judged solely on the basis of past performance, then the incentive is to hide risks in the left tail using a negatively skewed (or more generally, asymmetric) distribution for the performance. This can be generalized to any payoff for which one does not bear the full risks and negative consequences of one's actions.

Let $P(K, M)$ be the payoff for the operator over M incentive periods:

$$P(K, M) \equiv \gamma \sum_{i=1}^{M} q_{t+(i-1)\Delta t} \left(x_{i+t\Delta t}^{j} - K \right)^{+} \mathbf{1}_{\Delta t(i-1)+t < \tau}$$

where $X^j = (x_{t+i\Delta t}^{j})_{i=1}^{M} \in \mathbb{R}$, i.i.d. random variables representing the distribution of profits over a certain period $[t, t + i\Delta t]$, $i \in \mathbb{N}$, $\Delta t \in \mathbb{R}^{+}$ and K is a "hurdle," $\tau = \inf \left\{ s : \left(\sum_{z \leq s} x_z \right) < x_{\min} \right\}$ is an indicator of stopping time when past performance conditions are not satisfied (namely, the condition of having a certain performance in a certain number of the previous years, otherwise the stream of payoffs terminates, the game ends and the number of positive incentives stops). The constant $\gamma \in (0, 1)$ is an "agent payoff," or compensation rate from the performance, which does not have to be monetary (as long as it can be quantified as "benefit"). The quantity $q_{t+(i-1)\Delta t} \in [1, \infty)$ indicates the size of the exposure at times $t+(i$-1 $)$ Δt (because of an Ito lag, as the performance at period s is determined by q at a strictly earlier period $< s$).

Let $\{f_j\}$ be the family of probability measures f_j of X^j, $j \in \mathbb{N}$. Each measure corresponds to certain mean/skewness characteristics, and we can split their properties in half on both sides of a "centrality" parameter K, as the "upper" and "lower" distributions. We write $dF_j(x)$ as $f_j(x)dx$, so $F_j^{+} = \int_K^{\infty} f_j(x)\,dx$ and $F_j^{-} = \int_{-\infty}^{K} f_j(x)\,dx$, the "upper" and "lower" distributions, each corresponding to certain conditional expectation $\mathbb{E}_j^{+} \equiv \frac{\int_K^{\infty} x f_j(x)dx}{\int_K^{\infty} f_j(x)\,dx}$ and $\mathbb{E}_j^{-} \equiv \frac{\int_{-\infty}^{K} x f_j(x)dx}{\int_{-\infty}^{K} f_j(x)\,dx}$.

Now define $\nu \in \mathbb{R}^{+}$ as a K-centered nonparametric measure of asymmetry, $\nu_j \equiv \frac{F_j^{-}}{F_j^{+}}$, with values >1 for positive asymmetry, and <1 for negative ones. Intuitively, skewness has probabilities and expectations moving in opposite directions: the larger the negative payoff, the smaller the probability to compensate.

We do not assume a "fair game," that is, with unbounded returns $m \in (-\infty, \infty)$, $F_j^{+} \mathbb{E}_j^{+} + F_j^{-} \mathbb{E}_j^{-} = m$, which we can write as $m^{+} + m^{-} = m$.

Simplified assumptions of constant q and single-condition stopping time

Assume q constant, $q = 1$ and simplify the stopping time condition as having no loss in the previous periods, $\tau = \inf\{(t + (i - 1)\Delta t)): x_{\Delta t(i-1)+t} < K\}$, which leads to

$$\mathbb{E}(P(K, M)) = \gamma \, \mathbb{E}_j^{+} \times \mathbb{E} \left(\sum_{i=1}^{M} \mathbf{1}_{\Delta t(i-1)+t < \tau} \right)$$

Since assuming independent and identically distributed agent's payoffs, the expectation at stopping time corresponds to the expectation of stopping time multiplied by the expected compensation to the agent $\gamma \, \mathbb{E}_j^+$. And $\mathbb{E}\left(\sum_{i=1}^{M} \mathbf{1}_{\Delta t(i-1)+t<\tau}\right) = \left(\mathbb{E}\left(\sum_{i=1}^{M} \mathbf{1}_{\Delta t(i-1)+t<\tau}\right) \wedge M\right)$.

The expectation of stopping time can be written as the probability of success under the condition of no previous loss:

$$\mathbb{E}\left(\sum_{i=1}^{M} \mathbf{1}_{\Delta t(i-1)+t<\tau}\right) = \sum_{i=1}^{M} F_j^+ \, \mathbf{1}_{x_{\Delta t(i-1)+t} > K}$$

We can express the stopping time condition in terms of uninterrupted success runs. Let $\sum$ be the ordered set of consecutive success runs $\sum \equiv \{\{F\}, \{SF\}, \{SSF\}, ..., \{(M-1) \text{ consecutive } S, F\}\}$, where S is success and F is failure over period Δt, with associated corresponding probabilities $\{(1-F_j^+), F_j^+\left(1-F_j^+\right), F_j^{+2}\left(1-F_j^+\right), ..., F_j^{+M-1}\left(1-F_j^+\right)\}$,

$$\sum_{i-1}^{M} F_j^{+(i-1)}\left(1-F_j^+\right) = 1 - F_j^{+M} \simeq 1$$

For M large, since $F_j^+ \in (0,1)$ we can treat the previous as almost an equality, hence:

$$\sum_{i=1}^{M} \mathbf{1}_{t+(i-1)\Delta t<\tau} = \sum_{i=1}^{M}(i-1) \, F_j^{+(i-1)}\left(1-F_j^+\right) = \frac{F_j^+}{1-F_j^+}$$

Finally, the expected payoff for the agent:

$$\mathbb{E}\left(P(K,M)\right) = \gamma \, \mathbb{E}_j^+ \frac{F_j^+}{1-F_j^+}$$

which increases by (i) increasing $\mathbb{E}_j^+$, (ii) minimizing the probability of the loss F_j^-, but, and that's the core point, even if (i) and (ii) take place at the expense of m, the total expectation from the package.

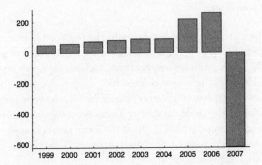

FIGURE 8. Indy Mac, a failed firm during the subprime crisis (from Taleb 2009). It is a representative of risks that keep increasing in the absence of losses, until explosive blowup.

Alarmingly, since $\mathbb{E}_j^+ = \frac{m - m^-}{F_j^+}$, the agent doesn't care about a degradation of the total expected return m if it comes from the left side of the distribution, m^-. Seen in skewness space, the expected agent payoff maximizes under the distribution j with the lowest value of ν_j (maximal negative asymmetry). The total expectation of the positive-incentive without-skin-in-the-game depends on negative skewness, not on m.

B. PROBABILISTIC SUSTAINABILITY AND ERGODICITY

Dynamic Risk Taking: If you take the risk—any risk—repeatedly, the way to count is in exposure per lifespan, or in the way it shortens the remaining lifespan.

Ruin Properties: Ruin probabilities are in the time domain for a single agent and do not correspond to state-space (or ensemble) tail probabilities. Nor are expectations fungible between the two domains. Statements on the "overestimation" of tail events (entailing ruin) by agents that are derived from state-space estimations are accordingly flawed. Many theories of "rationality" of agents are based on wrong estimation operators and/or probability measures.

This is the main reason behind the barbell strategy.

This is a special case of the conflation between a random variable and the payoff of a time-dependent, path-dependent derivative function.

Less Technical Translation:

Never cross a river if it is on average only 4 feet deep.[*]

A simplified general case

Consider the extremely simplified example, the sequence of independent random variables $(X_i)_{i=1}^n = (X_1, X_2, \ldots X_n)$ with support in the positive real numbers ($\mathbb{R}^+$). The convergence theorems of classical probability theory address the behavior of the sum or average: $\lim_{n \to \infty} \frac{1}{n} \sum_i^n X_i = m$ by the (weak) law of large numbers (convergence in probability). As shown in the story of the casino in Chapter 19, n going to infinity produces convergence in probability to the true mean return m. Although the law of large numbers applies to draws i that can be strictly separated by time, it assumes (some) independence, and certainly path independence.

Now consider $(X_{i,t})_{t=1}^T = (X_{i,1}, X_{i,2}, \ldots X_{i,T})$ where every state variable

---

[*] *Debate of author with P. Jorion, 1997, and Taleb 2007.*

X_i is indexed by a unit of time $t : 0 < t < T$. Assume that the "time events" are drawn from the exact same probability distribution: $P(X_i) = P(X_{i,t})$.

We define a time probability the evolution over time for a single agent i.

In the presence of terminal, that is irreversible, ruin, every observation is now conditional on some attribute of the preceding one, and what happens at period t depends on $t - 1$, what happens at $t - 1$ depends on $t - 2$, etc. We now have path dependence.

Next what we call failure of ergodicity:

Theorem 1 (state space-time inequality): Assume that $\forall t, P(X_t = 0) > 0$ and $X_0 > 0$, $\mathbb{E}_N(X_t) < \infty$ the state space expectation for a static initial period t, and $\mathbb{E}_T(X_i)$ the time expectation for any agent i, both obtained through the weak law of large numbers. We have

$$\mathbb{E}_N(X_t) \geq \mathbb{E}_T(X_i)$$

Proof:

$$\forall t, \lim_{n \to \infty} \frac{1}{n} \sum_i^n \mathbb{1}_{X_{i,t-1}>0} X_{i,t} = m \left(1 - \frac{1}{n} \sum_i^n \mathbb{1}_{X_{i,t-1}\leq 0} \right).$$

where $\mathbb{1}_{X_{t-1}>0}$ is the indicator function requiring survival at the previous period. Hence the limits of n for t show a decreasing temporal expectation: $\mathbb{E}_N(X_{t-1}) \geq \mathbb{E}_N(X_t)$.

We can actually prove divergence.

$$\forall i, \lim_{T \to \infty} \frac{1}{T} \sum_t^T \mathbb{1}_{X_{i,t-1}>0} X_{i,t} = 0.$$

As we can see by making $T < \infty$, by recursing the law of iterated expectations, we get the inequality for all T.

We can see the ensemble of risk takers expecting a return $m\left(1 - \frac{1}{n} \sum_i^n \mathbb{1}_{X_{i,t-1}=0}\right)$ in *any* period t, while *every single* risk taker is guaranteed to eventually go bust.

Other approaches: we can also approach the proof more formally in a measure-theoretic way by showing that while space sets for "nonruin" $\mathcal{A}$ are disjoint, time sets are not. The approach relies on the fact that for a measure ν:

$$\nu \left(\bigcup_T \mathcal{A}_t \bigcap_{\leq t} \mathcal{A}_i^c \right) \text{ does not necessarily equal } \nu \left(\bigcup_T \mathcal{A}_t \right)$$

Almost all papers discussing the actuarial "overestimation" of tail risk via options (see review in Barberis 2013) are void by the inequality in Theorem 1. Clearly they assume that an agent only exists for a single decision or exposure. Simply, the original papers documenting the "bias" assume that the agents will never ever again make another decision in their remaining lives.

The usual solution to this path dependence—if it depends on only ruin—is done by introducing a function of X to allow the ensemble (path independent) average to have the same properties as the time (path dependent) average—or survival conditioned mean. The natural logarithm seems a good candidate. Hence $S_n = \sum_{i=1}^{n} \log(X_i)$ and $S_T = \sum_{t=1}^{T} \log(X_t)$ belong to the same probabilistic class; hence a probability measure on one is invariant with respect to the other—what is called ergodicity. In that sense, when analyzing performance and risk, under conditions of ruin, it is necessary to use a logarithmic transformation of the variable (Peters 2011), or boundedness of the left tail (Kelly 1956), while maximizing opportunity in the right tail (Gell-Mann 2016), or boundedness of the left tail (Geman et al. 2015).

What we showed here is that unless one takes a logarithmic transformation (or a similar—smooth—function producing $-\infty$ with ruin set at $X = 0$), both expectations diverge. The entire point of the precautionary principle is to avoid having to rely on logarithms or transformations by reducing the probability of ruin.

In their magisterial paper, Peters and Gell-Mann (2014) showed that the Bernoulli use of the logarithm wasn't for a concave "utility" function, but, as with the Kelly criterion, to restore ergodicity. A bit of history:

- Bernoulli discovers logarithmic risk taking under the illusion of "utility."
- Kelly and Thorp recovered the logarithm for maximal growth criterion as an optimal gambling strategy. Nothing to do with utility.
- Samuelson disses logarithm as aggressive, not realizing that semilogarithm (or partial logarithm), i.e., on partial of wealth, can be done. From Menger to Arrow, via Chernoff and Samuelson, many in decision theory are shown to be making the mistake of ergodicity.
- Pitman in 1975 shows that a Brownian motion subjected to an absorbing barrier at 0, with censored absorbing paths, becomes a three-dimensional Bessel process. The drift of the surviving paths is $\frac{1}{x}$, which integrates to a logarithm.
- Peters and Gell-Mann recover the logarithm for ergodicity and, in addition, put the Kelly-Thorpe result on rigorous physical grounds.
- With Cirillo, this author (Taleb and Cirillo 2015) discovers the log as unique smooth transformation to create a dual of the distribution in

order to remove one-tail compact support to allow the use of extreme value theory.

• We can show (Briys and Taleb, in progress and private communication) the necessity of logarithmic transformation as simple ruin avoidance, which happens to be a special case of the HARA utility class.

Adaptation of Theorem 1 to Brownian Motion

The implications of simplified discussion do not change whether one uses richer models, such as a full stochastic process subjected to an absorbing barrier. And of course in a natural setting the eradication of all previous life can happen (i.e., X_t can take extreme negative value), not just a stopping condition. The Peters and Gell-Mann argument also cancels the so-called equity premium puzzle if you add fat tails (hence outcomes vastly more severe pushing some level equivalent to ruin) and absence of the fungibility of temporal and ensemble. There is no puzzle.

The problem is invariant in real life if one uses a Brownian-motion-style stochastic process subjected to an absorbing barrier. In place of the simplified representation we would have, for an process subjected to L, an absorbing barrier from below, in the arithmetic version:

$$\forall i, X_{i,t} = \begin{cases} X_{i,t-1} + Z_{i,t}, & X_{i,t-1} > L \\ 0 & \text{otherwise} \end{cases}$$

or, for a geometric process:

$$\forall i, X_{i,t} = \begin{cases} X_{i,t-1}(1 + Z_{i,t}) \approx X_{i,t-1}e^{Z_{i,t}}, & X_{i,t-1} > L \\ 0 & \text{otherwise} \end{cases}$$

where Z is a random variable.

Going to continuous time, and considering the geometric case, let $\tau = \{\inf t : X_{i,t} > L\}$ be the stopping time. The idea is to have the simple expectation of the stopping time match the remaining lifespan—or remain in the same order.

We switched the focus from probability to the mismatch between stopping time τ for ruin and the remaining lifespan.

C. PRINCIPLE OF PROBABILISTIC SUSTAINABILITY

Principle: *A unit needs to take any risk as if it were going to take it repeatedly—at a specified frequency—over its remaining lifespan.*

The principle of sustainability is necessary for the following argument. While experiments are static (we saw the confusion between the state-space and the temporal), life is continuous. If you incur a tiny probability of ruin as a "one-off" risk, survive it, then do it again (another "one-off" deal), you will eventually go bust with probability 1. Confusion arises because it may seem that the "one-off" risk is reasonable, but that also means that an additional one is reasonable. (See Figure 9). The good news is that some classes of risk can be deemed to be practically of probability zero: the earth survived trillions of natural variations daily over three billion years, otherwise we would not be here. We can use conditional probability arguments (adjusting for the survivorship bias) to back-out the ruin probability in a system.

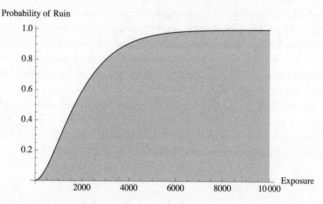

Probability of Ruin

FIGURE 9. Why ruin is not a renewable resource. No matter how small the probability, in time, something bound to hit the ruin barrier is about guaranteed to hit it. No risk should be considered a "one-off" event.

Now, we do not have to take $t \to \infty$ nor is permanent sustainability necessary. We can just extend shelf time. The longer the t, the more the expectation operators diverge.

Consider the unconditional expected stopping time to ruin in a discrete and simplified model: $\mathbb{E}(\tau \wedge T) \approx \mathbb{E}(\tau) = \sum_{i=1}^{\lambda N} i \left(\frac{p}{\lambda} \left(1 - \frac{p}{\lambda} \right)^{i-1} \right)$, where λ is the number of exposures per time period, T is the overall remaining lifespan, and p is the ruin probability, both over that same time period for fixing p. Since $\mathbb{E}(\tau) = \frac{\lambda}{p}$, we can calibrate the risk under repetition. The longer the life expectancy T (expressed in time periods), the more serious the ruin problem. Humans and plants have a short shelf life, nature doesn't—at least for t of the order of 10^8 years—hence annual ruin probabilities of $O(10^{-8})$ and (for tighter increments) local ruin probabilities of at most $O(10^{-50})$. The higher up in the hierarchy individual-species-ecosystem, the more serious the ruin problem. This duality hinges on $t \to \infty$; hence requirement is not necessary for items that are not permanent, that have a finite shelf life.

The fat tails argument: The more a system is capable of delivering large deviations, the worse the ruin problem.

We will cover the fat tails problem more extensively. Clearly the variance of the process matters; but overall deviations that do not exceed the ruin threshold do not matter.

Logarithmic transformation

Under the axiom of sustainability, i.e., that "one should take risks as if you were going to do it forever," only a logarithmic (or similar) transformation applies.

Fattailedness is a property that is typically worrisome under absence of compact support for the random variable, less so when the variables are bounded. But as we saw the need of using a logarithmic transformation, a random variable with support in $[0, \infty)$ now has support in $(-\infty, \infty)$, hence properties derived from extreme value theory can now apply to our analysis. Likewise, if harm is defined as a positive number with an upper bound H which corresponds to ruin, it is possible to transform it from $[0, H]$ to $[0, \infty)$.

Cramér and Lundberg, in insurance analysis, discovered the difficulty; see Cramér 1930.

A Note on Ergodicity*: Ergodicity is not statistically identifiable, not observable, and there is no test for time series that gives ergodicity, similar to Dickey-Fuller for stationarity (or Phillips-Perron for integration order). More crucially:

If your result is obtained from the observation of a time series, how can you make claims about the ensemble probability measure?

The answer is similar to arbitrage, which has no statistical test but, crucially, has a probability measure determined ex ante (the "no free lunch" argument). Further, consider the argument of a "self-financing" strategy, via, say, dynamic hedging. At the limit we assume that the law of large numbers will compress the returns and that no loss and no absorbing barrier will ever be reached. It satisfies our criterion of ergodicity but does not have a statistically obtained measure. Further, almost all the literature on intertemporal investments/consumption requires absence of ruin.

We are not asserting that a given security or random process is ergodic, but

---

*   Thanks to questioning by Andrew Lesniewski, who helped define what we mean by ergodicity, as the meaning here diverges from that in statistical physics.

that, given that its ensemble probability (obtained by cross-sectional methods, assumed via subjective probabilities, or simply determined by arbitrage arguments), a risk-taking strategy should *conform* to such properties. So ergodicity concerns the function of the random variable or process, not the process itself. And the function should not allow ruin.

In other words, *assuming* the SP500 has a certain expected return "alpha," an ergodic strategy would generate a strategy, say Kelly Criterion, to capture the assumed alpha. If it doesn't, because of absorbing barrier or something else, it is not ergodic.

D. TECHNICAL DEFINITION OF FAT TAILS

Probability distributions range between extreme thin-tailed (Bernoulli) and extreme fat-tailed. Among the categories of distributions that are often distinguished due to the convergence properties of moments are: (1) Having a support that is compact but not degenerate, (2) Subgaussian, (3) Gaussian, (4) Subexponential, (5) Power law with exponent greater than 3, (6) Power law with exponent less than or equal to 3 and greater than 2, (7) Power law with exponent less than or equal to 2. In particular, power law distributions have a finite mean only if the exponent is greater than 1, and have a finite variance only if the exponent exceeds 2.

Our interest is in distinguishing between cases where tail events dominate impacts, as a formal definition of the boundary between the categories of distributions to be considered as Mediocristan and Extremistan. The natural boundary between these occurs at the subexponential class, which has the following property:

Let $\mathbf{X} = (X_i)_{1 \le i \le n}$ be a sequence of independent and identically distributed random variables with support in $(\mathbb{R}^+)$, with cumulative distribution function F. The subexponential class of distributions is defined by (see Teugels 1975, Pitman 1980):

$$\lim_{x \to +\infty} \frac{1 - F^{*2}(x)}{1 - F(x)} = 2$$

where $F^{*2} = F' * F$ is the cumulative distribution of $X_1 + X_2$, the sum of two independent copies of X. This implies that the probability that the sum $X_1 + X_2$ exceeds a value x is twice the probability that either one separately exceeds x. Thus, every time the sum exceeds x, for large enough values of x, the value of the sum is due to either one or the other exceeding x—the maximum over the two variables—and the other of them contributes negligibly.

More generally, it can be shown that the sum of n variables is dominated by the maximum of the values over those variables in the same way. Formally, the following two properties are equivalent to the subexponential condition (see

Chistyakov 1964, Embrechts et al. 1979). For a given $n \geq 2$, let $S_n = \Sigma_{i=1}^{n} x_i$ and $M_n = \max_{1 \leq i \leq n} x_i$

   a) $\lim_{x \to \infty} \frac{P(S_n > x)}{P(X > x)} = n$

   b) $\lim_{x \to \infty} \frac{P(S_n > x)}{P(M_n > x)} = 1$

Thus the sum S_n has the same magnitude as the largest sample M_n, which is another way of saying that tails play the most important role.

Intuitively, tail events in subexponential distributions should decline more slowly than an exponential distribution for which large tail events should be irrelevant. Indeed, one can show that subexponential distributions have no exponential moments:

$$\int_0^\infty e^{\epsilon x} \, dF(x) = +\infty$$

for all values of ε greater than zero. However, the converse isn't true, since distributions can have no exponential moments, yet not satisfy the subexponential condition.

We note that if we choose to indicate deviations as negative values of the variable x, the same result holds by symmetry for extreme negative values, replacing $x \to +\infty$ with $x \to -\infty$. For two-tailed variables, we can separately consider positive and negative domains.

NOTES

———

The notes here are organized by themes rather than sequentially.

Ethics: Taleb and Sandis (2013), Sandis and Taleb (2015). See also Nagel (1970), Ross (1939); for the philosophy of action, Sandis (2010, 2012). Political ethics: Thompson (1983). Uncertainty and ethics: Altham (1984), Williams (1993), Zimmerman (2008). General: Blackburn (2001), Broad (1930). Climbing the mountain on different sides: Parfit (2011). Ethics and knowledge: Pritchard (2002), Rescher (2009).

While I lean towards virtue ethics, virtue for its own sake, for existential reasons, my co-author Constantine Sandis and I found, thanks to *On What Matters* by Derek Parfit (2011), who considers them all to be climbing different sides of the same mountain, that skin in the game falls at the convergence point of three main ethical systems: Kantian imperatives, consequentialism, and classical virtue.

Principal-agent and moral hazard in economics: Ross (1973), Pratt et al. (1985), Stiglitz (1988), Tirole (1988), Holmström (1979), Grossman and Hart (1983)

Islamic decision making under uncertainty: Unpublished manuscript by Farid Karkabi, Karkabi (2017), Wardé (2010). *Al ġurm fil jurm* is the main concept.

Eye for Eye not literal: The discussion in Aramaic that when a small man harms a big man, there is no equivalence, is mistranslated. *Gadol* refers to "hero" rather than "big" and *Qatan* to "puny" rather than small.

Rationality: Binmore (2008), and private communication with K. Binmore and G. Gigerenzer at the latter's Bielefeld festschrift in 2017.

Christians and pagans: Wilkens (2003), Fox (2006), among many. See Read and Taleb (2014).

Julian: Ammianus Marcellinus, *History,* vols. I and II, Loeb Classics, Harvard University Press. See also Downey (1939, 1959).

Ostrom: Ostrom (1986, 2015). Also, econtalk discussion with Peter Boetke with Russell Roberts, econtalk.org/archives/2009/11/boettke_on_elin.html.

Asymmetry and Scalability: *Antifragile.*

Selfish Gene: Wilson and Wilson (2007), Nowak et al. (2010). Pinker statement about the debate between Nowak, Wilson et al., and others who support the "selfish gene" approach, missing scalability among other things: edge .org/conversation/steven_pinker-the-false-allure-of-group-selection. Bar-Yam and Sayama (2006).

Fences make good neighbors: Rutherford et al. (2014).

Sacrifice: Halbertal (1980)

Dynamic inequality: Lamont (2009), Rank and Hirshl (2014, 1015). Also Mark Rank, "From Rags to Riches to Rags," *The New York Times,* April 18, 2014.

Ergodicity and gambles: Peters and Gell-Mann (2016), Peters (2011).

Inequality: Picketty (2015). Dispossession already in Piketty (1995).

Miscomputation of inequality: Taleb and Douady (2015), Fontanari et al. (2017).

Taxation for equality incompatible with fat tails: Such a tax, meaning to punish the wealth generator, is popular but absurd and certainly suicidal: since the payoff is severely clipped on the upside, it would be a lunacy to be a risk taker with small probability bets, with wins of 20 (after tax) rather than 100, then disburse all savings progressively in wealth tax. The optimal strategy then would be to go become an academic or a French-style civil servant, the anti-wealth generators. To see the cross-sectional problem temporally: Compare someone with lumpy payoffs, say an entrepreneur who makes $4.5 million every twenty years, to an economics professor who earns the same total over the period ($225K in taxpayer-funded income). The entrepreneur over the very same income ends up paying 75 percent in taxes, plus wealth tax on the rest, while the rent-seeking tenured academic who doesn't contribute to wealth formation pays say 30 percent.)

Kelly gambling: Thorp (2006), McLean et al. (2011).

Satisficing: It is erroneous to think that the axioms necessarily lead one to "maximize" income without any constraint (academic economists have used naive mathematics in their optimization programs and thinking). It is perfectly compatible to "satisfice" their wealth, that is, shoot for a satisfactory income, plus maximize their fitness to the task, or the emotional pride they may have in seeing the fruits of their labor. Or not explicitly "maximize" anything, just do things because that is what makes us human.

Violence: Pinker (2011), Cirillo and Taleb (2016, 2018).

Renormalization: Galam (2008, 2012). Renormalization group in Binney et al. (1992).

Thick Blood: Margalit (2002).

Bounded Rationality: Gigerenzer and Brighton (2009), Gigerenzer (2010).

Lindy Effect: Eliazar (2017), Mandelbrot (1982, 1997); also *Antifragile*.

Periander of Corinth: in *Early Greek Philosophy: Beginning and Early Ionian Thinkers, Part 1*.

Genes and Minority Rule: Lazaridis (2017), Zalloua, private discussions. Languages move much faster than genes. Northern Europeans are surprised to hear that (1) ancient and modern Greeks can be actually the same people, (2) "Semitic people" such as the Phoenicians are closer genetically to the "Indo-European" Ancient than to "Semites," though linguistically far apart.

BIBLIOGRAPHY

Altham, J.E.J., 1984. "Ethics of Risk." *Proceedings of the Aristotelian Society,* new series, 84 (1983–1984): 15–29.

Ammianus Marcellinus. *History,* vols I and II. Loeb Classics, Harvard University Press.

Barberis, N., 2013. "The Psychology of Tail Events: Progress and Challenges." *American Economic Review* 103(3): 611–616.

Bar-Yam, Yaneer, and Hiroki Sayama, 2006. "Formalizing the Gene Centered View of Evolution." In *Unifying Themes in Complex Systems,* pp. 215–222. Berlin, Heidelberg: Springer-Verlag.

Binmore, K., 2008. *Rational Decisions.* Princeton, N.J.: Princeton University Press.

Binney, James J., Nigel J. Dowrick, Andrew J. Fisher, and Mark Newman, 1992. *The Theory of Critical Phenomena: An Introduction to the Renormalization Group.* Oxford: Oxford University Press.

Blackburn, S., 2001. *Ethics: A Very Short Introduction.* Oxford: Oxford University Press.

Broad, C. D., 1930. *Five Types of Ethical Theory.* London: Kegan Paul.

Chistyakov, V., 1964. "A Theorem on Sums of Independent Positive Random Variables and Its Applications to Branching Random Processes." *Theory of Probability and Its Applications* 9(4): 640–648.

Cirillo, Pasquale, and Nassim Nicholas Taleb, 2018. "The Decline of Violent Conflicts: What Do the Data Really Say?" Nobel Foundation.

———, 2016. "On the Statistical Properties and Tail Risk of Violent Conflicts." *Physica A: Statistical Mechanics and Its Applications* 452: 29–45.

Cramér, H., 1930. *On the Mathematical Theory of Risk.* Centraltryckeriet.

Downey, Glanville, 1939. "Julian the Apostate at Antioch." *Church History* 8(4): 303–315.

————, 1959. "Julian and Justinian and the Unity of Faith and Culture." *Church History* 28(4): 339–349.

Eliazar, Iddo, 2017. "Lindy's Law." *Physica A: Statistical Mechanics and Its Applications.*

Embrechts, Paul, et al., 1997. *Modelling Extremal Events: for Insurance and Finance.* Berlin, Heidelberg: Springer-Verlag.

Embrechts, P., C. M. Goldie, and N. Veraverbeke, 1979. "Subexponentiality and Infinite Divisibility." *Probability Theory and Related Fields* 49(3): 335–347.

Fontanari, Andrea, Nassim Nicholas Taleb, and Pasquale Cirillo, 2017. "Gini Estimation Under Infinite Variance."

Fox, Robin Lane, 2006. *Pagans and Christians: In the Mediterranean World from the Second Century A.D. to the Conversion of Constantine.* Penguin U.K.

Galam, Serge, 2008. "Sociophysics: A Review of Galam Models." *International Journal of Modern Physics C* 19(03): 409–440.

————, 2012. *Sociophysics: A Physicist's Modeling of Psycho-Political Phenomena.* Berlin, Heidelberg: Springer-Verlag.

Geman, D., H. Geman, and N. N. Taleb, 2015. "Tail Risk Constraints and Maximum Entropy." *Entropy* 17(6): 3724. Available: http://www.mdpi.com/1099-4300/17/6/3724.

Gigerenzer, G., 2010. "Moral Satisficing: Rethinking Moral Behavior as Bounded Rationality." *Topics in Cognitive Science* 2: 528–554.

Gigerenzer, G., and H. Brighton, 2009. "Homo Heuristicus: Why Biased Minds Make Better Inferences." *Topics in Cognitive Science* 1(1): 107–143.

Grossman, S. J., and O. D. Hart, 1983. "An Analysis of the Principal-Agent Problem." *Econometrica*, 7–45.

Halbertal, Moshe, 2012. *On Sacrifice.* Princeton, N.J.: Princeton University Press.

Holmström, B., 1979. "Moral Hazard and Observability." *The Bell Journal of Economics*, 74–91.

Isocrates, 1980. Three volumes. Loeb Classical Library, Harvard University Press.

Karkaby, Farid, 2017. "Islamic Finance: A Primer." Unpublished manuscript.

Kelly, J. L., 1956. "A New Interpretation of Information Rate." *IRE Transactions on Information Theory* 2(3): 185–189.

Lamont, Michèle, 2009. *The Dignity of Working Men: Morality and the Boundaries of Race, Class, and Immigration.* Cambridge, Mass.: Harvard University Press.

Lazaridis, Iosif, et al., 2017. "Genetic Origins of the Minoans and Mycenaeans." *Nature* 548, no. 7666: 214–218.

MacLean, Leonard C., Edward O. Thorp, and William T. Ziemba, 2011. *The Kelly Capital Growth Investment Criterion: Theory and Practice*, vol. 3. World Scientific.

Mandelbrot, Benoit, 1982. *The Fractal Geometry of Nature*. Freeman and Co.

———, 1997. *Fractals and Scaling in Finance: Discontinuity, Concentration, Risk*. New York: Springer-Verlag.

Mandelbrot, Benoit B., and N. N. Taleb, 2010. "Random Jump, Not Random Walk." In Richard Herring, ed., *The Known, the Unknown, and the Unknowable*. Princeton, N.J.: Princeton University Press.

Margalit, Avishai, 2002. *The Ethics of Memory*. Cambridge, Mass.: Harvard University Press.

Nagel, T., 1970. *The Possibility of Altruism*. Princeton, N.J.: Princeton University Press.

Nowak, Martin A., Corina E. Tarnita, and Edward O. Wilson, 2010. "The Evolution of Eusociality." *Nature* 466, no. 7310: 1057–1062.

Ostrom, Elinor, 1986. "An Agenda for the Study of Institutions." *Public Choice* 48(1): 3–25.

———, 2015. *Governing the Commons*. Cambridge University Press.

Parfit, Derek, 2011. *On What Matters*. Vols. 1–3. Oxford: Oxford University Press.

Periander of Corinth. In *Early Greek Philosophy: Beginning and Early Ionian Thinkers, Part 1*. Loeb Classical Library, Harvard University Press.

Peters, Ole, 2011. "The Time Resolution of the St Petersburg Paradox." *Philosophical Transactions of the Royal Society of London A: Mathematical, Physical and Engineering Sciences* 369(1956): 4913–4931.

Peters, Ole, and Murray Gell-Mann, 2016. "Evaluating Gambles Using Dynamics." *Chaos: An Interdisciplinary Journal of Nonlinear Science* 26(2): 023103. Available: scitation.aip.org/content/aip/journal/chaos/26/2/10.1063/1.4940236

Piketty, Thomas, 1995. "Social Mobility and Redistributive Politics." *The Quarterly Journal of Economics* 110(3): 551–584.

———, 2015. *Capital in the Twenty-first Century*. Cambridge, Mass.: Harvard University Press.

Pinker, Steven, 2011. *The Better Angels of Our Nature: Why Violence Has Declined*. Penguin.

Pitman, E. 1980. "Subexponential Distribution Functions." *Journal of the Australian Mathematical Society,* Series A, 29(3): 337–347.

Pitman, J. W., 1975. "One-Dimensional Brownian Motion and the Three-Dimensional Bessel Process." *Advances in Applied Probability* 511–526.

Pratt, J. W., R. Zeckhauser, and K. J. Arrow, 1985. *Principals and Agents: The Structure of Business*. Harvard Business Press.

Prichard, H. A., 2002. "Duty and Ignorance of Fact." In *Moral Writings,* ed. J. MacAdam. Oxford: Oxford University Press.

Rank, Mark Robert, and Thomas Hirschl, 2015. "The Likelihood of Experiencing Relative Poverty Over the Life Course." *PLOS One* 10(7).

Rank, Mark Robert, Thomas Hirschl, Kirk A. Foster, 2014. *Chasing the American Dream: Understanding What Shapes Our Fortunes.* Oxford: Oxford University Press.

Read, R., and N. N. Taleb, 2014. "Religion, Heuristics and Intergenerational Risk-Management." *Econ Journal Watch* 11(2): 219–226.

Rescher, N., 2009. *Ignorance: On the Wider Implications of Deficient Knowledge.* Pittsburgh: University of Pittsburgh Press.

Ross, David, 1939. *The Foundations of Ethics.* Oxford: Clarendon Press.

———, 1930. *The Right and the Good.* Rev. ed., 2002, ed. P. Stratton-Lake. Oxford: Clarendon Press.

Ross, S. A., 1973. "The Economic Theory of Agency: The Principal's Problem." *The American Economic Review* 63(2): 134–139.

Rutherford, Alex, Dion Harmon, Justin Werfel, Alexander S. Gard-Murray, Shlomiya Bar-Yam, Andreas Gros, Ramon Xulvi-Brunet, and Yaneer Bar-Yam. "Good Fences: The Importance of Setting Boundaries for Peaceful Coexistence." *PLOS One* 9(5): e95660.

Sandis, Constantine, 2012. *The Things We Do and Why We Do Them.* Palgrave Macmillan.

Sandis, Constantine, and Nassim Nicholas Taleb, 2015. "Leadership Ethics and Asymmetry." In *Leadership and Ethics,* ed. Boaks and Levine, 233. London: Bloomsbury.

Stiglitz, J. E., 1988. "Principal and Agent." In *The New Palgrave Dictionary of Economics,* vol. 3. London: Macmillan.

Taleb, N. N., 2007. "Black Swans and the Domains of Statistics." *The American Statistician* 61(3): 198–200.

Taleb, N. N., and P. Cirillo, 2015. "On the Shadow Moments of Apparently Infinite-Mean Phenomena," *arXiv preprint arXiv:1510.06731.*

Taleb, N. N., and R. Douady, 2015. "On the Super-Additivity and Estimation Biases of Quantile Contributions." *Physica A: Statistical Mechanics and Its Applications* 429: 252–260.

Taleb, N. N., and C. Sandis, 2013. "The Skin in the Game Heuristic for Protection Against Tail Events." *Review of Behavioral Economics* 1(1).

Teugels, J. L., 1975. "The Class of Subexponential Distributions." *The Annals of Probability,* vol. 3, no. 6, pp. 1000–1011.

Thompson, D. F., 1983. "Ascribing Responsibility to Advisers in Government." *Ethics* 93(3): 5466–0.

Thorp, Edward O., 2006. "The Kelly Criterion in Blackjack, Sports Betting and the Stock Market." *Handbook of Asset and Liability Management* 1: 385–428.

Tirole, J., 1988. *The Theory of Industrial Organization*. Cambridge, Mass.: MIT Press.

Wardé, I., 2010. *Islamic Finance in the Global Economy*. Edinburgh University Press.

Wilken, R. L., 2003. *The Christians as the Romans Saw Them*. New Haven, Conn.: Yale University Press.

Williams, B., 1993. *Shame and Necessity*. Cambridge: Cambridge University Press.

Wilson, D. S., and E. O. Wilson, 2007. "Rethinking the Theoretical Foundation of Sociobiology." *The Quarterly Review of Biology* 82(4): 327–348.

Zimmerman, M. J., 2008. *Living with Uncertainty: The Moral Significance of Ignorance*. Cambridge: Cambridge University Press.

INDEX

———

expat employees, 101–2
funding and, 159
judgment of businessmen by others, 144
longevity of large firms, 99
losing an argument, 105–6
market manipulation, 63
peace and, 194
perks for management, 100n
products advocated by users, 63, 63n
sale of property to foreigners, 39n
salespeople, 53, 103
selling something knowing the price will drop, 54
simplicity, 161
"talking one's book," 63–64
theory of the firm, 100–101
whistleblowers, 109–10
See also companies; employees
business plans, 159
business transactions, 31–32, 32n
business transactions, legal approach, 32

Cambyses (king), 40, 63
Cameron, David, 178, 180
capital, Pikettism, 133–35
Capital in the Twenty-first Century (Piketty), 133
cars, automatic shifting, 74
Carthaginians, 87–88, 88n
Castiglione, Baldassare, 170
categorical imperative, *19*, 21
Catherine the Great, 106
Catholic Church, 200
Cato, 112
causal opacity, 25
caveat emptor, 55
celibacy, 110, 111
cellular automata, 91
charity, 182, 187, 242
Chernoff bound, 232
choice
  beer-wine asymmetry, 77
  of foods, 76–77, 167–69, 170, 171

paradox of, 152
"veto" effect, 76–77
Chopra, Deepak, 112
Christ. *See* Jesus
Christianity, 73, 77, 80–81, 82, 88n, 111, 120, 200–201, 202, 205, 206, 210
Christian minority, in the Levant, 201
churches, simony, 187–88
church-free religions, 202
Cicero, 54, 55, 151
Cirillo, Pasquale, 133, 138, 175, 194, 248
cities, 60, 61, 137
citizenship, 37
civil/ethical behavior, photos to encourage, 177
civil rights, 83
civil service, ethics of, 138–40
"classicists," 37–38
Classic literature, 37–38, 150–51
"class privilege," 185
Cleon, 113
clinical research, 149–50
Clinton, Hillary, 184–85
clubs, 58, 59, 60
Coase, Ronald, 100
Coase Theorem, 100
cognitive dissonance, 108, 151
Colette (writer), 158
collaboration, 145, 191, 195
collaborative animals, 192–93
collateral damage, 175
collection of units, 45
collective, 45, 188
collective behavior, 241
collectivism, self-interest under, 60–61
columns, in Greek architecture, 214
commerce, peace and, 194
Common law, 32
commons, 60–61
Commonwealth venue, 32
community, 60–61
companies
  expat employees, 101–2
  longevity of large firms, 99

NASSIM NICHOLAS TALEB spent twenty-one years as a risk taker before becoming a researcher in philosophical, mathematical, and mostly (very) practical problems with probability.